THE NEW WORLD RELIGION
AND
THE BELIEFS OF
THE ELITE

James Musker

ISBN: 9781980791256

CONTENTS

ACKNOWLEDGMENTS

I would like to thank Elena Dodevska for her excellent illustrations, and the unnamed 'pedantic maestro' for his advice and proofreading. Lastly thanks go to my wife for her commentary and giving me the space and time to write this book. I can be contacted on Twitter at 'New World Rel', and on Facebook at 'The Regeneration.'

PREFACE

There are numerous books trying to explain what is happening in our world today. The reasons for the wars, mass immigrations or why there is economic uncertainty. These reasons never seem to completely satisfy or answer the real deep motivations behind why any event actually happened. For example, why are we seeing an increasingly divided world where most people live in a state of 'buzzing confusion'? Why are we made to feel every insecurity which comes from a mainstream worldview? The explanations that are provided never seem to fully explain the true reasons behind anything that is happening today. There always seems to be a gap missing.

This book aims to look beyond the obvious, to the genuine motivating factors of the power Elite governing our planet. What are the actual inspirations behind what is going on in our world and what are the beliefs of these people? Why do they want more and more money, power, oil or whatever it may seem to be at the surface? This is surely only part of the story, it is not what really counts. It is the beliefs of the people themselves and what they really think and hold dear that matters.

There are so few books explaining the beliefs of the Cryptocracy (hidden government) and what they believe deep down. We are not able to understand world events because we don't understand the precise worldview of the actors involved. As a result, we can only guess at what is going on from imprecise knowledge. We know the long-term goal of the Elite is the New World Order: the development of a One World Economy, run by a One World Government with a One World Religion. These are the three main goals as we know from their writings. But why are they doing these things?

1

This book aims to explain the New World Religion, what it is, how it might emerge, and then relate this to the **ultimate goals** they are striving towards. Once you are able to understand their aims, many of the true motivations behind the machinations of the apparent chaos that we are going through in the world today will become clear.

This book is for those who are opened minded enough to consider the evidence and absorb difficult concepts which may counter current culture. It's conclusions in many places are profound and for those who intuitively recognise that things are not as they seem. At its heart, is the fact, which is proven numerous times throughout the book, that there is a Cryptocracy which acts as the parallel unseen government that runs our institutions and companies. They do this from behind the scenes of the supposedly democratically elected Politicians and global Financiers we see in the news. This book proves who they are, what they believe, and what their long-range goals are for humanity. All the necessary details are explained to enable you to gain an understanding of the complexity and vastness of the situation we are facing.

The United Nations is part of this story since they are the institution seeking to place over the Sovereign Nations a new set of rules which will enable them to take control. This is no secret. It is openly articulated in their literature, mainly: Agenda 21, Agenda 2030 and the Global Biodiversity Assessment. We will explore how all the groups of the New World Order, such as the Council on Foreign Relations, the Trilateral Commission and the Bank of International Settlements, are run by the same inner group.

The people who make up these groups have unusual beliefs, which we look at in some detail, and are succinctly summed up as being believers in the 'Luciferian philosophy'. All of these conspirators are verifiable members of secret societies as this is the easiest way to control and make policy for the inner initiates of the Cryptocracy.

The ultimate aim of the New World Order is the complete control of the world population with total power in the hands of a few families. In order to bring about this re-ordering of society they have engaged in a continuous effort of social engineering, to destroy the current religious and moral structures that have dominated for centuries. These traditional values and beliefs, which have become instilled in society at large, are worth holding onto as taught by the world's major religions since they keep the populace away from destructive tactics of the Cryptocracy. By removing the world's religions, or at least watering down their beliefs, and promoting a 'do as thou wilt' culture the elite are creating a cultural climate of moral relativism. The problem arises that when few boundaries remain, the people are left wide open to being indoctrinated to the politically correct view that they want. This is then used as a control mechanism.

Today the power elite are seeking to destroy the old religious beliefs and replace them with a 'new age religion' based on a form of Earth worship in which a person will be a 'Planetary Citizen' who will submit to the authority of the State without question and will love his slavery which would be seen as a matter of religious observance. Doing so will accomplish multiple objectives. The main thrust of which is the total control of humanity in the hands of the Cryptocracy at the expense of the people. This would also encompass the decoupling of western economies and the acceptance of lower standards of living to equal the living standards of the rest of the world. This is now being carried out in the name of a creed linked to saving the environment as detailed in the writings of Agenda 21 and other Sustainable Development publications.

The overall picture is also corroborated and mentioned in the writings and beliefs of Luciferians such as Albert Pike, Madame Blavatsky and Alice Bailey who make numerous references to the eventual collapse and destruction of Christianity to be replaced by the New World Religion. Their prediction is that as Christianity collapses, and its believers are killed, the rest of humanity will be led by the Luciferian Elite who will become united to worship the false light to make way for the New World Religion. This is their wish, but in reality, Christianity will indeed survive even during the Great Tribulation years. The eventual battles and end time prophecies mentioned in all the world's major religions also further corroborate this situation.

This is the least understood, fantastic and most complicated part of the dreadful New World Order to understand and so some prior knowledge of the subject would be helpful. The evidence for the New World Religion is backed up by quotes and information from all sorts of writings, comments and analysis. The overall picture is solid enough to be taken seriously.

It's comparatively easy to roll out the New Global Economy and Government when the populace is so easily deceived by the mythologies of the State and the media. All you need to do is to 'beat the drum' of Globalism and push through some unpopular laws telling the people all the time that there is some threat which means the State is looking out for their interests; and soon enough the Network will have the complete control they crave. But how are the Cryptocracy going to amalgamate all the World's religions into one belief system? How are they going to force Humanity to worship the Anti-Christ as a God?

This book's conclusions, by necessity, are partly a matter of faith. However, whatever creed you have, or if you are simply interested in how the World's religions might be transformed and changed over the next 100 years or so - or if you wish to find out about an alternative scenario - then this book is for you. Even if you are a hardened Atheist or Humanist not caring about religious beliefs, you will be able to see how the Elite are using religions as a social means of gaining power which will eventually lead to the enslavement of you and indeed all of us.

And, I'd best tell you straight away, so there are no illusions, that the social and political situation that we face is very grave indeed. We lurch from one crisis to another and are played like fiddles and manipulated to believe, behave, and think whatever the Elite wants. We are like putty in their hands - a pathetic sight to behold! Once robotics and trans-humanism become a viable proposition there will no longer be a need to maintain the charade any longer, and the last convulsion of the old social and economic system we currently live under, will give way to the emergence of the 'New International Economic Order.'

For those of us who are Christians this book is especially written for you since the viewpoint of the author conforms to this belief. He aims to prepare you, and all people for the deceptions coming our way. For those who don't have any beliefs, this is not just a Christian book on Theology and Conspiracy, but a book explaining the entire religious agenda and the beliefs of the Elite, and much more! There are many religious concepts within it, but not so many I hope, as to be too daunting! The book covers not only the view point of the New World Religion from a Christian perspective, but it also tries to do this from the view point of a Secular Humanist.

Surrey, March 2018

James Musker

CHAPTER 1

THE GREAT PLAN

Three 'legs' principle, Economics, Politics and Religion

Society is based on three identical legs; Economics, Politics and Society (Religion). If these pillars are nurtured Society will prosper but take away one of the 'legs from the stool' and Society would collapse. Each one is compatible with the other. At least this is the theory of the economist Peter Drucker. At the moment we are seeing an attack on all of these three pillars, in the UK, in the US, Europe and across the world.

Our current economic capitalist system is being moulded and transformed into the untested 'green economy' based on Sustainable Development and espoused by Agenda 21. This 'decoupling' of the global economy from the current price-based system, into an energy priced system of sustainable development based on environmentalism has been written about by the world's most influential economists, politicians and the UN amongst others.[1]

At any stage the 'financial plug' can be pulled by the 0.1% of the Elite who control the world's Banks. In fact, the 2008 Credit Crunch was sold to us as being a liquidity problem created by sub-prime

---

[1] See UN Environmental Program (UNEP) publication, *Decoupling Natural Resource Use And Environmental Impacts from Economic Growth* -2011 PDF at http://wedocs.unep.org/handle/20.500.11822/9816?show=full

mortgage debt, but the reality was that it was simply a withdrawal of money by the top financial Elite which created a serious liquidity problem which spiralled out of control as expected. This is not the first time this has been done. In 1929 the Great Depression is the classic example, as Milton Friedman, during a radio interview in 1996 said- **'The Federal Reserve definitely caused the Great Depression by contracting the amount of money in circulation by one-third from 1929 to 1933.'**[2]

Ben Bernanke picked up on this on 8th November 2002 in a speech in honour of Friedman's 90th birthday.

'I would like to say to Milton, regarding the Great Depression: You're right, we did it. We're very sorry. But thanks to you, we won't do it again.' (Fed website.)

Only a few years after this and the Elite are at it again! This time the reason for the Credit Crunch was part of an engineered power grab and consolidation to create lower interest rates across the West. So, when they are ready we will see the end of the current economic system of Capitalist supply and demand. It won't happen before they are ready since they have complete control of the central banking system, such as the Bank of International Settlements (BIS) which supplies the Banks with money for its lending, mortgages and debts, which they in turn lend to us, having been created out of nothing. A double fraud since the money is created out of nothing, and interest is charged on this capital which is then repaid a second time as the debt is down paid.

Our political structure is also being attacked, as slowly and imperceptibly the Elite Network are infiltrating more and more positions within governments and the largest and most important companies. The constitutional rule of law is being replaced by a system of autocratic regulations subject to neither external legal restraints nor any regularised mechanism of democratic oversight. In the EU, for example, laws are brought in as they see fit as overarching 'blanket' rules imposed on the whole continent without any real consideration for the local conditions of each country. Power is concentrated more and more into the hands of very few people, and with each passing year this is getting worse.

---

[2] Robin de Ruiter, *Worldwide Evil and Misery 2*. Kindle Loc 424.

The Cryptocracy (hidden government - which will be explained later), has complete control over the economy and almost complete control over the political sphere, and so, in a way, this battle has already been lost. To some degree, the New World Order has already arrived and is being assembled right in front of our eyes right now. It's strangle-hold is getting firmer, and its dictates are being implemented more boldly; for example, in the eventual harmonization of laws across continents. These laws can be more efficiently administered from a central location; the expansion of Eurozone influence into countries further east such as Azerbaijan and Georgia via the Eastern Partnership (EaP), the creation of the North American Union (NAU) and the death of cash via the emergence of the Special Drawing Rights (SDR) currency which are all indications of the continuing march of the New World Order.

The Political pillar was finally subjugated by the Milner Group and the Eastern Establishment with the Council on Foreign Relations who later on formed the Trilateral Commission, who completely infiltrated the US Administration from Carter's Presidency onwards, and the true puppet masters behind him, such as the intellectuals Zbigniew Brezinski and Richard Gardner, who sought to assimilate the US into the more 'global integrated world order'. This domination of the Executive Branch of the US government provided all the necessary political leverage and insider dealing to skew US and global economic policies to the benefit of the Network.

In 1979 Barry Goldwater, who is one of the only Trilateral Commission members to expose the conspirators wrote in his autobiography 'With No Apologies':-

"In my view The Trilateral Commission represents a skillful, coordinated effort to seize control and consolidate the four centers of power - political, monetary, intellectual, and ecclesiastical. All this is to be done in the interest of creating a more peaceful, more productive world community. What the Trilateralists truly intend is the creation of a worldwide economic power, superior to the political governments of the nation-states involved. They believe the abundant materialism they propose to create will overwhelm existing differences. As managers and creators of the system they will rule the future."

All subsequent Presidential administrations have been subject to this infiltration by the Council on Foreign Relations and Trilateral Commission. George H. W. Bush as Vice President under Reagan, Bill Clinton, George Bush, and Obama were all enabled by these insiders skewing political processes to their benefit. They are basically the same group with the same poisonous goals. Trump's Presidency has fewer Trilateral members but his administration is also administered by the same small Elite group.

The economic base of most major western countries had already been established by 1976 with huge companies in every major sector such as IBM, Coca Cola, CBS, Chase Manhattan, and Exxon - to name just a few, and these dwarfed American businesses even at this early stage.[3] Ever since the Network's interest have been gaining more and more of a hold on the global economy and now you can't even possibly begin to gain any foot hold in any market, or product without becoming an insider in some manner, normally to a large degree. In fact, the entire system has become rigged. If you want to do well in business you have to be an 'insider' who works for the establishment and will do whatever basically you are told to do - you have to become a puppet!

It is true that the 'old fashioned' capitalist economies have slowly been replaced by a Globalist Capitalist economy as the International Corporations have gradually joined up the world's supply lines. The old economy 'Made in' labels are no longer so relevant, since the products for those goods may have been sourced from all over the world, designed and assembled in another country with profits returned to yet another location. The largest shareholders and hence the owners of that company may themselves be from somewhere else, such as Qatar or Saudi Arabia for example. So you can see that the old-fashioned type of economy is no longer prevalent. This is globalism - an economy moulded and brought into line with legalised systems of regulating business. This, some may say, is the New Economic Order and economists and commentators have tried to explain this rise of the neo-liberal Global Economic Order in this manner, disassociating themselves from any conspiracy. The only problem with this is that Governments have been infiltrated by agents of the Trans-national

---

[3] Patrick Wood, *Technocracy Rising: The Trojan Horse of Global Transformation*, page 55. Kindle Loc 1271.

Corporations and not just lobbyists of the 'old capitalism'. In addition to which the bank bail outs and corporate cronyism in high places also points to the skewed system. Some, typically left Economists, have argued that there is no-group acting and moulding the political process, and hence this is all happen-stance when the evidence shows quite plainly that there is such a group. This can easily be discerned via the groups we investigate later on and by the bank bail outs and other activities of corporate favouritism. As profits have been driven into fewer hands by the process of globalisation, the bottom half of society has seen unprecedented wage stagnation and they are the group not benefitting from globalisation (hence Brexit and the Trump effect). Bring into the equation the emergence of robots in the next 30 years or so and the ultimate conclusion of the march of the Trans-national Corporations is a type of **monopolistic State economy**, exactly as the authors such as H G Wells, Aldous Huxley and George Orwell wrote about in the 1920s and onwards. (HG Wells, A Modern Utopia, Aldous Huxley, Brave New World and George Orwell, 1984.)

When the Network wants to change society at the economic and political level, they can at any stage, and fundamentally in any manner they see fit.

But Religion, as the other pillar in the three-legged stool model, is a trickier area over which to gain control, and is a more nebulous thing entirely since it's to do with human thought and the inner condition. As the saying goes: - 'You can take the man out of the religion, but you can't take the religion out of the man'. In other words, the Elite can try and force people to believe what they want, and lock people up if they don't conform, but since it's all in the mind, they can't take away the beliefs and thoughts of people. This is a serious problem to the Elite since they want control over the three Pillars - the Economy, Politics and Religion. They already have almost complete power over the Economy and Politics, but Religious faith and beliefs are more concealed and less malleable to the wiles of the Elites social engineering and psychological propaganda techniques. People who believe in a Religion or faith are **not as willing to go along with any agenda** the Elite want because they have a set of beliefs of their own and so they will be more resistant to the folly of what their rulers are trying to do. On a more rudimentary level the psychological conditioning which the Think Tanks are forcing on the populace will not be as effective. It was Edward

Bernays the 'father of public relations' from the 1920's onwards, who manged to make a science out of social conditioning and engineering, to manipulate the masses via public relations and advertising to believe and think whatever the government wants. Via their endless psychological studies and think tanks these means of mass social conditioning have been perfected and so the Elite can make us belief whatever they want even if it's completely false. We will still go along with the politically correct narrative even if the argument itself reveals a shocking level of double standards.[4]

In other words, those people who are totally secular and do not hold any beliefs are more susceptible to social engineering and propaganda, as opposed to those people who do hold beliefs who protest against the system. However, as Christianity proved in the first few centuries of the first millennium, their non-violent stand against the authorities of the day eventually won through. The world order in the end gave way to Christianity, which was an incredible achievement.

The reality is that the Elite are seeking to influence the World's Religions, and not just Christianity, but all of them, to try and make them converge and form a New World Religion - a syncretic religion with their State authority in the centre of it. Amongst the largest religious groups there are currently 2.4 billion Christians, 1.8 billion Muslims, 1.1 billion Hindus and 1.1 billion secular Agnostics / Atheists / non-religious people.[5] There are more people in one of these religious groups than there are in many countries, so if you think the Elite would not wish to affect or change religion you would be mistaken. Faith is an important part of controlling the populace and so if you can effect change across just one of these areas you will have gained power.

The most obvious group that the Elite would want to gain control over is Catholicism since they are comprised of 1.2 billion people making this the largest overall single grouping. Furthermore they supposedly take their lead from only one man, the Pope. The Pope can make Encyclicals, decrees, or wishes that he would want his flock to adhere to. If you want to affect those 1.2 billion then you only

---

[4] For more on this please see Edward Bernays, *Propaganda*, 1928.

[5] Number of people in each Religion- 'Major Religious Groups' Source Wikipedia.

have one man and his administration to go through. It shouldn't come as a surprise to notice that the Elite have managed to infiltrate and subvert Catholicism in a fundamental manner, and the direction they have taken it is to make Catholicism more 'green,' ecumenical and multi-faith.

The strategy is to have Catholicism as the ecumenical centre for Christianity, and try to make other denominations join forces with them. For interfaithism, which is the same term as ecumenical except for other religions, the strategy has been to syncretise them (join together), into the New World religion with Catholicism again at the centre with the Pope at the top. We should not be surprised to see that 'multi-faithism' is the direction the Catholic Church is going in. At Pope Francis' very first Ecumenical meeting he pushed the slow gradualist agenda of bringing the Muslims into the Christian fold.

"I then greet and cordially thank you all, dear friends belonging to other religious traditions; first of all the Muslims, **who worship the one God**, living and **merciful**, and call upon Him in prayer, and all of you. I really appreciate your presence: in it I see a tangible sign of the will to grow in mutual esteem and cooperation for the common good of humanity."

Emphasis added. Merciful is an obvious reference to Islam as having the same God. We shall cover this later.

Pope Francis' Encyclical in November 2015 was also a complete sign up to the establishment's Climate Change and green global agenda - a signing into Agenda 21. This 185 page Encyclical called for Catholics to confront environmental degradation and <u>climate change</u>, and contained a harsh critique of consumerism and irresponsible polluting living, with a plea at the end (as always!) for swift and unified *global* action. In other words he did exactly as the Elite wanted, no doubt cajoled by George Soros and his Open Foundation which we know from leaked emails has influence over the Papacy.[6]

But why would the Elite want to make Catholicism more 'green'? Well, as will be shown, it's for the purpose of bringing the World's religions into line with Agenda 21 and the new Sustainable Economy

---

[6] Soros influence of the Papacy
http://remnantnewspaper.com/web/index.php/articles/item/2718-the-pope-s-boss

they are trying to create. It's also, from a more religious perspective, about creating **'common ground'** into which all the Worlds' religions can be bolted and joined together. It's to create allegiance to Agenda 21.

Agenda 21

Agenda 21 is one of the most important political documents humanity has ever seen.[7] It was the main outcome of the United Nation's Earth Summit held in Rio de Janeiro in 1992, and it was the first time that the UN's vision for a centrally managed global society came into view. This contract will end up binding governments around the world to the United Nation's plan for controlling the way we live, eat, move, learn and communicate - all under the noble banner of saving Mother Earth. Agenda 21 is the action plan to inventory and control every human being on the planet, every country and piece of land, all water, all minerals, all plants, trees, animals, and all the means of production of any type. It also includes controlling all energy, and all information and educational establishments. It seeks to store all the world's information and data and have government involvement in every aspect of our lives. At the moment this new system is slowly being interwoven into policy decisions at the highest level and they are promoting it at every opportunity and so it seems more than likely that this is the direction in which they want to take humanity. Agenda 21 makes a mockery of the rights of the individual who would end up living in a collective, without any ownership of property or means of creating or storing wealth. It demotes mankind to a resource. It's full of the politically correct jargon on 'Sustainable Development', educational jargon and social adjustments – it's actually a kind of naïve wish list of the desires for humanity to grow into the Utopian New Age Society the Elite want for the world.

---

[7] A free download of the Agenda 21 PDF can be found here.
https://sustainabledevelopment.un.org/content/documents/Agenda21.pdf

The 350-page document basically assumes that people are not good stewards of their land and that government will do a better job. It really seeks to hand authority, decision making and sovereignty to a committee of unelected UN bureaucrats.[8] Individual rights in general give way to the needs of the community as determined by the state. This makes it a type of Communitarianism and from the point of view of the State, a collectivist economy. This is what it says - it is not a conspiracy theory! It says this in black and white. We can either disbelieve this as somehow a message to scare the populace, or they are publishing all sorts of documents all the time which are irrelevant and should be ignored! If this is the case then why are they continually promoting this Agenda? We need to take this seriously; the Elite take this seriously and have constructed an entire New World Economy based on it.

Dee Hock of Visa Credit Card fame (who we look at later in connection with URI) also stated:-

"We are at the very point in time when a 400-year-old age is dying and another is struggling to be born- a shifting of culture, science, society, and institutions enormously greater than the world has ever experienced."[9]

Christina Figueres, Executive Secretary of the UN said, "This is the first time in the history of mankind that we are setting ourselves the task of intentionally, within a defined period of time, to change the economic development model that has been reigning for at least the last 150 years, since the industrial revolution."[10]

The question is, changing the economy to what? To the New International Economic Order spoken of by the Trilateral Commission, Socialist International, a few other high level Elite politicians, and what the UN calls Agenda 21. This is their plan for this century and it involves the roll out of a centrally administered, globally controlled monetary system with its own new global culture. It is not democratic and it not based on supply and demand.

---

[8] See Agenda 21, page 347 section 40.8.

[9] Michael Waldrop, The Trillion Dollar vision of Dee Hock from First Company Magazine, October 1996.

[10] Read here: http://dailycaller.com/2015/02/05/climate-chief-world-economy/#ixzz4VZKVeEea

This New International Economic Order is really bad news for us, the normal man on the street because it's not based on individual freedoms, democracy and the rights of mankind, but is a top down enforced system, in which the government is all wise, and all powerful, where the people must serve the State. Overall Agenda 21 is the building of a Totalitarian State which has the element of top down authority. It will also be from bottom up, because people will **have to conform** to its dictates or else get locked out of the system, and not be able to have access to the infrastructure of society. For example, dissenters will be locked out of the energy grid, or have to conform to buying food from various State regulated shops or not have access to the Internet or Television. It's a bit like having your debit or credit card cancelled so you can't buy goods and services since you have been blacklisted. Or like having a bad credit score so you can't get a loan or mortgage - those people who do not conform to Society will be unable to live properly under its dictates. We are already seeing China build social credit scores including information on how likely this person is to adhere to the State's dictates. Politically active people dissenting against the system get worse scores than the 'socially responsible' non-dissenters.[11] In this manner they will control the masses via the roll out of this New Economy which in the final form will be an energy-based economy. If you refuse to behave by the dictates and laws coming from the top down you will be locked out and unable to access modern life.

There will also be no property rights of ownership, something which Agenda 21 only alludes to. The Global Biodiversity Assessment which expanded on Agenda 21 states that **usufruct laws** will be enacted. This will mean that licenses will have to be applied for 'rights' of ownership. This type of legal structure goes back to Roman times. The user or (*usus*) of the property is allowed to create a return and enjoy its fruits (*fructus*) but only according to the license which has been granted by the legal owner. This is how the UN will grab all the world's property and land, by making the values of the land worthless since the license involved will become so expensive

---

[11] For more on this check Social Credit Scoring see articles such as
http://www.wired.co.uk/article/chinese-government-social-credit-score-privacy-invasion)

and onerous the owners will be forced to sell.[12] Overall this is why farmers are being slowly squeezed out of their livelihoods to give way to the large corporate agri-businesses which is all part of their long-range plan - to control the food supply.

Eventually the economy which emerges will be one based on an 'energy currency' in which environmentalism and protecting the planet will be 'the excuse' used to enforce this. This will be the top down approach and regulation that Agenda 21 will bring in.

It is not irresponsible to believe in this - it is irresponsible to not believe in this, since the evidence points in this direction! It is not the case that conspiracists have made connections that are not there. It is the case that the media, and the political and economic commentators have not made the connections that are there! This is because they have bought into the propaganda and believed the media indoctrination. They are also guilty of under estimating the effects of secret meetings and societies where influential people make decisions to subvert the political process and activities of the governments they supposedly represent; and bring into effect a totally new political and legal framework in an under hand and crafty manner as part of their overall power grab.

Amending the World's Religions

In order to reach their controlled Scientific dictatorship they also need to amend the World's Religions. In HG Well's book, The Open Conspiracy: Blue Prints for a World Revolution, we can see the long terms plans of the Elite Network and how, in the end, it will culminate in a World Religion. *"The political world of the Open Conspiracy must weaken, efface, incorporate, and supersede existing governments. The Open Conspiracy is the natural inheritor of socialist and communist enthusiasms; it may be in control of Moscow before it is in control of New York. The character of the Open Conspiracy will now be plainly displayed. It will be a world religion."* Emphasis mine.

---

[12] See Global Biodiversity Assessment 12.7.5.

It's not only Christianity which is being affected and moulded. Islam, of the right type (good Islam) is also being brought into the 'Brotherhood of Man', the New World system, via the Organisation of Islamic Co-operation (OIC). The OIC was founded in 1969 and now has 57 member countries representing a total population of over 1.6 billion. From their website www.oic-oci.org it states:

"The Organization is the collective voice of the Muslim world. It endeavors to safeguard and protect the interests of the Muslim world in the spirit of promoting international peace and harmony among various people of the world."

Underpinning the OIC is the Cairo Declaration of Human Rights which is based on a strict interpretation of Sharia Law. Within its dictates there is no room for conversion to other religions and in general women in Islamic societies may not be treated as equally as in the west. But it doesn't matter to the international community that any of the 'rights' might be a bit far off from western human rights as long as the OIC and the countries it represents sign into the Green Agenda - they can believe what they want for the moment! The hidden government just want to make sure Islam is going in the right direction and signed into the Green Environmental agenda of Agenda 21, which of course it is, and so the OIC has been brought into the fold.

Hinduism has also signed into the agenda, but it has been fairly late on the scene which is interesting in itself, but then obvious, since Hinduism is a natural fit into the Pantheistic 'global environmental green movement' that they seek to espouse. Hindu writings such as the Upanishads and Vedas speak of the world being alive and teeming with life from the god-head. It is a religion filled with spiritual and poetic references to Mother Earth, where every living thing has an 'atman' which is the inner living soul, which is the closest concept to god who lives throughout all creation. It's a belief where trees, mountains and rocks can be made into shrines, and rivers are respected as a source and support for physical and spiritual life. It is an ideal religion for Agenda 21 which obliges believers to defend the environment and recognise that nature and ecosystems hold the fabric of the planet together via Mother Earth. In fact, India was the birth place of the New Age Religion via Madame Blavatsky which we look at in some detail later on.

For the Humanists, the Elite wish to **encase humanity in the material world** and so, they have been endlessly 'beating the drum' of Atheism and Scientism for decades. Even though we humans can only see about 5% of the entire spectrum of reality we are still taught that we have to see, feel and touch anything before we can believe in it. It has been their aim and goal to destroy the fabric of any faith and to replace it with the shifting sands of Scientism, and in so doing they are able to control vast numbers of humanity to whatever the beliefs are at that time, to suit the Elite.

The belief in a God has been reduced to the 100% certainty of what is true or untrue, even though any truth can never really be fully known. According to mainstream science God does not exist, because He is not provable. So people who believe in God are deluded and living under an ancient primitive superstition. Scientific principles can demonstrate many things but eventually if you dig deep enough into those principles there always comes a point at which something can't be explained and so we return back to Scientism for the answer. This therefore makes Science a belief in itself, just as is Religion. So modern Science has just as many unproven myths such as the Big Bang and Evolution as Religion. Although empirical evidence does indeed perhaps offer the most secure world view for the Secular Humanist, it does not offer ALL the answers and even Science admits this. That doesn't mean we should abandon reason and plum for any belief, but it does mean we should be even handed with the available evidence and make informed choices recognising there is a place for religious belief and scientific beliefs. To think otherwise would be being dishonest to the truth. We should therefore recognise that there is a place for belief and therefore, at the final analysis of life and deep down within the spiritual centre of your being or soul, you have to make a choice, to accept or reject God.

To the Elite, ALL of this knowledge must be skewed to the belief in no god. It makes their job much easier! If the masses are brought to believe in Lucifer it would by default substantiate the existence of God. And so, we have generally seen the ridiculing of anyone who believes in a God, and especially Christianity. In this manner vast sections of Western Society have given up on Christianity and turned to a secular humanist world view based on Science which as mentioned is itself a system based on belief. The only problem with this is that it's so easy to **make the State the authority** on knowledge and not the Bible and its revealed truth, or any other faith - and even if untrue, the fabrications of these faiths still have a place in modern society, and that is in **keeping people away from the clutches of the State.**

To the Elite their religion is Freemasonry, Luciferianism, (Hermeticism, and the Kabbalah); and for the masses it's Atheism. In the future the Elite wish to replace the World's Religions with their own system of beliefs. This will look like a type of Humanistic Pantheistic behavioural control religion, leading to the emergence of their pure Luciferian doctrine which is really their goal.

Before we can look at what the New World Religion will look like, we need to look at 'the theory' of New World Religion from its start. Later on, we discover who the Elite Cryptocracy are and their main beliefs. With all these elements in place the enormity of their plan for the 21st Century is revealed.

CHAPTER 2

THE ORIGIN OF THE NEW WORLD
RELIGION

The Bible teaches that Mankind is in a fallen state, removed from God and blinded by Satan. Ever since ancient times rulers have sought to enslave their subjects and rule over them for their own benefit. The culmination of this plan being the setting up of the One World Government. The first time this attempt was made back in the Bible days of Nimrod. In Genesis Chapter 11 we have the story of the **Tower of Babel**. A classic story probably written around the 8th Century by the Yahwist Bible Source {know as J}, which runs from Genesis 2:2b to the end of 1 Kings Chapter 2.[13] Material from this goes back much further and some stories are similar to what were well know Sumerian stories from the Third Millennium. Some academics insist the Yahwist source is post-exilic, but it is the Priestly (P) source which is later.

The Tower represents the Religious aspect, and the City of Babel represents the State, and so both elements of Religion and the State were in unity together as the world's first State Religion. Men spoke the same language and the people wanted to 'make a name for themselves' (Genesis 11:4) and be 'one race' (verse 6), unified in the making of a tower which would reach heaven to take over God.

In Genesis 11:3-9 it states:

---

[13] Richard Elliot Friedman, The Hidden Book In the Bible see Chapter 1. Harper Collins 1998.

They said to each other, "Come, let's make bricks and bake them thoroughly." They used brick instead of stone, and tar for mortar.

4 Then they said, "Come, let us build ourselves a city, with a tower that reaches to the heavens, so that we may **make a name for ourselves**; otherwise we will be scattered over the face of the whole earth."

5 But the LORD came down to see the city and the tower the people were building.

6 The LORD said, "If as **one people speaking the same language** they have begun to do this, then **nothing they plan to do will be impossible for them.**

7 Come, let us go down and confuse their language so they will not understand each other."

8 So the LORD scattered them from there over all the earth, and they stopped building the city.

9 That is why it was called Babel —because there the LORD confused the language of the whole world. From there the LORD scattered them over the face of the whole earth. (NIV)

God did not want the people to be **one,** and all have **one language** since this would have meant 'nothing they plan to do will be impossible to them' and hence it would have destroyed God's long-term purposes for mankind. Nothing will be impossible when man ends up speaking one language. He will become like god in terms of technological power and knowledge. The Tower of Babel Story is often interpreted as being the etiological story of how mankind produced different languages, but the deeper meaning is that with one language the dictates of the rulers could be forcibly administered and so it was the first attempt at a State authorised Religion united against God.[14] Mankind 'made a name for himself', in other words, Man had replaced God as the object of worship.

The Tower itself was built in the plain of Babylon, and it was a man-made structure which could be seen from miles away which became the focus for the outlying regions, in rebelling against God.

---

[14] See also Flavius Josephus, The Antiquities of the Jews. Chapter 4.

In the same way that God came down from heaven to sort the mess out, so it will be at the End Times when Jesus Christ returns to stop the New World Order from its path of man being worshiped as God and the Battle of man against God takes place - Armageddon. This is the completion of human History and what the conspirators are working towards – to make themselves and their god the object of worship, above God. The Tower of Babel, which has become stylised as the Pyramid, or Ziggurat, represents the **'un-accomplished'** work of Satan and his kingdom, the first attempt at World Government. It was put in tatters by God who in the end acted and did something dramatic. He came down to earth and scattered the people and divided their language.[15]

Nimrod was the theoretical start of the Elite ruling over mankind via secret hidden agreements normally via Secret Societies. The prediction of solar eclipses or astronomical observations could be very convincing for the conversion of the credulous masses. From ancient times these Societies or Cults created religions around them as a type of control mechanism to help with the functioning of government. In the ancient World there were many Secret Societies and the top men in them formed a Council which used to meet and so over time they all became connected. Every now and again throughout history we see the same Cult being expressed and emerging as a Philosophy or Secret group, and then it disappears again into the underground only to emerge later in a similar format. This cult is given the name 'Mystery Babylon' in Revelation and refers to all the religious and apostate beliefs of any non-Christian belief system.

The unifying principle at the highest levels of Mystery Babylon is the concept that by Initiation and via a secret knowledge the Elite are able and deserve to rule over the horde of masses, via the divine spark or fire of the intellect. For example, after Nimrod we have the Egyptian Pharaonic Cult (mentioned in Genesis and Exodus) which helped keep the Rulers in power and controlled the struggling masses below. The populace of Egypt lived in a highly stratified

---

[15] J Micha-el Hayes, Rise of the New World Order, The Culling of Man. Kindle Loc 1644 following. Or Glenn Beck
http://www.foxnews.com/story/2010/11/17/glenn-beck-lessons-from-tower-babel.html)

community with the Rulers at the top, then the Government Officials, then the Soldiers, Merchants, Craftsmen and Peasants, and the poor Slaves at the bottom. A related Cult emerged in Greece with Pythagoras in the 6th Century who plagiarised many concepts from the Egyptians (including their Maths), and 3 centuries later Plato, all of which then reached into Roman times and their Equestrian Orders. These secret societies went underground and emerged in various forms such as the Assassins, or Knight Templars and later on Rosicrucians. They have always existed and their presence on the world stage has always been central to how the world has been moulded. The men of the Inner Circle view themselves as descendants of this historical heritage and mystical inheritors of the great secrets.

This is Mystery Babylon, and the 'Spirit of Babylon' is still tying today to complete the work started by Nimrod (Revelation 17:5, Mystery Babylon). The EU even chose a picture of Bruegel's painting of the Tower of Babel for one of its posters and there is even the Bruegel Institute which is another economic think tank named after the painter. It is from the secret cult that we have, on the back of the One Dollar bill, the pyramid with the All-Seeing Eye coming down onto the pyramid or frustum to complete the work. The Triangle with the All-Seeing Eye is the Eye of Horus, and the star Sirius, The Great Architect of the Universe (TGAOTU) of Freemasonry. The words 'Annuit coeptis' on the one dollar bill means, 'He favours our undertaking', where Annuit means He favours, (and could possibly also refer to the Sumerian sky god Anu.) The 'He' referring to the All-Seeing Eye since the eye is there in the picture, and this cannot possibly be God or Jesus but is an occult motif. 'Novus ordo seclorum' means 'New order of the ages' and refers to the Great Plan which is what they call the New World Order. You don't have to stretch things at all to get to this logical conclusion! This is what it says! This is the ultimate completion of their Religion coming down to man on earth. So we can see that, at the Tower of Babel, Satan tries to take over the word via a world leader. Freemasonry has numerous references to Nimrod and Tubal Cain both of whom are portrayed as being bad in the Bible and yet for Freemasons they are portrayed as being good! Nimrod was a mighty hunter *against* God or else God would not have scattered them or forced them to change from what they were doing.

The equivalent parallel story to the Tower of Babel, is in Revelation where Jesus has to come down to prevent man from worshipping the Beast and God brings about the close of the age – 'the Regeneration' and later the New Heaven and New Earth (Revelation 22) with the New City of Jerusalem, not a Pyramid. Hence the book cover, you can choose between either the New City of Jerusalem, or, the Pyramid coming to earth. These are the only options - light and dark, good or evil, the Lord Jesus Christ as God, or Satan.

This is how things are today, the same evil 'Cult of Fire' is still in existence and - 'In her (Mystery Babylon) was found the blood of prophets and of the saints, and of **ALL** who have been killed on the earth.' Revelation 18:24 (NIV). This is one of the most important verses in the Bible to understanding who has been fighting Mankind since the Fall - the cult of Mystery Babylon. They have been responsible for all the deaths on the earth from the start.

The Temptation of Christ

The other scripture which helps to explain the New World Order and how the world is in the grip of the Devil, is the Temptation. Jesus is shown all the Nations of the earth and told that if he worships the Devil He would be given **all the Kingdoms of the world**.

Luke 4 verse 5 following: Then the devil, taking Him up on a high mountain, showed Him all the kingdoms of the world in a moment of time. [6] And the devil said to Him, "All this authority I will give You, and their glory; for *this* has been delivered to me, and I give it to whomever I wish. [7] Therefore, if You will worship before me, all will be Yours." [8] And Jesus answered and said to him, "Get behind Me, Satan! For it is written, 'You shall worship the LORD your God, and Him only you shall serve.'

This event presupposes that Satan owned all the nations already. Although God is in charge, Satan holds a huge amount of power over the affairs of men, he is the 'god of this world' and has been given authority over the world as a result of the Fall. It is Satan who is driving the New World Order forward and this is why it is taking so long to accomplish - many lifetimes and thousands of years in fact.

Also, according to this story, nation States are the best way for mankind to conduct their business and the Bible states they will always exist. It's not trading blocs or super-states that should be the manner in which nations conduct their business, and neither should it be a race to the bottom where the strongest out-competes the inefficient. It should be nation states in communication with each other pulling forward in the same direction for the good of Humanity. Not striving for a 'more global integrated society' for the Elite with the same regimented economic laws and greyed out beliefs - this is not the correct direction for humanity to be going in.

It is interesting to note just how important worship is, since presumably Jesus could have worshiped the Devil for a moment and then taken control of the entire Earth. The repercussions of this would have been disastrous because it would have meant Jesus circumvented the Cross and in so doing, created a worldly empire of worldly glory, but not a spiritual Kingdom which is what the Kingdom of God is: 'The Kingdom of God is within you' (Luke 17:21). There would have been no Atonement and so God would have become unable to commune with Man since there was no Cross, and as such it would have nullified not only the Prophecies of the Old Testament but the entire fabric of creation, since God spoke the Universe into existence and so his Word would have been nullified. 'Heaven and Earth will pass away but my words shall never pass away'. (Mark 13:31). Jesus was the Divine Logos, the Word. The severe consequences from this Temptation would have been un-imaginable, yet alone the fact that it would have made God a liar!

One World Government with a One World Religion

The Book of Revelation also predicts the emergence of a One World Government lead by a World Leader in which all the nations have to worship and receive the mark of the beast - (Revelation 13:7&8). And he (the anti-Christ) was given authority over every tribe, people, language and nation. All inhabitants of the earth will worship the beast...'

Mankind will not only worship the beast which is a Man, but it will be the Luciferian religion made manifest, which will be the most awful culmination point in all of human history. Later on, Revelation refers to the economy and how it will be impossible to buy food without being in the system of the beast. Revelation 13:7: 'no-one could buy or sell unless he had the mark, which is the name of the beast or the number of his name.'

(Daniel 2:35). But a rock, not made out of human hands, will strike the statute, which represents the beast system, and will become a huge mountain that fills the whole earth. This is the message in the Old Testament that God himself will overcome the beast system in the last days.

The Proto-Evangelium

The roots of the belief in the final encounter of God with Man at the end of time go deep and are important to review. The Patriarchs of Genesis, such as Adam, Seth, Methuselah, Noah and Lamech etc knew about **God's Redemptive Plan** because God had told Adam and Eve in the Garden that he would send a Saviour to bring mankind back to himself and eventually wrap up the Heavens and the Earth - they knew the full redemptive story. The **Proto-Evangelium** is God's statement to Mankind and the Serpent that "I will put enmity between thee and the woman, and between thy seed and her seed; it shall bruise thy head, and thou shalt bruise his **heel**." (Genesis 3:15, KJV). This is the first reference in the Bible, to the Saviour overcoming Satan. That the seed of the woman will overcome the devil -- an incredible prophecy only fulfilled by Jesus.

This why Masons roll up their trouser leg when they start the first Degree of Freemasonry as an Entered Apprentice, it is to expose the **heel** identifying themselves with the supposed uncompleted work that Satan will overcome God, in their view.

Entered Apprentice

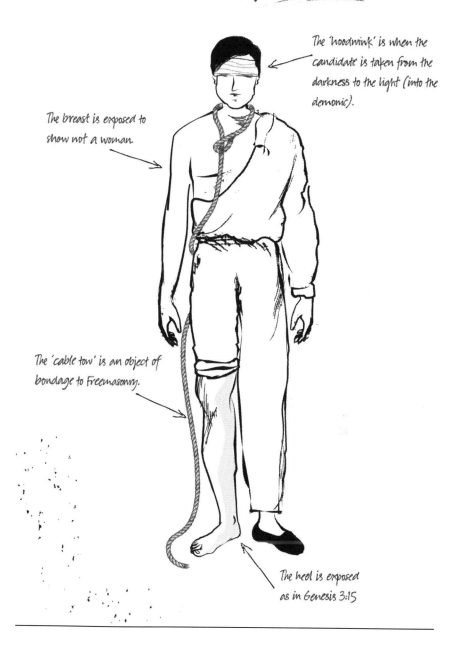

The 'hoodwink' is when the candidate is taken from the darkness to the light (into the demonic).

The breast is exposed to show not a woman.

The 'cable tow' is an object of bondage to Freemasonry.

The heel is exposed as in Genesis 3:15

The exoteric belief (outer belief) they are told is that God will overcome Satan, but as with all things Masonic it is always an inversion of the truth. As the initiate is led deeper and deeper into the demonic he will know that the esoteric (inner secret meaning) is that this is actually a way of acknowledging the narrative that Satan did pierce the feet of Jesus on the Cross, and in this manner, they are revelling in the work of Satan.

The Serpent would bite Jesus' feet and Jesus would bruise Satan's head. The teeth marks of the serpent were the nails of the cross. The letter W in archaic Hebrew is a picture of a nail, and is in the divine name, YHWH. 'The God of peace will soon crush Satan under your feet'. (Romans 16:20).

This knowledge of the Salvific purposes of God became warped, and so, during Nimrod's time, the religion which they set up became a counterfeit of the long-range Gospel story which became the world's first universal religion.[16]

The original story of the Proto-evangelium was subverted and twisted by Nimrod to form the first State Religion and this was the belief in Marduk, Shamash and Ishtar which was the **fertility Sun worshipping religion** which gave birth to all the later offshoot religions and secret societies. For example, Ra or Re in Egyptian religion, Baal in Syria, Philistines and Phoenicians, Bel (Assyrian) and Moloch (Ammonite) are all the same manifestation of the same Sun god. From Babylon these beliefs spread across the trade routes of the ancient world and so from this we have the main threads of the Egyptian, Greek, and Indian religions. This is why in Revelation the false religion is called Mystery Babylon, and is also represented by the sickle of Chronos or Saturn slashing throughout human history since the Fall.

So ever since the start of time Satan has tried to subvert the history of humanity towards the One World Government with

---

[16] Nimrod could refer to Tukulti-Ninurta 1243-1206 BC King of Assyria since he was the first person to rule over all Babylonia (cf Gen 10:10). See Interpreters Bible Encyclopaedia. The religion of the Ancient Near East was basically Polytheism - the belief in many gods, with Shamash being the Sun god, Sin the moon god, and Ninurta god of hunting, hence Nimrod being a mighty hunter *against* God. The date does seem rather late since the traditional Bible date reads nearer 2000 BC, but in any event this could easily refer to an earlier Nimrod.

himself at the centre and his subjects, as 'one race' plugged into the 'transhumanist hive network' which is now being set up. All of this in antipathy to God. Cain against Abel, man killing man in murder and war, until: "All who dwell on earth will worship him" - the beast. (Revelation 13:8). Empires have risen and fallen, countries have been formed and disappeared, Kings have made decrees and been deposed. All the while the unseen hand of Satan has been leading the Cryptocracy which has been directing mankind towards the ultimate conclusion of the One World Government with himself in the centre in anti-thesis to God. (Revelation 13:3b-4). "All the world marvelled and followed the beast. So they worshiped the dragon (Satan) who gave authority to the beast; and they worshiped the beast (the political government and the Anti-Christ) saying: 'Who is like the beast? Who is able to make war with him?'" (Revelation 13:4c).

This is what the Bible says; that deception upon deception will take man to the brink of existence and that the affairs of mankind have been directed towards a climactic end time. This is perhaps why Shakespeare wrote: 'All the world is a stage and all the men and women merely players.' He was referring to the entire 'cosmic play' which we see in this Biblical conspiratorial view of history.

It's interesting to note, at this point, that just about more is written in the Bible about the 'End Times' and the 7 Year Tribulation period than any other time, even including the years Jesus was on earth. Satan's final reign will only be 7 years, but the lead up to this time is happening now and has been ongoing for the last six thousand years. In the end, it is God who is in control, and God will always overcome evil since **God is sovereign.**

Prisca Theologia

Prisca Theologia is the occult belief that in antiquity God revealed a true religion to man and that all religions have a kernel of this truth embedded within. The word Prisca comes from the Latin meaning 'old', and theologia is obviously theology, so it means 'old theology'. This false belief is derived from the body of books supposedly written by ancient sages who were believed to pre-date even the Greek philosophers and to record divine revelations that paralleled God's revelation in the Bible. These sages included Zoroaster and the ORACULA CHALDAICA (Chaldean Oracles), allegedly representing the primordial wisdom of the Persians and Babylonians. It is also supposedly contained in the writings of Hermes Trismegestus in the Corpus Hermeticum, which preserves the wisdom of the Egyptian priests. Pythagoras managed to pass this ancient knowledge onto Plato and other writers such as Plotinus, Porphyry, Iamblicus, and Proclus, and this in turn survived to the post-Renaissance commentators. Obviously throughout time, the beliefs have become distorted and mixed with other concepts and diluted or amended according to the agenda of the writers themselves.

This belief is central to Occultism which is all about unearthing the hidden secret wisdom which used to exist in the past. It is related to the concept of an original religion either in the garden of Eden, or as a more occult Atlantis as a pre-diluvian civilization of immense purity and strength. This, we can recognize as being the **distorted Proto-Evangelium of Genesis**, which is the true source of walking with God. Later on, the belief of a world Saviour became distorted and distilled into the Babylonian Mystery Religion depicted at the Tower of Babel story. This is what Freemasonry tries to uncover and why Masons spend years reading occult books to try to get to the core of what the ancient beliefs were. This is because of their belief in the ancient religion - the Prisca Theologia, they seek to redefine Christianity towards a type of 'Hermetic Emanationism' and to return humanity to this theoretical golden age.

During the Renaissance writers such as Francis Bacon, with his book The New Atlantis - and Thomas More with Utopia, would pick up on this idea and develop it to something which eventually affected the development of the new country of Atlantis: America. In this manner the early developers of America were generally pushing this occult agenda for the 'New World' to be the first occult theocracy.[17]

---

[17] Manly P Hall, covers off this occultic belief in 'The Secret Destiny of America'.

What is the Great Plan?

Freemasonry is one of the most prevalent and easily discernible belief systems of the Elite. Many top Politicians and Statesmen within the Network adhere to this Religion. This does not necessarily mean that Freemasonry is of massive political importance, or has massive power, but it does mean that the Elite believe in it, or are indoctrinated into its tenets. **The Great Plan** of Freemasonry, (and one of their greatest secrets), is that The Great Architect of the Universe, (TGAOTU) which is their God, would eventually **establish the Kingdom of their 'God' on earth**. This Utopian plan originated far back into antiquity but was brought forward and emerged in its modern form around the 16th Century in England.

Albert Pike, (1809-1891) was a high-level Freemason and Confederate general who referred to Freemasonry as the 'custodian' or special guardian of these occult secrets and his writings reveal the hidden agenda of his institution, which is the formation of the Luciferic One World Government. This is only supposedly known to those initiates at the higher degrees. Those members of the outer order have to work to gain their knowledge and are subjected to various ordeals and 'levels' before they can receive the supposed deeper insight, and so they are completely ignorant of what their society does. It is like a cancer on humanity eating away at the worlds establishments and skewing them towards the Luciferian way of life of the Freemason. We explore this in Chapter 7.

Freemasonry's Kingdom of God is in complete antithesis to the Christian version of the Millennial Kingdom which arrives after the Seven Year Tribulation. This is the highest and most important part of the Great Plan but it does also include the development of the One World Government (the Political sphere) with Lucifer and his Anti-Christ ruling over mankind and the False prophet. (Revelation 17). The economy is represented by 'the beast' which is both the Anti-Christ and the economic system, since those in the beast system will be unable to buy or sell.

In order to achieve this, Albert Pike is **supposed** to have written a letter to Guiseppe Mazzini who was an Italian high Freemason explaining how the long-range plan of the Elite was to ferment three

World Wars the conclusion of which would be mankind under their Luciferian doctrine. This was written in 1871.

"We shall unleash the Nihilist and Atheists, and we shall provoke a formidable social cataclysm which in all its horror will show clearly to the nations the effect of absolute atheism, origin of savagery and of the most bloody turmoil. Then everywhere, the citizens, obliged to defend themselves against the world minority of revolutionaries, will exterminate those destroyers of civilization, and the multitude, disillusioned with Christianity, whose deistic spirits will from that moment be without compass or direction, anxious for an ideal, but without knowing where to render its adoration, will receive the true light through **the universal manifestation of the pure doctrine of Lucifer,** *brought finally out in the public view. This manifestation will result from the general reactionary movement which will follow* **the destruction of Christianity and atheism,** *both conquered and exterminated at the same time."* Emphasis added.

This letter was supposed to have been at the British Library and hung on the wall there but seems to have become lost, or there is a rumour that it was removed by Baron Rothschild when he became a Director of the Museum in 1977. Whatever the truth of this letter, Freemasonry is a vital part of the roll out of the New World religion. It's interesting to note that the political and religious institutions surrounding this roll out have many Freemasonry member within their ranks.[18]

Theosophy - The Great Plan

The Theosophists, such as Alice A Bailey, who is also a big part of this overall story, have written about the Great Plan, and it means the same as in Freemasonry. In fact in the Lucis Trust's 'Great

---

[18] Possibly, and probably this letter is most likely a hoax. Certainly it seems doubtful that the term Zionism was in use in 1871. The letter itself being dated 15th August 1871 it would have foretold both World War I and II, and even who would be the agents of World War III which will be according to this letter, and if it true, the Arab World against Political Zionism. William Guy Carr wrote this in his book 'Pawns in the Game' (Loc 220) quoted from Cardinal Caro y Rodriguez of Santiago, Chile, who saw this letter in 1925 from his book, The Mystery of Freemasonry Unveiled

Invocation' which the United Nations is keen to promote, there is in the last line of their 'prayer': 'Let Light and Love and Power restore **the Plan** on Earth.' What is the Plan? The plan for the Lucis Trust and Theosophy is the One World Government with the Church Universal which is emerging now and is a type of Apostate Christianity mixed in with all other world religions and given a green, Pantheistic 'gloss'. I quote from the Externalisation of the Hierarchy by Alice A Bailey, emphasis added[19]:-

"**Eventually, there will appear the Church Universal**, and its definite outlines will appear towards the close of this century. In this connection, forget not the wise prophecy of H.P.B. as touching events at the close of this century. This Church will be nurtured into activity by the Christ and His disciples **when the outpouring of the Christ principle**, the true second Coming, has been accomplished. No date for the advent do I set, but the time will not be long."

This is not the Christian Church which is being spoke of here, and Jesus is not 'the Christ principle' either, but the **Theosophic Church Universal in which all mankind will be United in diversity together**. It is the New World Religion, although as we will find out later this will be a religion slightly different to what the Theosophists think.

Theosophy teaches that the Hierarchy are acting from Shambhala, which is like their heaven, and 'impressing' their opinions on the leaders of the world for the good of humanity. But in reality Theosophy is the inversion of the true Plan from God and so evil masquerades as good, and the affairs of man are affected towards the full materialisation, or 'externalisation of the Hierarchy'. This will be the physical appearance of the terrible and terrifying demonic one world State which will lead to the religious, hive-mind, transhumanist, global police state.

Alice A Bailey further explains the strategy for the Plan in her book 'The Externalisation of the Hierarchy'.

*"1. The reorganisation of the world religions—if in **any way possible**— so that their out-of-date theologies, their narrow-minded emphasis and their*

---

[19] Alice A Bailey, *The Externalisation of the Hierarchy*, page 270 and 271.

ridiculous belief that they know what is in the Mind of God may be offset, in order that the churches may eventually be the recipients of spiritual inspiration.

2. The gradual dissolution—again if **in any way possible**—*of the orthodox Jewish faith, with its obsolete teaching, its separative emphasis, its hatred of the Gentiles and its failure to recognise* **the Christ***. In saying this I do not fail to recognise those Jews throughout the world who acknowledge the evils and who are not orthodox in their thinking; they belong to the aristocracy of spiritual belief to which the Hierarchy itself belongs.*

3. Preparation for a revelation which will inaugurate the new era and set the note for the **new world religion.** *"*

Emphasis mine. Here we have it DIRECT from her writings! She is saying that the two groups which pose the greatest threat to the externalisation of the New World Religion are orthodox, or traditional, Bible believing Christianity, and orthodox Judaism, and that **they should be removed** 'in any way possible' so that 'the churches may eventually be the recipients of spiritual inspiration.' It sounds like replacing true Christianity with their version of Apostate Christianity which is a polite way of saying Luciferianism. They are trying to replace the current Church with a different set of beliefs; and all this from the most important Spiritual influence on the United Nations, who, as we will see later on, have been heavily promoting precisely the agenda of Alice A Bailey. In fact, Robert Muller, Maurice Strong and other highly influential and important members of the UN admit that they have been heavily indebted to the writings and influence of Alice A Bailey who they see as their Prophet. Robert Muller has even openly said that the World Core Curriculum, which is a new set of educational suggestions, is based on the teachings of Alice A Bailey. All of this is covered later.

New Agers

The New Age religion is a re-worked and modernised version of Theosophy and its tenets are, to all intents and purposes, the same beliefs, and so the same ultimate goal of these myriad New age Religions is also the new Church Universal. This is not the Church of Christ, but the Church of THE Christ, in which man is seen as 'a god', which thereby completely denies the existence of a personal God. "A World Religion for the New Age... is needed to meet the needs of thinking people... and to unify mankind."[20]

The New World Religion is strongly supported by the Cryptocracy who wish to grey out humanity and make all people believe the same thing. The tools in their arsenal are the same they have used to coerce the Lesbian, Gay, Bisexual, Transgender (LGBT) agenda, and so the Cryptocracy's secret think tanks have been busy thinking up ways to create a new system of beliefs with themselves at the top as the Gods, and the masses at the bottom as their drone-workers. This fits in precisely with their beliefs which go back to Plato who expounded the theory of the state with the Elite in control dictating their wishes to the masses below. Influential leaders from all walks of life, prominent people such as famous scientists, celebrities, rock and pop stars, artists, law makers, economists and educationalists have been pushing their agenda in subtle ways, or not so subtle ways if it's the music industry. On the one hand, the New World Religion, on its surface offers a great appeal for modern man as he struggles to make sense of his world which is increasingly looking in peril. If only we could create peace, they profess, and, if only we could somehow be one, then we could all get along, and amalgamating all the world's religions into a simple new religion could well be the answer! In this way we can stop all the wars, economic and political bickering and be 'unified in diversity'. Many intellectuals are drawn to this concept as a harmless way forward for mankind, in which a universal religion emerges with open-arms that excludes no-one and is all inclusive of everyone's needs and beliefs, and into which the 'family of Man' can be brought into the Brotherhood of Man.

It seems like a good idea, and it could possibly be a good idea, except for several major flaws which make it completely untenable. The main arguments being that is it disingenuous to the person's original religion, and secondly it will be yet another control mechanism, but this time completely State authorised. Not to mention that if you believe your religion is, as Jesus said, 'the way, the

---

[20] Lola Davis, *Toward a World Religion for the New Age*, Coleman publishing 1983.

truth and the life, and no-ones comes to the Father but by me' (John 14:6) then there are not many ways you can support this concept. The New World Religion battle lines have been drawn in the sand - the concept that all paths lead to God is an anathema. We cover this off in Chapter 12.

The Reason for the New World Order

Have you ever wondered why the New World Order is coming into existence? The Cryptocracy already have practically all the power and influence across the 3 areas as previously mentioned - the Economy, Government and Religion, so why do they have to change to the New system?

The old-world order, which is the current, Capitalist, democratic, freedom of speech, political system we enjoy now, HAS to be replaced with a system whereby the Cryptocracy can eventually be worshipped, but at outset a new Religion or Creed is the only method whereby their policies can be carried through for generations to come. The ultimate goal of the Cryptocracy is actually to overthrow God, but to get to this point they have to set up a new creed. However good any one person is, or however persuasive the culture is en-masse, the only long-term method in which a policy can be carried through inter-generationally is via a Creed or Religion. That is why they are bothering to do it! If they could have people worship them under the current political and social structure they would just do this, although they also need their precious One World Government, however there is little chance that they are able to bring people to worship them as gods under this current political system - people just won't buy it, we are too far removed from where they want us to be. "We the people" would make too much of a fuss - we don't want to worship other people as Gods, that's abhorrent to us. No-one wants to worship a man, any Christian, Jew, Hindu, Muslim, humanist, atheist etc, anyone you care to mention will not worship a man. But with a creed which supports and is interwoven into the fabric of Agenda 21 this will enable a new global culture to emerge and be administered. This is why the Cryptocracy have to bring in the global police state and push their religious agenda by making us as slaves in order for us to worship them eventually. And this is the reason why the New World Order, at-its-heart, and the New World Religion is mainly a spiritual endeavour promoted by Satan. The Cryptocracy have to set a Creed in place, they are not so naïve to believe that they can carry out their long-range plan for humanity without an accompanying belief system to prop up their Scientific dictatorship. This is why the New World Order is emerging in the first place - for us to worship them so the purity of their Luciferian World Religion may be seen by the masses and believed by them for the good of humanity. It's them instead of Christ.

CHAPTER 3

WHO ARE THEY? – AN OVERVIEW

There are several different layers of people, organisations, institutes, secret societies and corporations all working within a complex, part hidden structure which make up the Cryptocracy. Some groups have websites which provide an explanation of their activities, as a front, which allows people to look at half-truths, spewed out to keep the average enquirer unaware, or dismiss the groups as being harmless. They are therefore 'hidden in plain sight' which is one of Freemasonry's maxims. The Elite hide behind numerous covers, but the motive is always the same, **the eventual total enslavement of humanity for the Network. They already control practically all the worlds wealth (via access to Banks) and in order to consolidate their power, the Elite will take extreme and inflated measures to protect their interests and agendas.** They have no national affiliation to any one country, in fact it is their desire to eliminate the concept of national boundaries altogether. They are extreme globalists and have no problem selling out the little man for themselves and their greedy business partners. These groups listed below are never analysed by the mainstream media since this is controlled by these groups. Neither are they ever held accountable by governments or law enforcement agencies from around the world, again because they are controlled by them.

The complexity of the groups is all part of the deception and illusion. It's almost as if there are so many groups and secret societies that one feels like giving up – but this is to put you off! In essence they are a cartel of international bankers and corporate industrialists, primarily, but not exclusively in North America and Western Europe. There are a smattering of members in Japan, Australia, Hong Kong and elsewhere but overwhelmingly the list of members from these groups show the US and the UK as being their home. Predominately the Inner Circles of the Cryptocracy are white Anglo-Saxon Protestants, and Ashkenazi Jews. In the Network which surrounds them there are members from every religion, Catholics, Buddhists, Hindus, Muslims, Shinto and other religions, and so the old argument that the hidden government are made up of Jews and no other groups is incorrect and something that the Cryptocracy like to propagate.

The 0.1% are inter-related to each other by a complex network of relationships such as directorships, or non-executive positions, or working in government, or having met as they progressed in their careers and were recruited into the hidden system. Some people are obviously more connected to the highest initiates than others, but they are the insiders of the insiders, an un-approachable, secret cabal of chums, working steadily towards the accomplishment of the Great Plan. It is the influence and power of the Elite that is of interest and sets them apart from the masses. They have wealth inherited from family and influence in both political and business spheres. In many cases this influence is indeed hereditary because within the Network it's as much who you know, as what you know, and the only way to be a trusted member of the inner circle is to have been born into it.

However, having said this, the people within the groups change over the years and the Network morphs and adapts all the time. The CFR, UN and the Trilateral Commission are possibly the most important groups we can see but we can't see the full picture since we aren't privy to all the information. One feels like one is getting closer to the truth if you could just find out which group is pulling the strings, but Satan can use whoever he wants, how he wants, and when he wants, and so the picture is extremely complex. In Eustace Mullins' book 'The World Order' he wrote that there were 5 men ruling the world at the time of his publication in 1992, and he **supposedly** knew of 4 of them, and they were, Baron Guy de Rothschild, Evelyn de Rothschild, George Shultz and Robert Roosa. Evelyn de Rothschild and George Shultz are still alive and certainly both of them are right at the very top of the pyramid, but who the ultimate person or family is behind the conspiracy no-one has yet managed to find out and they won't either, since they are really far removed from the media. George Shultz, for example, is a Trustee of the United Religions Initiative which is perhaps the most important part of the roll out of the New World Religion.

The groups below are the ones they allow us to know about, and information about them is freely available on the Internet using Google, Start Page or other search engines. How easy would it be for them to have their own meetings completely in secret which we have no idea about? Of course, they can do this at any time, and with the flow of information almost completely captured through their media, and other outlets, they can leak only the relevant information they want leaked as part of their Hegelian dialect. Controlling the flow of information on whatever they want us to know about and we will be none the wiser. Such are the groups below which will hopefully provide a starting point for much further study. In fact, entire books have been written about each one of them, for example on the CFR, Bilderbergers, the Tavistock Institute, Bohemian Grove and Skull and Bones to name just a handful. If you had to sum up the rulers of the World in a phrase it would be 'Deep State' or 'Shadow Government', this is a 'catch-all' phrase which encapsulates who and what is running everything. The term Network is a good one because it provides a greater understanding of the relationships between the politicians, bankers and heads of the corporations as they jockey and vie together to get what they want whilst all the time progressing towards the one world government which is a pre-requisite, mandatory belief. But these people are traitors and conspirators against us, conspiring to bring about policy changes we have not voted for and undertake their unfair and disastrous policies, which are damaging and murderous.

Political Groups

Rothschild/ Rhodes/ Milner/ Rockefeller related groups

The Council on Foreign Relations (CFR) is the most powerful group within the United States and it advises American politicians about policy and international issues, which makes it therefore a type of high level think tank but one with enormous clout. They act similarly to how an occupying foreign power within a country might. Their agents have infiltrated high office across the entire US governmental system and they seek to carry out the precise dictates of the New World Order conspirators. CFR members started the CIA and the National Security Council, and are like an enemy within the country and they seek to destroy American sovereignty, her borders and to bring the country to its knees in order to bring it into the New World Order. Practically every important decision has come from their headquarters, which are Harold Pratt House in New York. They effect change by infiltration and by promoting their own members to positions of power within the structure - be it the CIA which they run, the US military which they have almost complete power over, or the President himself and his inner circles. All are infiltrated with CFR agents. This is truly the shadow government of the United States.

They are linked to the British Royal Institute of International Affairs having grown out of the Institute of International Affairs and effectively merged with 'The Inquiry' group started by Woodrow Wilson and his handler Colonel Edward Mandell House. Most of its members are close to the Rhodes groups. The CFR was started in 1921 and the Presidents who were CFR members were: Wilson, Harding, Coolidge, Hoover, Roosevelt, Eisenhower, Nixon, Johnson, Ford, Carter, Bush Snr, Clinton and Bush Jnr. Obama membership is not confirmed but it is known that Michelle Obama was a Chicago CFR member.

Presidents who were not members of the CFR are: Truman, JFK, Reagan and Trump but they were, and are, easy to manage in their own ways.

Both sides of the political establishment, Republican or Democrat have been CFR members. Truman, JFK and Reagan were surrounded by CFR agents at outset and certainly by the end of their terms all of them had carried out policies born from the Harold Pratt House, New York; the true seat of the government of America.

The President is therefore surrounded by a Network of members who dictate policy to the President for the benefit of the hidden government. They have his ear and use special 'handlers' with sophisticated psychological intelligence techniques to make the President sign off on any dictate that the Cryptocracy want. This is how it works! It's not, 'you are our puppet and you will do as we say, or else', they use far more clever means to get what they want. Policies come from the CFR and are 'sold' to the President who enacts them. If he asks for advice and 4 out of 5 of his advisors are saying, do this, then he's likely to do precisely as they suggested.

Lastly Donald Trump is not a CFR member and neither does his administration have that many CFR or Trilateral connections within his administration, however he has surrounded himself with bankers, oil men and high-level business men and financiers, who to all intents and purposes represent the same interests as the CFR. It's as if he has 'by-passed' the CFR and Trilateral Commission and has gone straight to the corporates. The Cryptocracy don't need to make policy in the normal way, via their inner circle of members of the CFR, since they already hold enough power to affect all the changes necessary via these other channels. At the same time this gives the US establishment and CFR distance to allow Trump to make a fool of himself and the Presidency as part of their strategy to belittle the function of the President, all the while getting the media to destroy him. Fundamentally it's about destroying the post of the President in preparation for the eventual roll out of the New World Order. The Elite can watch and mock!

The President of the CFR is Richard Haas who has openly written about there being a 30-year War from 2001. Rick Warren is a CFR member and he is a preacher pushing a type of syncretic Christianity to set up an ecumenical church.

Total number of CFR Members slowly grows each year and is now over 5,000.[21]

The **Trilateral Commission** has many members who are in the CFR, and is probably the most important and powerful international group affecting high level policy making and the roll out of the New World Order. It was originally started by David Rockefeller in 1973 to foster better business relations between the US, Europe and Japan, but has slowly morphed into being the shadow world government.

---

[21] Council on Foreign Relations website: https://www.cfr.org/ Suggested reading Servando Gonzalez, *Psychological Warfare and the New World Order.* Or *Shadows of Power*, James Perloff. A List of their members is on their website, alphabetically: - https://www.cfr.org/membership/membership-roster-a-f

Once they had infiltrated the Carter presidency and all subsequent presidencies, they have dedicated themselves to passing laws to introduce their **'New International Economic Order'** written about by Zbigniew Brzezinski which is a type of Technocratic State. Many important decisions which further the New World Order on a global basis is derived from this group. For example, European and UN Immigration policy is headed by Peter Sutherland who is a Trilateral member, and has been at the forefront of the deliberate policy of encouraging migration everywhere to divide people up. By greying out the identities of countries and then pitting people against people, this diverts attention away from them and divides us up into powerless segments of society. This is no co-incidence and all part of the destruction of cultural identity in order to bring to fruition their own new version of 'greyed out' humanity.

Total number of Members of the TC: 390.[22]

Bilderbergers: this a Political Group, meeting in total secrecy (but not so much now) intent on developing the world into the one world government with their members at its head. Started by Joseph H Retinger, and Prince Bernard it had David Rockefeller as one of the early members. They are basically a link between the European and US elite. The sort of thing they are discussing is whether they should assassinate Ron Paul, and when they should cause stock market crashes. At least this is what they have leaked to the world via Daniel Estulin and Jim Tucker.

They publish the whereabouts of their meetings a few days before which has enabled some activists to hold meetings close by.[23]

Total number of members of the Bilderberg Group: 150.

---

[22] Trilateral Commission website: http://trilateral.org/ Patrick Wood has been documenting the Trilateral Commission from its inception. Please see *Technocracy Rising and the Trojan Horse of Global Transformation*. A list of members is on their website.

[23] Bilderberg website http://bilderbergmeetings.org/frequently-asked-questions.html James Tucker Jim Tucker's *Bilderberg Diary: Reporter's 25 Year Battle to Shine the Light on the World Shadow Government* or Daniel Estulin *The True Story of the Bilderberg Group*. A List of Members is on their website, eg steering committee list: http://www.bilderbergmeetings.org/steering-committee.html

The **Group of 30**. Founded in 1978 as a financial and economic group with heavy weight Central Bankers from across the world's most important economies they meet to discuss global issues. It is another group receiving funding from the Rockefeller's who helped to start it up. The current chairman of the group of Jean-Claude Trichet who is also a Trilateral Commission steering group member.[24] Total Number 30.

Round Table Groups

Royal Institute of International Affairs: Chatham House: this is the old English establishment started by the Cecil Rhodes group around 1905 and its aims were to further the Empire for the Elite and ideally to have the entire world ruled by Britain and the controlling Corporate Elite of the day. Its History was documented by Carroll Quigley, an American Historian of huge significance who was given access to their records and exposed their aims and distortions of History. All of this is provable and explained in the next chapter. The RIIA is related to the CFR which is related to the Trilateral Commission, the conspirators work together.[25]

Total number of RIIA members: 3,000.

United Nations is the de facto shadow world government in the making and one of the avenues through which Agenda 21 is being pushed. There are 3 layers to the UN. The General Assembly may be compared to being the Parliament. The second layer is the bureaucracy which is made up of a technocratic group of sub organisations or programs, such as the UN Development Program (UNDP) or the World Health Organisation (WHO). These agencies are in charge of administering the UN conventions and bringing their

---

[24] Group of 30 website: http://www.group30.org/ Criticism by Andrew Gavin Marshall of Boilingfrogs.com see http://www.occupy.com/article/global-power-project-group-thirty-and-its-methods-financial-governance#sthash.mvgYQ8DO.70ez7gqe.dpbs

[25] RIIA website (Chatham House): https://www.chathamhouse.org/ A List of corporate and other members is on this website.

policies into effect. The third layer, which has only formed in the last 30 years or so, are the plethora of NGOs and private agencies pushing their versions of world government to the people. The UN is controlled by US and UK interests, and Britain can generally count on there being 54 out of the possible 192 country votes since those ex-British colonies which made up the Commonwealth can be relied on to vote as directed. Normally the US also has a coalition of countries behind it anyway. Also, the top 5 permanent countries on the UN Security Council hold a veto over the rest which hardly makes the original set up of the UN equitable.

Religious NGOs only make up about 10% of the total number. Since there is no particularly strong central authority in the UN, this lack of accountability enables these private NGOs to make changes to countries to bring in the New World Order as they see fit without proper oversight.

In the future it is possible that the UN will be disbanded and replaced by another institution with another name more in keeping with the concept of the Earth Mother religion, such as the 'Earth Trust'. This is alluded to in some of their writings.

Total number of Employees 44,000.[26]

NGOs

Non-Government Organisations are normally foreign corporations based in countries abroad, and when you think about it, they will only do what they are told to do by their foreign controllers. In this respect they are like an enemy within a country, they may do good on the one hand, but then there is normally some other agenda going on in the background. Generally, they promote Globalist trends to make the country closer to the West. What better way to effect political change than a private organisation which is not accountable to any Government or to the UN? The number of NGOs each Elite member, such as Henry Kissinger, is involved with is listed by the

---

[26] United Nations, see Ioan Ratiu, *The Milner Fabian Conspiracy*, chapter 6 page 193 following. Print on demand publishing.

Institute for the Study of Globalization and Covert Politics (ISPG).[27] Even a cursory glance of this list says volumes about who is effecting change across the globe. The top members by way of the total number of NGOs they are involved with are, Henry Kissinger (110), James Woolsey (86), George Shultz (74), and the Rockefeller family (69): the number would be higher if the Foundations were included. Thomas Pickering (57), the Rothschild family (54): this would be higher as well if employees from NGOs were included, the Bush family (54), Madeleine Albright (54), Maurice Greenberg (53), Paul Volker (51), Brent Scowcroft (50), and George Soros (49). Obviously, this is not evidence in itself that there is a high-level conspiracy in operation, just because these politicians and Statesmen are involved in many NGOs, but if, for a moment, you take the view that these NGOs are fronts for global government then you will actually be closer to the truth. Why would they be effecting changes if it weren't in line with their systems and beliefs which we already know about? The same names we see heading up the most important parts of the new world order global agenda, just happen to be the same names we see heading up the most NGOs!

Foundations- by way of size in terms of Funding

Bill and Melinda Gates Foundation is a self-serving NGO run more like an extension of US Shadow Government policy, than a philanthropic charity.[28] Its 3 Trustees are Bill and Melinda Gates and Warren Buffet, and it is involved in global health care programs and education. They do some good if you believe their reports, but in the final analysis it's a corporate take-over of the poor countries and in America, an indoctrination into the Common Core Standards

---

[27] With acknowledgment and thanks for their research, please see the Institute for the Study of Globalization and Covert Politics (ISPG) website: https://isgp-studies.com/

[28] Bill and Melinda Gates Foundation https://www.gatesfoundation.org/jobs

education program.[29] This educational strategy is all about collecting data and ramming Sustainable Development indoctrination to youngsters.

Open Society Foundation is George Soros' shadow government foundation and they fund, aid and advise subversive groups to carry out their wishes. They are all over the world but most transparently in Eastern Europe. Practically everyone knows of their subversive undemocratic operation in those countries, but they are powerless to do anything. Serbia, Georgia, Ukraine, Kyrgyzstan, Macedonia and many others have been directly politically affected for the worse by the policies of George Soros. Other countries such as the UK, Malaysia, Thailand and many others have suffered under George Soros' harsh trading activities. George Soros has also been accused of finding and funding US Presidential candidates to do his bidding. In Albania the evidence garnered from the appointment of Miroslav Lajcak via the supposed leak of Hillary Clinton's email is revealing and shows that Soros had enough power to affect this outcome. Soros is an important figure in the New World Order.[30]

Rockefeller Foundation has more NGOs under its influence that any other single family measured in terms of the total number of NGOs. The Rockefeller family have been heavily involved with the roll out of the New World Order from around 1880 and have used this foundation (from 1913) as a front and means to effect change and implement policy in a wide range of activities. They have funded anything and everything which has advanced their vision of the New World Order, as they seek to create monopolies and dominate countries under their control. We can trace their activities in the areas of medical health, population sciences, agriculture, arts and humanities, social sciences and International relations. They have used their wealth to fund other groups and start institutions to bring in the changes they desired. For example, David Rockefeller funded

---

[29] Bill and Melinda Gates Foundation helped fund Common Core State Standards Initiative https://weaponsofmassdeception.org/2-common-core-fake-standards/2-1-the-real-history-of-common-core

[30] George Soros website:
https://www.opensocietyfoundations.org/people/george-soros Criticism
http://humanevents.com/2011/04/02/top-10-reasons-george-soros-is-dangerous/

the CFR, RIIA, World Bank, Brookings Institute and many other New World Order institutions, often pretending on the one hand to be from the right and Republican (like Nelson Rockefeller, {because it's good for business}) but all the while supporting and subverting institutions and nations using Socialist, Fabian methods. In other words, they were really from the left.[31]

Carnegie Endowment for International Peace is a think tank set up in 1910 by Andrew Carnegie. Norman Dodd as part of the Reece Committee (between 1952-54) conclusively showed that the Foundation, (via their own historical documents) was involved with the long-range plan of setting up World War I to affect society in the manner in which the Cryptocracy wished.[32] Quoted from G Edward Griffin's interview in 1982 with Norma Dodd: "the trustees... raised a specific question.... Is there any means known more effective than war, assuming you wish to alter the life of an entire people? And they conclude that, no more effective means to that end is known to humanity, than war. So then, in 1909, they raise the second question, and discussed it, namely, how do we involve the United States in a war?" This is what the Carnegie Endowment were involved in.[33]

They are linked to the Council on Foreign Relations and Bilderbergers.

Other foundations, such as the Ford Foundation and William J Clinton Foundation are significant in the overall picture of how the agenda for the takeover of the world is being mastered by private hands with enormous finances.

---

[31] For more on the Rockefellers see Gary Allen, *The Rockefeller File*. 1976.

[32] The Reece Committee report of 1953 (United States House Select Committee to Investigate Tax -Exempt Foundations and Comparable Organizations) is a very important document since it shows with excellent evidence that the foundations were involved in a conspiracy to undermine democracy and the United States. A copy of the report can be found here https://archive.org/details/DoddReportToTheReeceCommitteeOnFoundations-1954-RobberBaron

[33] The Norman Dodd interview by Edward Griffin can be found on You Tube: search for Norman Dodd interview by G Edward Griffin.

United Nations linked Banks

The World Bank set up in 1944 at Bretton Woods is a Bank that lends money to help Countries build up their infrastructure and modernise their economy to stop world poverty. In reality it has been used as a subtle method of bringing countries into the New World Order 'fold' lending money for capital projects which the country has no chance of repaying. In fact, not a single country has managed to repay its loans.[34] It is an instrument carrying out the orders of the Cryptocracy to enslave poorer countries with so much debt that they can be controlled.

Total number of Employees: 9,000

International Monetary Fund (IMF) lends to countries whose credit worthiness has shrunken so low that 'standard' lending methods are not available to them, so they are the lender of last resort.

Total number of Employees 2,400

Bank of International Settlements is the Central Banks own Bank which means it is at 'the apex' of the Global Banking system and so it is in charge of making sure the flow of money is maintained to all the Central banks.[35] As Caroll Quigley wrote: - 'the international bankers would control and manipulate the money system of a nation while letting it appear to be controlled by the government.' This is the bank that controls all the other Central Banks which means that this is probably the most important financial institution that exists, yet how many people have even heard of it? The fact that it is never mentioned in the media and does not advertise its activities even to Governments or Finance Ministers just shows how much they control financial power and how weak the supposed democratically elected Ministers really are. It is an extremely secret Bank that ALL the most important central Bankers go to discuss their next financial moves and to ensure that they keep control and ownership of the system and that is working for their benefit, not for the benefit of humanity as a whole, but for

---

[34] Zoe Young, A New Green Order, Pluto Press 2002 page 21 quotes Michael Rowbotham from *Goodbye America*, Globalisation and debt and the Dollar Empire.

[35] Carroll Quigley, *Tragedy and Hope*. Page 324 Apex of system BIS.

their own private interests. The entire worlds' central banking welfares are reflected at these meetings, although there are only 60 of the most important Banks which gather in Basel every other month to hold their secret meetings, all the other banks have to follow suit or else face consequences.[36] Current members are:- William C Dudley (Fed), Janet Yellen (Fed), Mario Draghi (ECB), Mark Carney, (BoE), Stephen Poloz (Canada) and other central Bankers from China, Brazil, Japan, Germany, France and other nations. In the past other members have included Mervyn King who was head of the Economic Consultative Committee (ECC), Ben Bernanke and Jean-Claude Trichet to mention just a few. With historic links to the Nazis, and massive collusion, this is the prototype of the future World Bank in charge of the possible global 'SDR' currency leading into the Technocratic energy currency of the future.

Total number of Employees: 632

European Union (EU) / The European Council / The Council of Ministers. The EU was set up as a Milner-Fabian, Eastern Establishment (US) project to control Germany and Europe. It is the de facto Technocratic State into which all the outlying areas are to be brought into subjugation, subverted, subdued, and in 'Borg like' fashion brought into the New World Order. A study of its history will reveal the same groups and characters outlined in this section; groups which are working towards the total subjugation of European Sovereignty and Nationality in every way. The European Council is run by a small number of conspirators who can dictate whatever policies the Cryptocracy want via their secret agreements and subtle manipulations. Europe's culture, history, heritage, financial acumen and sense of fair play must be destroyed and greyed out according to the maniacs who run it, in order to bring it into their New World Order system. So far, they are doing a good job in doing precisely this, flooding Europe with immigrants, stealing Sovereignty from nations by whatever means possible, whilst all the while bankrupting an entire Continent via their deliberately flawed economic policies.

The UK voted 52 to 48 to leave the EU but you can guarantee that the Cryptocracy will have planned these conclusions years ahead,

---

[36] See Adam Lebor, *Tower of Basel: The Shadowy History of the Secret Bank that Runs the World.*

and so the negotiations are a contrived foregone conclusion. In other words, the outcome will be precisely as the hidden government had planned. Most likely the owners of the UK want the nation returned back to a US amalgamation (something which is alluded to in the writings of Carroll Quigley) and which makes sense since the UK and the US are the top conspirators in the New World Order.[37]

Total number of Employees: 46,356

Le Cercle or the Pinay Group are a group of aging right-wing politicians, intelligence officers and ideologues based in Europe. They are considered a sister wing to the Bilderbergs. They promote their warmongering 'war on terror' by brokering weapons deals, arranging false flag attacks and otherwise subverting the democratic process. They probably have links and possibly control the secret 'stay behind' armies of Gladio which were set up as subversive armies which could go into action in case of a Communist invasion by Russia. The trouble was that the army was so secret they became a seditious division outside of European governments almost like another secret service within NATO. Norman Lamont has been Chairman of the Group since 1996.[38] As an aside, since we know the entire Cold War was a scam with the Cryptocracy controlling investment and information to the Russian elite all the way through from 1917; the very fact that they set up Gladio as resistance to a Russian take over, makes it a scam on a scam - they controlled the Cold War but still had to set this group up and used it to further their causes. At the moment Gladio are one of the possible culprits who are funding, aiding and directing ISIS.[39] Alan Clarke mentioned in his 'Diaries' that Le Cercle was funded by the CIA.

Total number of Members unknown (perhaps region of 50 to 200.)

---

[37] The US and UK hidden governments being together as co-conspirators is a fact mentioned throughout *Tragedy and Hope* by Carroll Quigley, see for example pages 950- 956.

[30] https://wikispooks.com/wiki/Norman_Lamont

[39] Gladio: See Simon Cottrell, *Gladio, Nato's Dagger at the Heart of Europe: The Pentagon-Nazi-Mafia Terror Axis*. ISIS funding see https://wikispooks.com/wiki/Operation_Gladio/B or website search ISIS + Gladio

Political Puppets and Scape Goats

Neo Conservatives (Neo Cons) is the political ideology that says that American national interests are above every other country, and so they can basically do as they see fit to other nations. They essentially believe they are above the State and that the people somehow owe them a living, and that they can do exactly as they want because they have the power. The writers of the Project for the New American Century (PNAC) were heavily involved in 9/11 and the subsequent fake anthrax scare that eventually led to the war they wanted with Iraq.[40] They are also heavily influenced by the CFR to which most of them belong. Neo Cons are a true danger to the world constituting some of the most flawed thinking in politics ever seen in modern times. This is why they have become the 'fall guy' for their New World Order controllers, their political beliefs are so outrageously flawed they are obviously being controlled for another purpose, and they don't mind being used for this purpose.

Globalists: a big term and not that easy to narrow down as a 'group', but they are people or Politicians who do not ask too many questions but are willing to push forward the agenda of the big corporates more than their own official government. They don't have problems selling out the 'little man' to the needs and profits of big companies. Globalism has brought many ills, as well as some good things, but eventually it will lead to a 'greyed out society' where the global culture predominates, and people everywhere are the same, holding the same beliefs, having the same income, and living in the same police-state conditions. Corporations and governments will act together in a monopolistic synergy. This is the conclusion of the globalists, but to them this doesn't matter, as long as they are making a dime along the way.

Puppets: this is an interesting 'group' because they don't have any particular allegiance and aren't members of any of these groups with spiritual links such as Freemasons, but they go along with what they are told to do, or are easily manipulated to perform the tasks that the

---

[40] The type of anthrax was finally and conclusively proven to have come from an Army research lab in Maryland, US. See article
https://www.livescience.com/13229-anthrax-attacks-2001-genetics-110314.html

super Elite want them to do. They fall into 2 sub-groups, i) they know they are being manipulated but don't mind, or are in the pay of the group or ii) they don't know they are being manipulated and so they are in essence victims. Sometimes the super Elite may have some information against them which enables them to be managed and manipulated and so they are blackmailed to support their agenda.

Zionists support Israel, often at whatever the cost, with their 'Israel first America second' ideology. In the Unites States there are many high-level Politicians who have a political philosophy much more closely aligned to the needs of Israel than the US. You've heard the expression that the Jews run the planet, and this is indeed true to an extent but only since they are pushed forward as visible scapegoats for the controllers behind them. The Cryptocracy are not all Jews but the inner circle of the CFR is predominately made up of Ashkenazi Jews who are by definition Zionists and who therefore have the interests of Israel above America.

The Pilgrims Society - British and American- was started in 1902 and is an Anglo-American club of top elite politicians, members of royalty and business men who meet at annual dinners to foster good relations and fellowship. Heavily linked to the Milner and Eastern Establishment, members of the club have been Henry Kissinger, David Rockefeller, John D Rockefeller, Jacob Schiff, Elihu Root, Averell Harriman, Joseph Kennedy, the Dulles brothers, Nelson Aldrich, Margaret Thatcher, Queen Elizabeth and Philip, and Prince Charles just to name a few. Some seriously heavy weight players. The UK Ditchley Foundation could perhaps be said to be a lead into this higher group.

Total number of Members: not known probably 1500.

Davos: the world's foremost businessmen and politicians get together and go skiing and talk globalism for the **World Economic Forum**. It's a gathering of 'would-be-New-World-Order-yes-men' to get into the club and be given their marching orders.

Secret Services: CIA, MI6, Mossad, Europol and other Secret agencies are all doing the bidding of the New World Order controllers. They are **immune to prosecution**, and above the law in every way, they kill, conduct false flags, create hoaxes, and change governments as directed. They advertise themselves as working for the interests of the country they represent but in reality they are doing the bidding of the highest members of the Cryptocracy. They are like a secret society but with weapons, and they are directed by shadowy individuals for purposes clandestine in the extreme. The secret services have been infiltrated by the master illusionists and to believe otherwise is naïve in the extreme. The CIA are the private army of the Council on Foreign Relations. In effect there are 2 CIAs - those who work for the Cryptocracy and know it, and the second group who are trying to protect the American people and don't know it.[41] They pretend to be protecting us from the Arab Terrorists or Islamic Fundamentalists, as they are now called, but, in reality, it is they who are conducting all the events and false flags. The War on Terror is a giant hoax because there is no enemy as will be explained later on. No doubt there might be some good people within their ranks actually doing some good to help the man on the street but this seems highly unlikely. They are protecting the New World Order controllers and making sure their dictates are carried out. In the UK they swear allegiance to the Crown and not to the people, the Crown being the visible tip of the iceberg of the Cryptocracy. You can't have a surveillance police state without violence.

Vote Rigging: MI5/6, the CIA and other secret agencies are in charge of rigging the Elections to the precise results the Cryptocracy desire. They can easily change the number of votes by altering the Electronic counting machines or altering the result by adding or removing the Postal Votes in any constituency they want. In this manner Elections are completely contrived and worthless, enabling the Cryptocracy to create hung parliaments or landslides to their advantage. It is all the same! We seem to forget that institutions can easily be bought. We naively believe that Electoral Commissions or fraud detection agencies are working for our interests to make sure foul play does not occur, but any institution can be infiltrated, blackmailed, or its employees paid to occlude any result and provide protection and cover up facilities if difficulties arise. In the US, fraud via electronic vote rigging is well documented and there is evidence for this from the voting machines which can be easily hacked.[42]

---

[41] For more on the 2 CIA theory / fact, see Servando Gonzalez, *Psychological Warfare and the New World Order*, Chapter 6 Location 2707 following.

[42] Vote rigging articles
https://www.computerworld.com/article/2511508/security0/argonne-researchers--hack--diebold-e-voting-system.html (E-vote hacking.)

Enmeshed within the software are bugs, holes and back door programs which can be used to hack and alter the vote. The media then 'mop' up with the official explanation to make sense of why 'a particular group' voted in this surprising direction this time around (to make up for the exit polls showing different results). A few innocent interviews from Voters explaining why they voted in this bizarre manner and the scam is complete.[43] This is also how the Cryptocracy maintains and keeps control of Parliament, allowing only their people to get into office and only those people who have the Elite's interests at heart into even higher office. You didn't really think Democracy works the way they tell you!

Drugs: CIA involvement in drug running is well documented with links from the East India Company, the Russell family of Skull and Bones and others, through Laos and Vietnam, Mexico and elsewhere. The drugs of the Cryptocracy are Opium and Heroin, and this is how some of them made their money in the past and one other reason why Vietnam and Afghanistan took place. Money can be laundered in any number of ways such as via the secret services, government agencies or casinos in Las Vegas for example, or even through the International cabal of Bankers themselves.

Think Tanks

Think Tanks are a vitally important element to the success of the New World Order plans since they are the engineers of the social conditioning of the masses. They are the groups advising the rest of the apparatus on how to promote and engineer an entire society in

---

http://people.howstuffworks.com/vote-tampering.htm (How to)
http://www.spokesman.com/stories/2016/dec/26/us-elections-still-vulnerable-to-rigging-vote-stea/

[43] In the UK we saw this strategy with the re-election of Theresa May (June 2017) where students were interviewed afterwards as an explanation for the surprising exit poll results. To confuse it further some students even admitted they had voted twice. http://www.independent.co.uk/news/uk/politics/student-jeremy-corbyn-vote-twice-fraud-general-election-electoral-commission-home-university-a7846516.html

which the Elite are in total control. They have perfected the Science of 'Mass Psychological processing' which means they use propaganda, indoctrination and a huge array of deep subconscious words, symbols, cyphers and subtle manipulation in order to make us believe what they want.

The **Tavistock Institute** was started in 1947; the aim of the think tank is to break down the psychological strength of the individual and render him helpless to oppose the dictates of the New World Order. Any technique which helps break down the family unit, or 'traditional' family values, or the principles of religion, national sovereignty, patriotism and sexual behaviour are used by the Tavistock scientists as methods of crowd control. Just because they are thinking a lot doesn't make them impotent![44]

The Club of Rome think tank was founded in 1968 in Italy and is in charge of the long-range depopulation program of bringing the world's population to around 500 million. Their Neo-Malthusian belief that billions of people needs to be culled is truly Satanic and their belief that the Earth cannot sustain all the people shows a complete lack of faith. Their books such as *'Limits to Growth'* (1972) and *'The First Global Revolution'* (1992) identify humanity as the enemy and the hoax that is climate change as the method of gaining power over national governments. Mikhail Gorbachev, who is an important figure in the roll out of the New World Religion became a member of the Club of Rome at about the same time he became President of the USSR.[45]

Brookings Institute was founded in 1916 and is another think tank in charge of global economics and development, politics, and social sciences. It is based in Washington with links to the CFR.[46]

Aspen Institute: This think tank was originally called the Aspen Institute for Humanistic Studies. It was started by Aldous Huxley in 1949. It has been heavily involved with promoting and teaching humanism to international corporates as part of its indoctrination to

---

[44] TAVISTOCK http://www.tavinstitute.org/ Daniel Estulin, Tavistock Institute, or John Coleman, The Tavistock Institute of Human Relations; Shaping the Moral, Spiritual, Cultural, Political and Economic Decline of The USA

[45] Club of Rome website: https://www.clubofrome.org/

[46] Brookings Institute websigte: https://www.brookings.edu/about-us/

push Sustainable Development and the New International Economic Order as spoken of by the Trilateral Commission to which it has strong ties.[47]

Institute of Strategic Studies: "Its mission is to promote the adoption of sound policies to further global peace and security and maintain civilised international relations."[48] It's a New World Order weapons talking shop - so much for global peace!

European Council on Foreign Relations is another think tank specialising on European and wider political intrigues.[49] It is a private institution part funded by George Soros' Open Foundation and other related groups. It has links to the Bilderberger Group.

There are hundreds of other think tanks worthy of further research such as the Stanford Institute for Economic Policy Research, the Rand Corporation, Bruegel Institute, Civitas, Quilliam and the Henry Jackson Society just to name a few more. They are all working toward nefarious purposes for the furtherance of the controllers strangle hold on humanity - their methods are subtle and their reach totally pervasive.

Spiritual / Occult Secret Societies

The Cryptocracy are interested in Religion, Luciferianism and secret societies. Every person in the Cryptocracy has links to one of these groups below. The very nature of what they are doing has to be done in secret, and be unknown to the masses, and so secret societies are a vital method of advancing their programs, communicating and forming policy. In order to maintain that secrecy, they use oaths and secret agreements. Hence the profusion of secret societies.

---

[47] Aspen Institute website: https://www.aspeninstitute.org/ Links to Trilaterals see Patrick Wood Technocracy Rising, the Trojan Horse of Global Transformation, page 119.

[48] From IISS website http://www.iiss.org/

[49] EUROPEAN Council on Foreign Relations http://www.ecfr.eu/

Freemasons: since Freemasons are a Secret Society it is not always possible to know who is or isn't within this group. They are in all walks of life and only in the upper levels do they know what the true agenda is - they are Luciferians as will be explained in Chapter 7. On a local and national level they are not that important to the overall picture. They are a recruiting ground for people to gain admission into the higher groups, but the main issue is that once you are a Freemason you are in 'the Club' and from here can be put into higher positions of power within the structure.

Illuminati: This is a very broad category and has become something of a mainstream term for the politically enabled insiders who are developing the New World Order. To all intents and purposes these people are high level Freemasons, OTO members, Palladium or Knights of Malta, and, as such their political agenda and philosophy is totally different to the man on the street. Originally the Illuminati came from Bavaria, Germany, and writers such as Robison and Barruel in 1797 warned Europe of this dangerous subversive group, but no-one paid much attention to them. The Illuminati were exposed in 1785 and 'officially' disbanded in 1786 with all their papers published they were outlawed, although there is evidence that they managed to survive and re-emerged later in the US as Skull and Bones.[50]

---

[50] Evidence that the Illuminati survived is:- the Illuminati were sworn to infiltrate and take over all the governments of Europe and elsewhere to form the One World Government. (See: Perfectibilists – Terry Melanson, p 32). If they were supposed to have died out in 1786 why did John Robison, years later write his book, Proofs of a Conspiracy in 1797, if there wasn't a threat? And in that very same year, in France, why did Augustin Barruel write a very similar work if the conspiracy had faded away? John Robison's book was even sent and read by George Washington who admitted the Illuminati existed, the first President of the United States wrote: - "It is not my intention to doubt that the doctrine of the Illuminati and the principles of Jacobinism had not spread in the United States. On the contrary, no one is more satisfied of this fact than I am." From: *The Writings of George Washington*, Volume 14, 1798-1799, New York, G. P. Putmans Sons, 1893, p. 119.

Adam Weishaupt himself wrote: 'The great care of the Illuminati after the publication of their secret writings was to persuade the whole of Germany that their Order no longer existed, that their adepts had all renounced, not only their mysteries, but as members of a secret society.' All of this proves once and for all that the Illuminati survived the 'purge' of 1786 to 1799 and went further under-ground. In 1832 the same group emerged in Yale University as Skull and Bones with the same German writing found in its corridors and many of the same rituals

Skull and Bones 322: these are a group from Yale University who are like Freemasons on steroids and they have managed to gain a lot of power and control within the American political system, such as John Kerry and George Bush who ran as Presidential Candidates against each other in the 2004 Election. So it was illuminati insider 1 or illuminati insider 2! They are the same! Averell Harriman, one of the 'wise men', were also Bonesmen with McGeorge Bundy. 322 is their special number which is a reference to Genesis 3:22 that 'they are gods'. 22 is also a Master Number which means it is imbued with more power than other numbers. 3 x 22 = 66. The group is indirectly linked to the Bavarian Illuminati via the Germanorden Society. In fact, between 1786 when the Bavarian Illuminati officially ceased to exist and the creation of Skull and Bones in 1832, is a period of time of only 46 years. This is not a long enough a period of time for their teachings to have disappeared and when the Tomb, which is the name for the Skull and Bones building, was raided there were the same German writings present. The Illuminati had re-emerged as Skull and Bones via William Russel and Alphonso Taft in 1832. Many Secretary's of War have been Skull and Bones - Alphonso Taft, his Son Howard Taft who was also the 27th President, Henry L Stimpson, Averell Harriman as Secretary of Commerce and of course the Bush family. Prescot Bush who funded Hitler, both George's and Jeb Bush were all members of this deeply conspiratorial, undemocratic and sinister Satanic cult. They promote their fellow Bonesmen into positions of power, above any others and in this way, have become a central group with enormous power.[51]

Total active number: 300 (15 are recruited each year but most are not active after University.)

Knights of Malta: this secret Society is an extremely high-level group with links to the Papacy. Practically every CIA Director has been a Knight of Malta. Members of this groups are: Henry Kissinger, Tony Blair, Queen Beatrix of the Netherlands, Jose

---

(eg Regent Ritual.) This secret society is still in existence today. Many recent US Presidents and high level American politicians have been Skull and Bones members, and this fact is provable.

[51] See Anthony C Sutton, *America's Secret Establishment: An Introduction to the Order of Skull and Bones*. 2004. List of Skull and Bones members see:
https://en.wikipedia.org/wiki/List_of_Skull_and_Bones_members

Barrosso, Silvio Berlusconi, Bush Snr, Bush Jnr, Jeb Bush, Michael Chertoff, Noam Chomsky, Gustavo Cisneros, Bill Clinton, Kenneth Copeland (Evangelist), Lord Christopher Walter Monckton, Rupert Murdoch, Stephen A. Schwarzman (Skull and Bones), Ted Turner, Archbishop Desmond Tutu, Zbigniew Brezinski, and David Rockefeller.[52]

I draw your attention to Kenneth Copeland who is a TV Evangelist and most likely a heretic with statements that we can 'all be as god'. Ted Turner crops up later on in our study as a promoter of the New World Religion. Lastly of interest is to note is Lord Monckton - does that make him a shill that's he's on the list?

Jesuits: the Society of Jesus was started in 1534 and is another secret society which swears allegiance to the Black Pope. The Black Pope is in charge of many paternal organisations including the Knights of Malta with its links to highest levels of government such as the CFR and the CIA. The Jesuits are another group working for the Great Plan and part of their aim is to slowly and imperceptibly bring Christian denominations together into Catholicism and then into the New World Religion.

Order of the Garter- although a tiny group it is 'the fish head that stinks not the tail'. It is the most prestigious order of British chivalry with many members of the Royal family and approximately 24 other 'companion members' worldwide who have been recruited or born into high level political and influential positions. (It used to be 13 as a Coven). The group below this is the Privy Council. UK high ranking political members are promoted to these roles for good service to the Establishment.

Collegiate Fraternities such as Alpha Phi Omega or Phi Beta Kappa are secret societies. In the US there is some evidence that they are another recruiting ground for the Elite. (Ralph 'Waldo' Emmerson, who was a Dark Green Religionist we look at later, was a Phi Beta Kappa member).

Bohemian Grove are an important group and are mainly made up of US Republicans, although there are a large number of Democrats and upper echelon businessmen within their ranks, as well

---

[52] For a list of the Knights of Malta see:
http://www.biblebelievers.org.au/kmlst1.htm

as leaders of Industry, Banking and Commerce. Each July they meet up in the woods of northern California for a two week vacation. But in reality, it's a networking and business meeting where ideas can be aired without fear of reprisals. They worship or pretend to respect Molech, an Ammonite Old Testament god (1 Kings 11:7) and have an annual 'fake human sacrifice ritual' called the Cremation of Care. The sacrifice of passing children through the fire as an offering is mentioned in numerous places in the Bible such as Leviticus 18:21, II Kings 23:10 and Jeremiah 32:35. Of course the members of Bohemian Grove say they are doing nothing of the sort, but once you start wearing hooded robes at night wandering around a forest grove, and bowing to a 42 foot high Owl chanting 'Oh Great Owl of Bohemia' it is not illogical to wonder if these people really are Satanists! There are numerous books about this group although there is cause for concern that perhaps the infiltration by Alex Jones and Mike Hanson into their ceremony with a video camera was NOT for real, but part of some deep con or Hegelian dialect.[53]

The concept of the United Nations, was born at one of their meetings.[54] (The League of Nations previously did not include the US.)

Is it possible that at these parties there are hidden cameras to video the goings on, such as homo-sexual activity, which can be used later for bribery and skewing political processes?

Religious Groups

The Parliament of World Churches was started in 1893 and was the world's first truly inter-faith attempt at bringing the world's

---

[53] The video of the Bohemian Grove filming can be found on You Tube. Mark Hanson, *Bohemian Grove: Cult of Conspiracy* 2012. A List of Bohemian Grove members can be found in the internet, such as https://en.wikipedia.org/wiki/List_of_Bohemian_Club_members

[54] Article by Terry Melanson quotes from The Annals of the Bohemian Club For the Years 1907-1972 - volume V, William C Bacon .
http://www.conspiracyarchive.com/2013/12/11/united-nations-and-the-war-years-in-bohemia/

religions together. (Please see the Appendix for the Chronology of the New World Religion.) Ever since there have been regular meetings promoting the concept of interfaith dialogue or interfaith 'pathways' leading to some sort of progressive conclusion. It's not harmful for religious groups to get together and discuss things, but unfortunately there is also evidence of a slant towards syncretising the world's religions as well. The Parliament is also guilty of promoting precisely the agenda the Elite would like them to promote - namely the Climate Change hoax and the subsequent Marxist doctrine of Agenda 21 along with religious reverence for the Earth.[55]

World Council of Churches (WCC) is an ecumenical group seeking to unify Christian Churches into one body or group. They are not an interfaith group but were infiltrated by the Russian secret services and are part of the overall conspiracy.[56]

Alliance of World Civilisation is a UN think tank promoting cross cultural activity in mainly the areas of education, youth, migration and media to create greater understanding between the Islamic world and the West. They actually seek to counter the 'clash of civilisations' narrative between the west and Islam, but instead are highlighting the clash; one between moderates and extremists. In this subtle manner they are trying to 'cure religious fundamentalism' by making the State the authority to decide what is extremist and what is allowed. In the final analysis what they are actually saying is that if your belief system makes any absolute claim to be the truth you must be an extremist. The UNAOC was proposed by Jose Zapatero of Spain and endorsed or sponsored by Recip Erdogan of Turkey.[57]

United Religions Initiative. The formation of the New World Religion is well underway through the networking and development of a syncretic, civic, world religion under the auspices of the United Religions Initiative (URI). They are the largest most important inter-faith group forging alliances with religions at local level to unify all faiths and traditions. Of course, they will completely deny this, saying that they just wish to foster better relations within religions by holding interfaith meetings and ceremonies to develop better

---

[55] Parliament of World Churches website https://parliamentofreligions.org/

[56] World Council of Churches website https://www.oikoumene.org/en

[57] Alliance of World Civilisation website https://www.unaoc.org/

understanding. Bishop Swing started this group with the blessing of Robert Muller who said it would be larger than the United Nations. Initially the strategy was to build alliances amongst the world religious leaders but obviously they were resilient to such a syncretic attempt and the strategy failed. They are now building URI alliances, called 'co-operation circles', amongst grass roots believers across the world. On the one hand, they pretend to be a grass roots institution since they are most active with people on the ground level, but in reality they are a group thoroughly endorsed, mandated and pushed along by the United Nations. URI even has George Shultz as one of their Trustees.[58]

No doubt many people within URI are well meaning and have a genuine heart and desire to see unity amongst the different religions, especially in regions where there is conflict, but the reality is that slowly the syncretic civic religion with its new ceremonies, formulae and beliefs is being set up to promote exactly the Sustainable Development of the New World Order. Chapter 12 explains the vital role of URI as the engine for the development of the New World Religion and the long-term goal of global governance.

Tony Blair Institute for Global Change used to be called the Tony Blair Faith Foundation which was an inter-faith organisation seeking to promote peace by breaking down religious differences between the faiths. It took the view that the differences between faiths are based on the distortions of faith rather than the faiths themselves, which all teach respect, justice, and compassion. In other words, it seeks to fit all religions into the same grouping in particular Islam which it seeks to promote as 'Good Islam' and demote 'Bad Islam' whilst saying that the bad aspects of Islam are a result of people distorting the doctrine of the faith of Islam. The foundation was accused of *"promoting one and only one religious confession, which a universal, global political power would impose on the entire world."* [59] The new version has become more political and less religious and seeks to

---

[58] United Religions Initiative (URI), George Shultz
http://www.uri.org/about_uri/presidents_council

[59] Tony Blair Faith Foundation: from Professor Michel Schooyans of the Catholic University
https://www.theguardian.com/commentisfree/belief/2009/may/13/tony-blair-faith-foundation

'combat false populism', which probably refers to whatever version of state sanctioned truth they want us, the people, to adhere to.[60]

The Deep State

Overall these Individuals within Political or Religious institutions in general terms make up the 'Deep State', which is a melting pot of high level politicians, corporatist, oligarch investor trillionaires, financiers and academics, who have cosy links to the Banking industry, Government or the pharma-media-military industrial complex and allied industries. In this book they are variously called the Elite, the Super or Power Elite, the Network, or the Cryptocracy; these are just words for the same group which constitute the secret hidden government which is running everything in our world today. Their main method of gaining power is to infiltrate institutions and subvert them from within to do their bidding. They are particularly good at doing this with large institutions since it's easier to create a fifth rank from within a large institution than a small group. They are generally unelected, unaccountable infiltrators who advance their agenda completely outside of any democratic structure as 'deep moles' behind the governments they supposedly represent. They are the ruling class behind the governments of today. They exist and are real people; just because it seems difficult to believe that such a group operates does not mean that they do not exist! They are Conspirators and they constitute the 'Illuminati' and are the reason for the terrible events we see in the daily news.

They make a disgusting mockery of the normal man on the street as they revoltingly tread down people, society and culture to their aggrandisement and our destruction. We will never know fully who they are at the top of the pyramid, but somewhere there is high level communication between the Cryptocracy and the Devil. This is what the Bible says, and the writings of Luciferians concur with this. **Satan wants to control the world, and so he must control the leaders**

---

of the Cryptocracy. Satan himself can easily get the Cryptocracy to do what he wants since their intellect is no match against his, because they are not submitted to Jesus Christ. This is what Satan is doing, through the politicians and statesman right at the top of our world. Satan is effecting changes to bring about the destruction of humanity and to thwart the plans of God. But we have the victory through Jesus Christ! Christians today should point out what is happening and expose the Cryptocracy: Have nothing to do with the fruitless deeds of darkness, but rather **expose them.** Ephesians 5:11.

Oaths of Allegiance

One of the best methods that Satan has to effect these changes is via the taking of Oaths. Most of these institutions have Oaths which the members must take to become entered into the group - Freemasons, Skull and Bones, Knights of Malta, Jesuits, Order of the Garter, College Fraternities all take serious blood curdling oaths as part of their ceremonies. When they do this, they fall under the power of Satan.

Other groups do not have to swear a spiritual oath formally, such as Trilateralist Commission members, Bilderbergers, Bohemian Grove, Le Cerle, Group of 30, and other political structures used by the Cryptocracy; but they are made aware that if they divulge any information they will be ostracised from the club and never be invited back. They like to invoke the 'Chatham House Rules' which means that they can talk freely without report and that whatever they say cannot be divulged to anyone else. The Milner Groups such as the Institute of Affairs, or RIIA for the UK, and the CFR are private clubs and they also swear allegiance to the club and to their superiors.

As mentioned in the next Chapter, Cecil Rhodes intended for his groups to be run along Freemasonry and Jesuit terms with the chain of command being from the top down along narrow lines to maintain the absolute control they desire. Later on, it was agreed for them to be semi-secret since if they were entirely hidden it would be difficult for them to effect changes fast enough - this is what they called the 'open conspiracy'.

Right or Left it doesn't matter

It doesn't matter if they are from the right or the left of the political spectrum: they all swear allegiance and normally take an oath to their superiors to follow through on the 'Great Plan'. They are only really interested in following through on the dictates of the Cryptocracy who they serve. As they progress and go higher up within the structure they are subject to more and more tests of loyalty to make sure they will not go against their masters. At the top are the Illuminati Initiates involved in arcane occult ceremonies, rituals and sacrifices. They derive their power from Satan, and his followers have his mind. For example, Skull and Bones members perform evil rituals with coffins, skulls and mock blood which all allude to the devil.

When they write their autobiographies, they have become so deceived and brainwashed into Luciferian deceptive thinking that they daren't expose them (and neither do they want to) but only hint at them in veiled whispers. If you read their autobiographies, you will see a few of these undertones but nothing that tangible. That is because after a lifetime of serving the Cryptocracy, which has showed them every favour imaginable, they have become so completely compliant owing their very existence to their masters, that they will never betray its trust or break that oath of oblique allegiance they took years before. Not to mention the fact that the publishing houses which sell their books are owned and controlled by them anyway so any attempt to get information out in this way would be thwarted.

The Bible concurs that the practice of making oaths is wrong. 'Nor shall you make an oath by your head, for you cannot make one hair white or black'. Matthew 5:36.

CHAPTER 4

HISTORY PART 1

Rothschilds

The belief in charging interest as a compensation for the potential loss of capital was instituted in Judaism from around the First Millennium BC and was codified in Deuteronomy 23:19-20.

"You shall not charge interest to your brother—interest on money or food or anything that is lent out at interest. **To a foreigner you may charge interest**, but to your brother you shall not charge interest, that the LORD your God may bless you in all to which you set your hand in the land which you are entering to possess."

From around the time of the first Crusades the Knight Templars and Jewish money lenders in Europe became a problem to the Governments of Europe as they became too powerful.[61] At a time when Christianity forbid the charging of usury, the power and influence of the Jewish money lenders grew.

---

[61] In 1215, the Catholic Church held the Fourth Lateran Council which passed laws instituted across Europe to try and reduce the powers of the Jews and their charge of 'exorbitant interest'. Then in 1253 the French Government expelled them and this trend spread across Europe for the next two hundred years directly or indirectly caused in part by what was seen as unfair lending practices. England 1290, France again in 1306, Saxony 1360, Belgium 1370, Slovakia 1380, Austria 1420, the Netherlands 1444 and Spain 1492.

In 1689 William and Mary of Orange from Holland were put into place in England as the new King and Queen, funded and aided by Jewish money lenders such as Gaspar Fagel. In 1694 the Jewish Bankers had managed to gain control of the Bank of England and King William made the first Bond loan for £1.25 Million but the precise identity of the money-lenders was a secret. This was the start of a new type of the lending, namely, getting Governments and their people into debt so that private individuals can gain power over them.

It was into all this background of secretive money lending and banking that the Rothschild family started their meteoric rise to become the master controllers of all time.

The House of Rothschild long-range strategy

As will be shown in the short section below the Rothschild family have become the owners of about half the entire Worlds Wealth estimated by Credit Suisse to be $280 trillion.[62] They have hidden their money in trusts, offshore companies and via their trusted agents. Currently this is controlled by the head of the family Sir Evelyn de Rothschild (born 1931) who is also the Queen's Financial Adviser, as well as the Vatican's. At this level, being a Financial Advisor to some degree, places you in a position of authority, since you have the ability to make investment recommendations and put them into effect. This puts him in a position of enormous power – to control both the Queen's and the Vatican's wealth and well as their family's vast financial resources, not to mention the many paid agents who hold wealth for them. The House of Rothschild have been advising the Vatican since 1823 and the British Royal family for a similar length of time.

The Rothschild's family have heavily been involved in the creation of the current economic and political system we have today, and if you research deep enough you can often see them or their agents managing the outcomes of important historical events.

---

[62] World's wealth. https://www.credit-suisse.com/corporate/en/articles/news-and-expertise/global-wealth-report-2017-201711.html

The Rothschilds are comfortable **not** to be in the limelight and choose on purpose to work in the shadows, and this is the blinding brilliance of their plan! They chose to remain hidden, out of view and unaccountable, which means that it's extremely difficult to pinpoint anything on them. And this is also why it's so difficult for Governments to resist their gradualist plans for world domination as one of the top families of the Cryptocracy. By stealth and infiltration, the invisible hands directed through their secret societies and fronts have gained influence over institutions which they can bend to their will in their ongoing pursuit of global power.

The Rothschild dynasty found out early on that lending to governments and nations was much more lucrative and safer than lending to Individuals. If governments could not repay their debts they always had the back stop of raising more taxes against the populace. If a country did not want to get into debt with them they would use their considerable power to get their agents into positions of influence or use corrupt politicians to get the governments to agree to their debts all the while creating the money supply out of thin air.

They then set up countries to fight each other and funded them making sure that the victor would honour the debts of the loser. In this manner, they would build up two powers of approximate equal strength and then finance both sides. They then had a third power, which for Europe was England, as a kind of insurance policy should one of the countries step out of line. If they wanted to sway any battle one way or the other they brought England into the fray. This was the 'Balance of Powers'. This is how Nathan Rothchild's England became the supreme power in Europe. The outcome of a war could always be determined by checking which side was favoured by England. This is why England was always on the winning side. This could also be the reason why today Britain has a special place in the Cryptocracy's activities, and possibly why the owners of the UK want the country out of the European Union. Or possibly joined back into the US as the 'Oceania' of George Orwell.[63]

By the turn of the 20th century it was said that the Rothschilds controlled half the property of the world. The House of Rothschild

---

[63] George Orwell, *1984* the 3 fictional states. Oceania, Eurasia and Eastasia. See https://en.wikipedia.org/wiki/Nations_of_Nineteen_Eighty-Four

works to a long-term plan - their threats cannot be brought about instantaneously since it takes time, effort and a lot of political manoeuvring to get countries to fight against each other. This is part of the reason why the timeframe for the development of the New World Order is so long, it takes time to make good on all the necessary threats made in the past. For example, when Russia stood against the Congress of Vienna in 1814 to create a centralised European State the payback for this only happened with the destruction of the Tsar in 1917, over a hundred years later.

In this way debt is used by them as political leverage to gain control and power. If a country fails to accept a loan there are wars and invasions or regime change or assassinations to oust that Government until a Rothschild controlled Bank promoting usurious practices is installed. The fact that these banks are the World Bank or the IMF doesn't matter since the Cryptocracy control this as well as everything else.

A Short History

Instead of providing an in-depth history of the Rothschilds for the last 270 years we are going to look at some of the most important business events that show how they managed to infiltrate and take over many countries in the 18th and 19th Century. It is this legacy which gives us the dire situation we are in today. The Rothschild family have Ashkenazi Jewish heritage.[64] This was a diaspora group which moved into Germany among other countries, and it is from this group that the most powerful Jews and all Prime Ministers of Israel are derived.

The founder of the Rothschild dynasty was **Mayer Amschel Bauer** (1744-1812) who was born in Frankfurt, Germany. In 1783 he became a successful Banker to Count Frederick II of Hesse-Cassel and his son Prince Wilhelm IX, Langrave (Count) of Hesse-Hanau in

---

[64] From the Bible the oldest son of Gomer was Ashkenaz from Genesis 10:3 and it is from him that we have the descendants of the Ashkenazi Jews. So the list goes Noah, Japheth, Gomer, and his first born was Ashkenaz (Gen 10:3).

1801.[65] Amschel Bauer changed his name to Mayer Amschel Rothschild.

He had 5 Sons who were dispatched to continue their domination of world banking using the principles learnt by their Father. His first son, Amschel, stayed in Frankfurt, his second son Solomon was sent to Vienna. In 1798 he sent his third son Nathan Rothschild to London and it was he who was to become the most successful of his brothers. The fourth son Karl went to Naples, and the fifth, Jacob went to Paris. All of them were Freemasons. In the early days by being 5 brothers in different countries each one could help the other if difficulties arose, and in those early days of Banking they certainly did. Banks were formed and went bankrupt on a regular basis and whilst others banking families perished the Rothschilds above all survived, helping each other out when times were bad, and colluding together when times were good. All the while they were infiltrating their agents into every imaginable scenario behind the scenes in order to gain greater profit and greater power.

In the end it became the case that they no longer lent to Countries which were able to pay back their loans, or even countries which were sympathetic to their long term aims, but that they lent to countries which they controlled via their agents who could direct the course of events for those countries. In Rothschilds day, before banking regulation and antitrust laws existed, it was indeed possible for small groups to gain controlling interests in enough financial institutions that it could be argued that they 'controlled' a nation's money supply. Mayer Amschel Rothschild in 1790 supposedly made the infamous declaration, to the effect of, "Let me issue and control a nation's money and I care not who writes the laws."[66]

The Rothschilds take over France

Amschel Mayer Rothschild had links to the Bavarian Illuminati of Adam Weishaupt. He was not a member of the Illuminati, presumably because they did not allow Jews into the group, but both

---

[65] Terry Melanson, *Perfectiblists, The 18th Century Bavarian Order of the Illuminati*, Trine Day. The Bavarian Illuminati. Page 21.

[66] There has been some debate if he said this or how he said this.

his patrons of Frederick and Wilhelm Hesse-Cassel were indeed members of this subversive group. In fact, they were not the only connections Amschel Rothschild had to the Illuminati, there were other financiers and contacts who he would have undoubtedly have come into contact with.[67] In Walter Scott's History of Napoleon, he states that the French Revolution was planned by the Illuminati and funded by European Bankers.[68] It is partly from this publication that the belief has emerged, that the Rothschilds financed the Illuminati.

The Rothschilds take over Britain

During the Napoleonic Wars (1803-1815) the 5 Rothschild brothers supplied gold to both Wellington's army and Napoleon's, funding both sides which was excellent business for them since the debts themselves were guaranteed by the government of that country.

They also set up a postal service across Europe so that confidential war correspondence could be intercepted and disclosed to the Rothschilds, so they could stay one step ahead of everyone else. As the story goes, after the Battle of Waterloo one of Rothschild's couriers managed to get back to England a full day before the others. Nathan Rothschild sold all his stock making his competitors think that the English had lost the war. The stock price collapsed, and then Nathan bought up all the shares at heavily discounted prices. When news of a British victory broke, the share price rocketed, making the Rothschilds a 20 to 1 return on their investment.

Nathan Rothschild became the richest man in Europe and had complete control over the British economy, so much so that he reformed the Bank of England. He openly bragged that during his 17 years in England he had turned his £20,000 stake given to him by his father to £50 million. An incredible sum for 1815 and even a good fortune in today's money.

---

[67] Terry Melanson, *Perfectiblists, The 18th Century Bavarian Order of the Illuminati,* Trine Day. Page 334-336.

[68] Walter Scott, *The Life of Napoleon,* volume 2 of his 9-volume history. It might be too much of a stretch to say that the Rothschilds financed the Illuminati since they were not members of the Bavarian Illuminati since their names are not on the list.

The Rothschilds save the Bank of England. The Rothschilds caused the 'Panic of 1825' which was the world's first major stock market crash. The Bank of England took the economy off the gold standard of the time to use the fiat money system to flood the market with cheap debt which created a deflationary spiral. This was at a time when there was already a lot of debt in the system and the government had been encouraged to take out huge loans to keep the economy and payment of war loans afloat. This was the start of Bank of England being the lender of the last resort. In the end Nathan Rothschild rescued the Bank by suppling gold from the Banque of France, which they also owned, to keep the Bank of England afloat. The significance of this event should not be underestimated since it put the control of the Bank of England into the hands of the Rothschilds.[69]

This situation continues to this day, and the Rothchild offices at St Swithin Lane which were bought in 1809, is only a minute's walk from the Bank of England in Threadneedle Street in the City of London.[70]

Every high-level member in the Bank of England is hand-picked from a very narrow selection of businessmen, 'illuminati economists' or academics who are the 'insiders of the insiders', controlled via secret groups, meetings and disinformation. They are chosen because they can be manipulated normally by way of polite mutual assurances. There is no need for heavy handedness, and anyway practically ALL of them have been Freemasons or members of other secret societies which is another control mechanism, 'insurance plan' which they can always use in the background if they have to step in and make any serious alterations. In the US the same insider technique has been employed and practically ALL of the Federal Reserve Chairman's have been Jewish. They have also only been one step away from the Rothschild family, who enabled their careers in the top Banking establishments they own. Being Jewish is not a prerequisite, but there is a link between the Fed inner circle and the CFR inner circle who

---

[69] See Larry Neal report on the Panic of 1825 at
https://files.stlouisfed.org/files/htdocs/publications/review/98/05/9805ln.pdf

[70] St Swithin Lane office
https://www.rothschildarchive.org/collections/treasure_of_the_month/march_20
16_nathan_mayer_rothschilds_bill_case_1831

run the political aspect, and that is that both are drawn mainly from Ashkenazi Jews.[71]

The Rothschilds take over America

The First Bank of the United States 1791-1811

In 1791 Alexander Hamilton, who was a Rothschild agent, set up the First Bank of the United States much to the disgust of Madison and Jefferson who saw it as a sell out to the European Banking powers. The Bank had a 20-year charter after which it was not renewed, but the Rothschilds would take revenge. In 1812 Nathan Rothschild single-handedly managed to get the British to try to re-take the United States as a colony and so Britain declared war on the US. The aim was to win the battle for control of American banking and reinstate their hidden hand. But they didn't expect that the British would be so busy fighting Napoleon that they would not be able to gain a solid victory and so the war ended in 1814 with America undefeated. The US was then saved by the incredible foresight of Stephen Girard who bought the First Bank for a third of its value and saved the fledgling America from becoming subsumed back into the 'British Empire'.

The Second Bank of the United States 1816-1832

In 1816 both Madison and Jefferson had previously voted to keep foreign banks out of the US, but they suddenly changed their minds possibly fearing further war with Britain. The House of Rothschild thereby secured the Second Bank of the United States with another 20-year charter which was exactly what they wanted.

The Panic of 1819. The Rothschilds had only been in control of the Second Bank of the United States for 3 years and in that time managed to create the first US property boom and bust. It's easy when you know! You flood the market with lots of cheap money so debt flows freely, and property prices soar, and then you suddenly

---

[71] List of Fed Chairmans see
https://en.wikipedia.org/wiki/Chair_of_the_Federal_Reserve

withdraw money, raise interest rates and clamp down on debts, and lo and behold, there's a crash! In this manner the Rothschild foreclosed on houses, farms and businesses and many people were made bankrupt and ruined. It was an obvious power grab, but America was not going to be taken over so easily and so, when in 1832 the Rothschilds approached Congress four years early to get to get another extension on the bank, they were declined.

For the next few years President Andrew Jackson tried to wrestle control of American banks back from the Rothschilds. The Rothschilds responded by pulling back the money supply causing another economic depression. They then tried to have him assassinated in 1835. Richard Lawrence who attempted to assassinated him, bragged that 'some influential people in Europe' had protected him and he didn't go to jail.

Andrew Jackson eventually succeeded in breaking the Rothschild's grip on American banking and the third Bank Charter was not enacted. He famously said that he would 'kill the Bank.' He was referring to the banking conspirators who were trying to take over America since he did not want that to happen. But in 1857 the Rothschilds and associated banking conspirators, *still* did not have the financial control of the United States they desired, and so it was decided to create an incident which would allow the establishment of a Central Bank. Wars are expensive, and governments need money to win, so to bring the country down, they instigated the American Civil War which was over slavery.[72]

In 1913, under the auspices of the Federal Reserve, they would be able to set up their third bank in America, the Fed. Jackson is still hated today by the Network and in 2015 there was a media fuelled attempt to remove him from the $20 bill. The answer why is not lost to history, as the controlled, biased media would like to tell us. The

---

[72] Canada and Mexico weren't strong enough, to fight the US and England and France were too far away. Russia wasn't under their control until much later on in 1917. So they decided that the contrived American Civil War which ran from 1861 to 1865 would be about slavery (slave rights), even though only approximately a third of Southerners held slaves and, incredibly, four of the Northern states held slaves anyway. On both sides of the conflict there were Rothchild agents - in the north, August Belmont worked for the Rothschild's from outset (Wiki), and in the South there was John Slidell and Baron Frederick Erlanger.

reality is Andrew Jackson fought the Rothschilds and won. But over 180 years later they still feel aggrieved by this and propagate the idea that Andrew Jackson was somehow undeserving to be on the note. This is just a bit more evidence to show how the Cryptocracy works to a long-range plan, not to mention how petty they are, that they have to slate the name of someone who's been dead for 180 years! Andrew Jackson should be considered a hero, and he was the first and only American President to pay off all the national debt.[73]

Federal Reserve conspiracy

Paul Warburg, as the main conspirator lead the cabal of bankers who created the Federal Reserve, and this time it would not be a charter, but an act of law signed off by Woodrow Wilson. He later said he had destroyed his own country.[74] The Federal Reserve Bank was formed in 1913 under very suspicious circumstances. Paul Warburg took the Hegelian dialect to a new level of duplicity saying that he didn't want the Federal Reserve Bank to exist since it would be bad for the people. But he instigated it and stood to gain from it.[75]

The Rothschilds were involved in numerous other financial transactions which enabled them to gain power. They financed Brazil

---

[73] January 1835 p 63 MS King, *Planet Rothschild*, Volume 1. Articles on this see:-

https://www.washingtonpost.com/news/the-fix/wp/2015/03/06/why-is-andrew-jackson-on-the-20-bill-the-answer-may-be-lost-to-history/?utm_term=.042cc37453c8

https://www.washingtonpost.com/news/wonk/wp/2015/06/18/why-the-u-s-government-needs-to-remove-andrew-jackson-from-the-20-bill/?utm_term=.0f7cb7b5e42b

[74] Quote of Woodrow Wilson. "I am a most unhappy man. I have unwittingly ruined my country. A great industrial nation is controlled by its system of credit. Our system of credit is concentrated. The growth of the nation, therefore, and all our activities are in the hands of a few men. We have come to be one of the worst ruled, one of the most completely controlled and dominated Governments in the civilized world no longer a Government by free opinion, no longer a Government by conviction and the vote of the majority, but a Government by the opinion and duress of a small group of dominant men." -Woodrow Wilson, after signing the Federal Reserve into existence.

[75] See G Edward Griffin, *The Creature from Jekyll Island*, and Eustace Mullins, *The Secrets of the Federal Reserve*.

in 1824; when they wished to become free from their colonial masters of Portugal, it was agreed that they would have to pay £2 million as compensation. It was the Rothschild family who provided this, but Brazil struggles to repay this debt. Again, political leverage can be brought to bear on whoever is in power. In 1875 the Suez Canal loan for £4 million was agreed on a hand shake between Benjamin Disraeli and N M Rothschild.

In 1896 the concept of Zionism and the creation of a Jewish State was pushed along by Theodore Herzl who even wrote his book, 'Addressed to the Rothschilds' (also known as 'The Jewish State'). As is typical of the Hegelian dialect, Baron Edmond de Rothschild took the opposite view in public and thought it a bad idea. They then positioned themselves to take advantage of the creation of Israel and the famous Balfour Declaration which set up the plan to create Israel as the Jewish State. This was the plan of the Cryptocracy and the Declaration was written by Arthur Balfour and Alfred Milner who were both inner members of the Rhodes / Milner secret society.

By the end of the 19th Century, the Rothschilds had a controlling influence in Britain and all her colonies, China, the U.S, most of Europe, South America and parts of Asia. Only Russia was the main power left out of their financial sphere. From about 1900, the apparent role of the Rothschilds diminished as they pushed their agents forward as front men to do the work whilst they remained in the background. This involved the recruitment of John D Rockefeller, Andrew Carnegie and John Pierpoint Morgan all of whom were helped by the Rothschilds at some stage in their career progression. The Rockefeller-Rothschild link is a fascinating one, since at first it appears they were competitors, and later on it seems likely that the Rockefellers are subordinate to the Rothschilds. Perhaps the Rothschilds were attracted to the industrial espionage system that the Rockefellers ran – most things were written in code, and they had secrets contacts everywhere.[76] The emergence of the Milner group meant that the overall agenda of the Cryptocracy could be advanced through those various power bases, and political

---

[76] Rockefeller industrial espionage - a point made by Gary Allen in *The Rockefeller File* p 23 (Seal Beach 1976.) Quoted from Servando Gonzalez, *I Dare call it Treason*, Kindle Loc 251.

institutions which they controlled via the fronts and secret societies they ran.

Between about 1880 and 1933 the 'robber barons' in America, who had made vast fortunes in heavy industry, such as oil and steel or building the railway infrastructure, slowly shifted their interests to international Banking.[77] Banking was the obvious business where they could maintain and grow their wealth and expand their power base.

The rise of Standard Oil via John D Rockefeller and the subsequent joining up with the likes of John Pierpoint Morgan and Paul Warburg as agents for the Rothschilds made a financial power house of unprecedented influence and political importance.[78] Carrol Quigley wrote in 'Tragedy and Hope' that: 'The greatest of these dynasties, of course, were the descendants of Meyer Amschel Rothschild...'

There were less than a dozen Banks who controlled America and after the Second World War, they set up other financial institutions to occlude their presence. Ever since this time, these same coalesced groups have been grabbing power across the world and they have succeeded in skewing political and economic processes for over the last one hundred years.[79]

When big corporations and governments collude together to do business, this is the definition of Fascism. This is how the corporations have been using tax payers' money to fund the difficult aspects of any deal, but at the same time ripping out the massive profits for themselves.

Despite this, not everything went their way (in the early days), and when taxation started in America in 1913 they sought new ways to hide their money. This started the tax-free Foundations, the most influential (at this time) being the Rockefeller, Carnegie and Mellon Foundation which were used as instruments to further their final goal of world government under their control.[80]

---

[77] Carroll Quigley, *Tragedy and Hope,* p 71+72.

[78] Ibid page 532.

[79] Ibid page 545.

[80] Ibid page 938.

In 1917 Trotsky and Lenin manage to overthrow Russia. They were funded and helped along by the Rothschild banking-agent, Jacob Schiff, of Khune Loeb Bank in New York. This was a totally pre-meditated conspiracy in which Communism was used as the excuse to excite the people and overthrow the weak government.[81] The Schiff family and the Rothschilds shared a house in Frankfurt in 1785 and were therefore very well connected close family friends.

After the Bolshevik Revolution, Standard Oil of New Jersey brought 50% of the huge Caucasus oil field, even though the land had theoretically been nationalized. In 1927, Standard Oil of New York built a refinery in Russia and provided loans to the Bolsheviks[82] throughout the Cold War years, the Rockefellers seem to have been able to go anywhere and meet whoever they wanted, perhaps even deposing Nikita Khrushchev in 1964.

The Cryptocracy ran Russia as well as the US and everywhere else, exactly as they do so today, but in order to advance their plans for humanity they have to create their myths which they sell to us as a means of maintaining power and keeping control. If the truth ever came out and enough people knew what they were doing their entire system would fall apart. So they keep lying to us!

In 1987 Edmonde de Rothschild (1926-1997) set up the Global Environmental Facility which was a lending institution linked to the World Bank and IMF to provide funds to help countries become more 'green' and advance the environmental agenda. We know this from James Hunt's expose at the 4th Wilderness Conference in 1987. This was the same strategy the Club of Rome alluded to that they needed some unifying principle, or excuse, in order to gain further power. This was the same environmental strategy which lead to the global warming and CO_2 anthropogenic hoax we have mentioned before. The Global Environmental Facility (GEF) (also called the World Conservation Bank) was set up to facilitate governments to borrow money from this 'bank' to help them deal with environmental

---

[81] See Antony C. Sutton, *Wall Street and the Bolshevik Revolution*, published by Arlington House in New Rochelle, NY, 1974.

[82] Then Standard Oil floated a loan of $75 million to the Bolsheviks and marketed Soviet Oil to Europe.

issues.[83] If any of these countries are unable to repay these loans they may donate land to the fund and in this way, the conspirators have gained even more land.[84]

Secret Funds: there exists in various locations funds which are beyond the reach of global Tax Authorities. These funds are used to further New World Order objectives. The **Trident Fund** set up in Reno, Nevada is apparently beyond the reach of the IRS and OECD authorities and as such, money seeking new tax avoidance havens has flowed into these Rothschild Trust enabled Funds.[85] Data from the World Bank, IMF, UN and other New World Order agencies have said they expect there to be between in the region of US$21 to US$31 trillion in hiding in these types of arrangements. This is almost certainly the tip of the iceberg. This is the Cryptocracy's 'money under the mattress' in case some unforeseen event occurs and causes them to lose power. They can create new money or bring this back into the normal economy. Real misers always have a secret stash no-one knows about!

Conclusion of the Rothschilds

In this manner the Rothschilds became the World's Bankers and this came with all the power and influence to make and break governments, nations and anything which stood in their way. This is the true History of the last 270 years, how the Rothschild bankers and allied co-conspirators have stealthily and craftily infiltrated governments and institutions as part of their subtle drive to seize power. They have done this to take decision making away the elected individuals and place this into the hands of the very few. This is the true story of our time.

---

[83] For more on the Global Environmental Facility see '*A New Green Order*' by Zoe Young (Pluto Press 2002.)

[84] It is said that 30% of land is already in the hands of these conspirators. See https://www.bibliotecapleyades.net/sociopolitica/esp_sociopol_rothschild37.htm

[85] See article https://www.bloomberg.com/news/articles/2016-01-27/the-world-s-favorite-new-tax-haven-is-the-united-states Or web search: Trident Fund Reno.

Our politicians are in the pockets of these extremely powerful individuals and the groups they control, and they will do exactly as they are told since they are insiders working for their benefit. If there is a financial crash, they never hold them accountable, and instead of letting them go bust, bankrupt and be brought to justice for fraud, they give them other people's money; bailing them out with tax payers hard earned cash. The bankers ruin economies, wreck lives with their 'mistakes', which make us suffer, and then they have our governments use our money to bail them out. The 'them' being the multi-trillionaire bankers and financiers. It is all a power grab to consolidate mankind into their systems. We will never escape this problem. This is why, in the Bible, it says that 'money is the root of all kinds of evil.' 1 Timothy 6:10.

HISTORY PART 2

Carroll Quigley (1910-1977)

Carroll Quigley was an academic American Historian who was given access to the private papers and writings of the Royal Institute of International Affairs from 1940 to the early 1960s. His research and subsequent books prove conclusively, and with very good evidence, that there is indeed a world political conspiracy under way which has severely altered the history of the world, to their benefit rather than the national interests of each nation which they supposedly served. At every step of the 20th Century you can see the 'invisible hand' of the Elite Network above our governments which is made up of the Cecil Rhodes group and the Rothschild power base, together, forming a conspiratorial cabal intent on world government. Once you know about this group and can track their beliefs and methods, they can be seen manipulating world events to gain themselves more power; but for the nations they represented, this resulted in less power and less democracy. To write a single academic book about the history of the 20th Century without knowing about this Network is a terrible shame because it makes all their work disinformation.

'Illuminati Historians' are everywhere giving us the conspirator's version of events as they unknowingly push the completely false and contrived version of what really happened, because they don't know about the Milner group and secret societies, or they choose to downplay their power and impact to such an extent as to be an irrelevance. Even though the reality of this tiny, but vitally important subversive group, is right in front of them, they have been indoctrinated into the sanitised untrue version of history from their teachers, university professors and others.

Although Carroll Quigley was a believer in the positive aspect of the concept of the New World Order, he didn't like the fact that it should be kept secret and thought that people deserved to know what was happening. On the one side Carroll Quigley thought that the group was a good thing, and that they were trying to help humanity to a create a more integrated global system, but on the other side, he seemed to think that their goals and methods were deplorable. In this respect Quigley shows himself to be an insider who is more of a reluctant whistle blower than a conspiracy historian.

But at every step Quigley supports them, with their version of History, and always gives them the benefit of the doubt. He was not a believer in God, which is a point Dr Stan Monteith makes in his lectures and writings, and so he couldn't see the spiritual significance of this.[86] It is from Carroll Quigley that we know about Cecil Rhodes' secret society which is what his book the Anglo-American Establishment is all about. He also expounds the Council on Foreign Relations and explains the History and methodology of JP Morgan, the Rockefeller Foundation, and allied conspirators. His book *Tragedy and Hope* was published in 1966 but was censored and re-emerged only years later.

---

[86] Stan Monteith went through all Carroll Quigley's notes to check what he said was correct. He thought it was **Alfred Zimmern** who divulged the conspirators' History to Quigley. Zimmern was a fellow Historian and founding circle member of the RIIA. See the 'Brotherhood of Darkness' lecture on You Tube from mins 40 following. https://www.youtube.com/watch?v=-YUQcmvItuY&t=2494s

Cecil Rhodes (1853-1902)

Cecil Rhodes is one of the most seminal individuals in how our world became ruled by just a handful of men. He is central to understanding the development of the Cryptocracy in modern times and by what methods they manage to keep control since he started the *Society of the Elect*, a secret society which created all the political groups of today.

His father, Francis, was a Church of England Vicar. He went to a grammar school in Bishops Stortford and later on, was schooled by his father for a period of time before he was sent to South Africa to work on his older brother's cotton farm. It was thought that the hotter weather of South Africa might suit him since he had poor health with heart and lung problems.

Working the land wasn't a lucrative trade and Rhodes moved to the now famous Kimberley diamond mines where he made many innovative improvements to the rather primitive working conditions at that time. From around 1871 to 1874, he quickly amassed a considerable fortune in the diamond trade. Later on, he was funded by N M Rothschild which enabled him to take over and consolidate the smaller diamond mines and start the DeBeers company in 1888, which is still in existence today. He also turned his hand to gold mining and politics becoming the Prime Minister of Cape Colony, South Africa from 1890 to 1896. His company, the British South Africa Company, also acquired Rhodesia which became modern day Zimbabwe.

John Ruskin

In 1873 Rhodes returned to England briefly to study at Oxford University. There he was heavily influenced by John Ruskin who was first and foremost an artist, but he was also a writer, occultist, Freemason and notably, a Fabian Socialist. He was also a racist and Malthusian eugenicist devoted to the creation of a master - slave society based upon the principles of eugenics largely derived from Plato's Republic.

Plato's Republic

In this book we have the concept of the Elite ruling Man; the Police enforcing the rules, and the Masses who are the Slaves do all the work. This is the three tier system Plato thought would work best. Why the Elite have gone along with this crazy idea seems extraordinary![87] But Ruskin envisioned a race of 'human thoroughbreds' led by the **British socialist elite ruling class**, whose sole purpose was ultimately to dominate, own and rule the world under a Globalist Government using the British Commonwealth of Nations structure as their preferred model.

Rhodes was impressed with all this rhetoric and became a devotee of Ruskin. He was also influenced by the colonial historian John Seeley. Having a vast fortune at his disposal he set about drafting a secret program for world domination with himself and his friends as rulers. To guarantee this funding after his death (since he had poor health) he wrote a Will bequeathing funds for Political Scholars whereby future leaders could be indoctrinated into the Globalist, Socialistic one world government via the Rhodes Scholarship. In this manner, and under the leadership of mentors such as Harold Laski, many politicians (eg Callaghan) have been indoctrinated into the global political belief system of the Cryptocracy ever since. In 1877 he wrote the first of seven wills that he composed over his lifetime, the aim of which was **for expansion of the British way of life and creation of a world system of Government under their control.** Here is a section from Rhodes first Will, the addendum, which is called the 'Confessions of Faith'. It is provided without alteration and in full to gain a bit more understanding. Emphasis added.

I look into history and I read the story of the Jesuits I see what they were able to do in a bad cause and I might say under bad leaders.

At the present day I become a member of the Masonic order I see the wealth and power they possess the influence they hold and I think over their ceremonies and I wonder that a large body of men can devote themselves to what at times appear the most ridiculous and absurd rites without an object and without an end.

Let us form the <u>same kind of society</u> a Church for the extension of the British Empire. A society which should have members <u>in every part of the British Empire</u>

---

[87] Plato: the Elite's political beliefs relate more to Plato's philosophy than a studied system of political science.

working with one object and one idea we should have its members placed at our universities and our schools and should watch the English youth passing through their hands just one perhaps in every thousand would have the mind and feelings for such an object, he should be tried in every way, he should be tested whether he is endurant, possessed of eloquence, disregardful of the petty details of life, and if found to be such, then elected and <u>bound by oath</u> to serve for the rest of his life in his County. He should then be supported if without means by the Society and sent to that part of the Empire where it was felt he was needed.

To and for the establishment, promotion and development of a Secret Society, the true aim and object whereof shall be for <u>the extension of British rule throughout the world</u>, *the perfecting of a system of emigration from the United Kingdom, and of colonisation by British subjects <u>of all lands</u> where the means of livelihood are attainable by energy, labour and enterprise, and especially the occupation by British settlers of the entire Continent of Africa, the Holy Land, the Valley of the Euphrates, the Islands of Cyprus and Candia, (Crete) the whole of South America, the Islands of the Pacific not heretofore possessed by Great Britain, the whole of the Malay Archipelago, the seaboard of China and Japan,* **the ultimate recovery of the United States of America** *as an integral part of the British Empire, the inauguration of a system of Colonial representation in the Imperial Parliament which may tend to weld together the disjointed members of the Empire and, finally, the foundation of so great a Power as to render wars impossible and promote the best interests of humanity."*

So here we have it, DIRECTLY from the man himself calling for the formation of 'British rule throughout the world' via a 'secret society' based on the Jesuits and Freemasonry! The primary function would be focused on Global Government by whatever means the British Empire could, to bring about world governance. Therefore, will any Rhodes Scholar be rooting for World Government? Is this what the evidence leads us to? Yes, every Rhodes scholar, without fail, is a 'one worlder'. The most famous would be Bill Clinton, James Woolsey (ex- head of the CIA), Strobe Talbot, Susan Rice (head of the NSA under Obama), James Fulbright, (Edwin Hubble) and Dean Rusk amongst others. They are, what could be termed 'inner circle members' fully on board with the complicated business of destroying world-wide democracy and making policy for the benefit of the Cryptocracy's long-range plan.

The Secret Society of The Elect

This was Rhodes' vision, to take over the whole world for his British friends with them in power and the people as slaves below, as in a feudalist state. His 'Society of the Elect' was based upon the concept of a secret society which means they do things hidden and in private.

Cecil Rhodes founded the Society of the Elect in 1891.

The Inner Members or the Core Elect, were 4 in number. There was Cecil Rhodes (Freemason), and then the Junta of 3 who were William Stead (Theosophist), Reginald Brett 2nd Viscount of Esher (Atheist) then Baron Nathan Rothschild (Ashkenazi Jew) and later on Alfred Milner (Freemason). These men formed the inner core of the group. Cecil Rhodes was a homosexual and Reginald Brett was a pederast.[88]

Behind these 5 were The Society of the Elect who were made up of about 28 members including members such as Alfred Beit who helped Rhodes with money and Arthur Balfour, later to be the Liberal Prime Minister (1902-5). Others were Lionel Curtis who formed the Royal Institute of International Affairs (RIIA) and founded the American counterpart of this, The Council on Foreign Relations.[89] Curtis was a major advocate of world government.[90] Waldorf Astor and Lady Nancy Astor were also within this inner circle.

---

[88] Maurice Brett / MI6 link Wikipedia entry on Reginald Brett. For more on his life see *The Enigmatic Edwardian: Life of Reginald, 2nd Viscount Esher'* by James Lee-Milne. Reginald Brett had incest with his son Maurice Brett who went on to found MI6 during World War 1.

[89] CFR: Carrol Quigley, *Tragedy and Hope* p 951.

[90] See Lionel Curtis book, *Civitas Deit, The Commonwealth of God*, written in 1934-37.

Alfred Milner (1854-1925)

Rhodes died early and his secret society was continued by Alfred Milner. **It was under Alfred Milner that the strategy of creating practically all the political apparatus which we still have in position today was formed.** The influence and power that is contained within this machinery is, and was concentrated at the heart of their Society and has been from around 1915. This is a fact which has enormous significance since it means that all of our political institutions were populated by people who have sworn oaths to work for the hidden hand and the Great Plan, which therefore means that all our institutions are being subverted from within by secret society members. The evidence for this is also irrefutably corroborated once you can gain the necessary 'height' to see the Cryptocracy's decisions and understand how they think, behave and what they really believe.

The Beliefs of the early Milner Group

Practically all of the members were **Freemasons** and the links to occultism are undeniable. If they weren't Masons, they were Theosophists such as William Stead who was one of the original Junta of 3, the inner core of the group. Arthur Balfour was supposedly a Christian, but he was also President of the Society for Psychical Research in 1893 which makes him an occultist. Other members of the group were, Rudyard Kipling who was a Theosophist, and H. G. Wells who was Freemason, and propagandist for the New World Order. Wells' writings do expose some elements of their plan because in those days it was a more 'open conspiracy', they even called it that themselves revealing some information in a book of the same name, 'The Open Conspiracy'. Nowadays they have to be more guarded, but at the same time they are a lot bolder as well. The only Bible believing Christian amongst them was the Methodist William Booth of the Salvation Army and he should be excluded because he was in the outermost circle and didn't have any true effect on the society.

Other Milnerites were, Jan Smuts, Prime Minister of South Africa and John Buchan the adventure novelist (39 Steps), who was the private Secretary to Alfred Milner from 1901 and later on became the Governor of Canada. It was Nathan Rothschild who appointed Lord Alfred Milner to head up the Secret Society for which Rhodes' first will made provision.

The Milner group goes international

Between around 1900 and 1915 the Society consolidated its power with The Inquiry group in America and linked up with the 'Eastern Establishment' in the US; with the likes of John Pierpont Morgan and the Warburgs, and Lazards who were the American counterparts to the British establishment. The 'Anglo-American establishment' as Carroll Quigley called it, was truly born. It is fair to say that previous to this there were other groups with similar aims, but Milner's group is by far the most important since **they created every piece of political machinery which we have in place today**. The list of these institutions was provided in the previous chapter.

In 1909 Milner founded the Round Table. This was named after King Arthur's Round Table, but the group had different names at different times. Under Rhodes it was called the Society of the Elect, or the dream of Cecil Rhodes, or the secret society of Cecil Rhodes. In the second and third decade of its existence it was called the Milner Kindergarten, and from 1910 the Milner Group. It has also been called the Times crowd, the Rhodes crowd, the Chatham House crowd, the All Souls Group, and the Cliveden Set in the 1930s. The outer circle of the group was called The Association of Helpers whereas the real centre of the organization was The Society of the Elect.[91] Oxford University and All Souls college was a form of recruiting ground.[92] This Round Table was instrumental in the setting up of World War 1 under Sir Edward Grey.

---

[91] Carroll Quigley, *The Anglo-American Establishment* p 4.

[92] Ibid page 91.

Chatham House, International Institute of Affairs

Lionel Curtis was an Inner Initiate of the Society of the Elect and under him and with Alfred Milner the group's secret society truly went International with the Royal Institute of International Affairs (RIIA) founded in 1919 in London, the Council on Foreign Relations (CFR) founded in 1921 in New York, and the Institute of Pacific Relations (IPR) founded in 1925.[93] By 1927 the Royal Institute of International Affairs had offices in over 7 countries: United States, Canada, Australia, New Zealand, South Africa, Germany and India. They then secretly infiltrated all these countries to become the world's shadow government. The Council on Foreign Relations lead to the Trilateral Commission. **All these groups are linked as a Secret Society.**

In the UK it is my estimation that most Prime Ministers are members of this group. This is conjecture. Out of the last 8 British Prime Ministers 5 of them have been to Oxford University which is where Rhodes scholars go for their indoctrination and is where the conspirators consistently recruited members for the Great Plan. As mentioned in Caroll Quigley's book The Anglo-American Establishment page 91, he states that they recruited from All Souls, Oxford University. The following UK Prime Ministers went to Oxford: Wilson, Thatcher, Blair, Cameron, and May. Callaghan was tutored under Harold Laski at the London School of Economics that other haven the network uses to recruit and indoctrinate future politicians. The LSE was set up, run and funded by the Rockefellers, so he qualifies as being in the inner list as well. Which leaves only Major and Brown standing outside. Both of them came to power almost as aberrations once their ubermensches had stepped aside. Boris Johnson also went to Oxford along with a plethora of other politicians all of whom should be treated as being suspects for being Secret Society members of the Rhodes Group. This is conjecture, we simply don't know, since it's a secret. But lists are available online for Freemasons, Skull and Bones, Knight of Malta and other groups, and practically all politicians will be a member of one type of secret society or another, and this is a fact – but you will never see this mentioned in the press but it is of vital significance to understanding what is happening in our world today.

---

[93] Ibid pages 190-192.

Council on Foreign Relations

The CFR was founded in 1919 and is the American branch of the Royal Institute of International Affairs. It was felt that the word *Royal* was too much of a giveaway so it was dropped. The group was made up of experts from the American delegation to the Versailles Peace Conference who were most closely associated with J.P. Morgan and the Rockefellers. The CFR headquarters is at Harold Pratt House, New York, and were acquired with Rockefeller funds just like the United Nations building. Ever since, the CFR conspirators have been directing foreign relations and dictating policy to the President and his administration. The reason why US Politicians do exactly as they are told is because they are controlled and put into place by the same controlling secret group.

David Rockefeller admitted in his book, Memoirs page 408 that the CFR **"continues to influence the formulation of American foreign policy."** He doesn't say it dictates it, but to all intents and purposes the CFR is above, and in control of the US administration, although it is at least 2 or 3 rings out from the centre of power according to G Edward Griffin.[94] We also know this from Hillary Clinton's frank comment where she admitted more than she really intended, that they didn't now have to go far to receive their orders from the 'mother ship' that is the CFR. There was a new office at Washington not New York so it was close by. This really is the shadow government of the US. We can see their actions all over the history of the past 100 years and yet few history books are concentrating on who is and isn't a member of the CFR and so the nuances of what really happens are completely lost because historians are not critical enough of the advisers surrounding the levers of power. From the Treaty of Versailles in 1919, to the financial and military build-up of Hitler, to the UN, the destruction of Eastern Europe, to the CIA, to Fidel Castro, to Iran, to the EU, 9/11 and Afghanistan: at every stage of these events you will see CFR members

---

[94] See G Edward Griffin's lectures 'Rings of Power' on You Tube
https://www.youtube.com/watch?v=uzMKO56E5Ak

affecting the outcome. This is a fact. But you have to look, and you have to know who is a CFR member and who isn't. You can guarantee that the CFR conspirators will be present skewing the political process and the outcome. For those struggling with this entire concept it might be worth researching any of the above events and making notes about which President or politicians, and advisors were, or were not, CFR members. You will notice an alarming pattern: that the CFR conspirators were cleverly making policy towards the direction they wanted for their agenda.[95]

CFR / Trilateral Commission

As Japan started to gain prominence in the 1970s it was felt by David Rockefeller that they should be brought more into the fold. This was originally discussed but rejected at a Bilderberg meeting and so he started the Trilateral Commission. The US/UK, Europe and Japan would make up the 3 areas. The symbol for the Trilateral Commission is three Sixes, (666) with three (illuminati) triangles.

The Fabian Society link

In the UK the parallel organization to the Milner group was the Fabian society whose symbol is a wolf in sheep's clothing. Whilst the Fabians dominated the Labour movement and the left, the Milner group operated among liberal and conservative circles, so the middle and right. George Bernard Shaw was an early member of this group which attempts to stealthily bring about world domination for the Socialists. This gradualist approach (like a tortoise which is another symbol they use) is the best and surest way to get the change they desire, but it does take a long time to slowly and imperceptibly work society into their direction and this is where the spiritual element lies. The New World Order moves at a different pace to a man's lifetime, it slowly morphs. Perhaps the reason why they put up with this slowness is that they believe in Reincarnation, that they will bear the fruits of their work when they come back again in the future. The Fabian group has links to Theosophy the most obvious link being

---

[95] For more on CFR collusion see Servando Gonzalez, *Psychological Warfare and the New World Order*.

Annie Beasant who was a Fabianist and close friends with both George Bernard Shaw and Bertrand Russell.

How do they do it? How does a Secret Society work behind the scenes?

The Anatomy of the Secret Society

The way all secret societies typically work is that they have a central command of 1 or 2 top authoritative key-men and then around 4 other people who make up the Inner Core of the group. Then further out from this there is another group with a larger number, and then an even greater number: the broad masses who are really a cover for the inner groups. In this manner, orders from the top can be disseminated to the members who are indoctrinated to obey, and all the time it is a secret who is directing what is happening. You have the Key men, then the inner core, and then the cover ruling body, and then outside of them the Outer Circle who generally don't have a clue what is going on. In the example of the Milner Group the outer circle was called The Association of Helpers, the broad masses of the group.

It is like an onion, with the central core dictating ALL policies and actions out to the other groups within the structure. Cecil Rhodes was a Freemason and he did mention setting his Society up along Jesuit grounds. It is also possible that he might have read about Adam Weishaupt who started the Illuminati and decided to copy his political infiltration system of 'rings within rings within rings' directing other rings, as mentioned by G Edward Griffin.[96] Certainly, he claimed that the society should be based on the Jesuits, and the concept of a secret society, within a secret society directing other secret societies, was an illuminati control method which probably dated back to the Islamic Assassins and the Knight Templars. They were the first to perfect the infiltration technique of the deep mole.

The hidden hands of the conspirators' manoeuvre behind Politicians and Policy makers but unfortunately very few have

---

[96] See G Edward Griffin's lectures 'Rings of Power'.

managed to infiltrate their ranks and expose them as they are a closed shop. The reason for this is that once within the Secret Society the centre keeps control and stops people from getting to the top by **constant testing**, surveillance and fear. By teaching their followers to depend on the hierarchy for truth and encouraging people not to think for themselves and be completely dependent on the network for 'orders' as Hillary Clinton alluded to, they can allow only those very few they fully trust to get to the true centre of power. The degrees of progression within a Secret Society are the perfect method to keep control and in ever increasing degrees of complexity, the top can control the up-coming initiate until they are certainly they are someone who will never betray their secrets.

This is why time after time we see the unusual and bizarre actions of politicians who, 'by mistake,' make errors for the benefit of the Elite. This is the problem we have today, that **these people with their secret rules are still meeting behind closed doors directing the affairs of every single government** to their aggrandisement and our, the normal man on the streets' demise. Eventually, and inevitably, not that far into the future, the Network will have completed their last third revolution which is Religion (or Society or Culture) and will have the complete control they crave over Humanity. They will not need to hide any longer, and so their dictates can be brought into fruition without any detrimental objection from the people. One of these dictates will be for Man to worship Them in the form of the New World Religion they are setting up now: this is what the Bible says after all. In the next Chapter we look at some of the methods they use to control us, and how eventually they will manage to bring total brainwashing into effect.

CHAPTER 5

SOCIAL ENGINEERING OF THE MASSES

Propaganda, Propaganda and more Propaganda!

Media Control

The Cryptocracy keep control by creating mythologies which they sell to the people. The TV you watch, the Newspaper and articles you read on the Computer are all used as subtle 'infecting devices' to administer their 'viruses' or memes to affect your beliefs as a method of advanced mind control. The news on the TV is used as a vehicle of propaganda; the information you receive about world current affairs and politics is completely biased. If you don't believe this I suggest you think about these questions. Why is it that all news channels report exactly the same story in the same manner, and even in the same order? Why is it that we are always the good guys? Have you ever noticed any element of 'doublespeak'?

The Mainstream Media (MSM) provides just enough information to trick people to think they are receiving the truth. The News is often more about informing opinion and controlling the agenda than telling us what is really going on. There are hundreds of examples of media distortion and dis-information. But in reality, what we receive has been heavily filtered and made 'agenda friendly' to what the Cyrptocrats want us to know about, believe or think. In this way they can indoctrinate us subtly to create the managed society they want.

There are only two *major* Global News Agencies, namely Reuters and the Press Association who disseminate most of the news we see today. These two press agencies (and the few others that exist) circulate and control, to a large extent, all the worlds news. These corporations have become heavily amalgamated over the past 30 years. In the US, there are currently only 6 companies disseminating all media coverage which makes it easier to handle and pump the same untruths.[97] Is it possible that one group has control over all of these agencies? People like Rupert Murdoch (News Corp) and Ted Turner (Time Warner) are close to the centre of power and command the 'Media trick' that is going on every day. They distribute the news we see on a daily basis which means it goes through the same channels from where they pump the Elite's politically indoctrinated, sanitised version to us.

They propagandize on behalf of these powerful interests and they do this without the crude intervention of being told what to write or how to write, but by placing their indoctrinated people into places of power as the editors and the journalists. In this way the news conforms to the institution's policies and the entire process continues as 'a loop' in which only those who conform to the media held view and are willing to tow the establishment's beliefs are allowed into that role. That what they say is destructive, untrue, disinformation, anti-human, anti-God, anti-family, anti-parent matters not in the least! We toe the line unblinkingly and are easily manipulated to provide the necessary indoctrination to the masses, but they do this subtly, so we don't notice. **They aren't so stupid to indoctrinate us with us knowing.** That would be a silly thing to do! They have to indoctrinate us without us knowing, and this is they are managing to do very successfully.

Intellectual gatekeeper Noam Chomsky, says in his book *Media Control*, we are, after all the 'bewildered herd', too stupid to know what is right for us and even if we did know what was right, we wouldn't have any ability to affect that change anyway.[98] They want us to remain as spectators, atomised, and unable to form organisations which might

---

[97] These media corporations in the US currently are, GE (Comcast), Disney, News Corp, Time Warner and National Amusements who own CBS and Viacom. No doubt this will change again as further mergers take place.

[98] Noam Chomsky, *Media Control*, page 17.

upset the status quo. The Elite tell us completely false information about just about everything, so we can be ill informed, and this in turn means that we cannot make a meaningful contribution to the running of our society, even if we wanted to.

This is just another terrible flaw of the modern political apparatus, that we are unable to make a meaningful contribution to policy and the running of society. The Elite think they are above the system and can dictate whatever they want to us because they are the ones with the power. This makes it the rule of the jungle, or the force of the strongest, and not any form of meaningful democracy (even if voting did work). The people at the top with the power, who own the society, can dictate, via the media, whatever they want to us. We will believe and be none the wiser because we are, after all, the 'bewildered herd'. The media themselves have to be deeply indoctrinated in the values and interests of the corporate nexus, which in turn are deeply indoctrinated by the Elite who own them. It is all a method of control.

'Propaganda is to a democracy what the bludgeon is to a totalitarian state.' This refers to the fact that in the current society Propaganda takes the place of State violence as the method of bringing everyone into line.[99]

On the internet the situation is a little more complicated since there are some websites which have managed to get around the censorship of companies like Google, Yahoo and Microsoft which are obviously fully paid up members of the Great Plan agenda. This is the alternative media, which, by its very definition should be reporting the alternative view to the mainstream. They themselves are not always able to explain the dire political situation we are in and have been infiltrated by mainstream journalists and shills. The alternative media is the same, there are shills in every corner of it, telling us false information leading us up the garden path to something totally incorrect which diverts attention to what really is going on. Such as aliens, moon bases, ancient lost secrets, and all sorts of nonsense. However, some truthful information does manage to get out to the public domain about what is happening.

---

[99] Ibid; page 20.

So the Cryptocracy don't need MK Ultra (German for mind kontrol) or some such deep esoteric system to get their views into our heads, they have the Media with their subtle programming. This is exactly as it says in the Protocols of the Elders of Zion 12:4.

Not a single announcement will reach the public without our control. Even now this is already being attained by us inasmuch as all news items are received by a few agencies, in whose offices they are focused from all parts of the world. These agencies will then be already entirely ours and will give publicity only to what we dictate to them.

The Protocols were written in 1903 and provide a blueprint for the take-over of the world, to anyone who reads them. They could well be a fake in terms of not relating to Jews, and subsequently being used as a method of whipping up Anti-Semitism, but what matters is that their schemes have been used by the Cryptocracy as a blueprint to advance their plans. The amalgamation of newspapers and media corporations in general started at the turn of the 20th century and has been ongoing for the simple reason of controlling the media. The question that next arises is why would they be indoctrinating us if there wasn't an agenda?

The Destruction of Western Society

In 1933 H G Wells wrote in his book 'The Shape of Things to Come': 'When the existing governments and ruling theories of life, the decaying religions and the **decaying political forms** of today, have sufficiently lost prestige through failure and catastrophe, then and then only will world-wide reconstruction be possible.'

In other words, is it the 'Order ab Chao' which means Order out of Chaos spoken of by the Freemasons which, of course, H G Wells was a member. They want to smash everything up and from this bring about the New World Order with its New World Religion and the New Economic International Order which is Sustainable Development. 'When the existing government... and decaying political forms... have lost prestige' in the above quote, is exactly what we are seeing with the slow but steady destruction of religion and politics. For example, the office of the President of the US and other government institutions are to be slowly eroded so we have no faith in them, so they can bring in their new system. The ridicule and reduction of government to a joke.

Once 'the decaying religions… have sufficiently lost prestige through failure and catastrophe then and only then will world-wide reconstruction be possible.' This is their agenda, to destroy the traditions of the past. In order to get there, they have to change our society and our behavior, and to change our behavior, they have to change our morality.

Morality

The greatest single influence on human behavior, apart from the basic biological drive, is morality; the system of values which defines right and wrong behavior in society. Morality is so important to the successful functioning of society that even the most basic early hunter-gatherer societies organized themselves along some form of moral principle.[100] Humans have a strong inbuilt predisposition to obey and respond positively to authoritative control. It is society, as a whole, which gives the individual that sense of who they are, and therefore how they are to behave and even who they are to be when they grow up. The content of this moral ideology is vital to the success of any functioning society, so if you want to destroy society, as the Cryptocracy do, you have to destroy the fabric of the society's morality. In the West, the morality we have today was originally built on Christianity and so they desire to see this morality trampled and replaced with a state authorized morality. This is part of the reason why they want to destroy Christianity – they don't like moral absolutes since it forces a belief in God and the Judgement. And the Cryptocracy can't bear to see Christianity since it offends their religion which seeks to overthrow God with the belief in Lucifer. Another further reason is that Western Society has permeated more countries and effected global society and culture more than any other custom, and so, in order to bring about the changes they seek, they

---

[100] Christopher Hallpike, *Do We Need God to Be Good*. Chapter 2. Circle Books 2016.

have to destroy Christianity. They seek to bring it to total collapse, and basically ridicule Christianity into submission. In this respect it does indeed seem as if the Elite wish to destroy Christianity more than any other faith. But they also seek to reduce mankind to a type of 'greyed-out' humanity where all cultures and beliefs are the same, and so, in order to do this, they keep pushing the boundaries of what is morally acceptable to such an extent that society will become a 'do as thou wilt culture'. This may seem all quite theoretical but actually once your eyes are opened to it you will see it everywhere.

For example, the one area and 'cell' that the Cryptocracy cannot infiltrate is the family unit. This is quite a problem to them since they need to gain control of everything that is going on and bring it into subjugation. This is why one of the Cryptocracy's main PSYOPS has been the continual erosion of anything to do with the family unit and marriage. If they can break it down and make it a weak irrelevance to society then they will have won. This is why we see the mainstream media 'advertising' Divorce as an acceptable and allowable necessity for the 'modern man'. We never see the mainstream media up-sell the family unit as being something to be supported and encouraged through thick and thin! But we see them continually promote the Single-family unit as being an equally acceptable form of being brought up – which of course it may be – and herein lies part of the problem. They've even made this a political issue! It may not be as good a unit since there is one adult and not two, which should by definition be better? (Unless one member is beating up every other.) But they won't say that, because in reality they want us to be weak, divided, poor, with one income, and over-stretched with time so we cannot mount any meaningful opposition against them.

This is also why we also have the homosexual PSYOP, which is the promotion of the belief that being a homosexual, or a lesbian is EQUALLY as valid as being a hetero-sexual. In fact, we are even seeing the media telling us that if you are a homosexual or lesbian you are someone very special, and a lot more interesting than heterosexuals! What does this do to society? It makes society freer and looser and more tolerant on the one hand, which is a good thing, but that is the bait. On the other hand, it knocks down the family unit and introduces a serious level of moral relativism, which is the hook. The belief that you really can do what you want without consequences.

If sexual choices are equally as valid, (as they are being taught / indoctrinated) then this leads onto questions if their gender choices are equally as valid. This in turns leads onto questioning a child's gender choice. This is why children today are being asked if they are comfortable being a boy or a girl, which concludes with the question if they want a sex change! It helps to destroy the fabric of society by making it more morally relative, more fluid, and less a convention of society. Do you think they would be pushing this agenda if there wasn't some reason for it? And why are the Cryptocracy interested in promoting this anyway?

It is to push moral acceptability to the extreme. Of course, there is also the 'side agenda' of ridiculing Christianity and other 'traditional' faiths which say that homosexuality is wrong, and the family unit is right. It's just another method of encouraging people to give up on their beliefs and thereby subduing the population to think what they want you to think.

This is why on the TV, in the newspapers, and from media celebrities, you can witness the slow backward progress of society into a broken state in which anything can be tolerated. We all become uncaring about our situation and uninvolved with other people as we sit behind our screens busy with artificial bureaucracies on bureaucracies which is yet another part of their overall tactic. Our spirits dying, our world view entirely conforms to that dictated by the internet, films and TV, all of which are carefully and craftily manipulating us into an unnatural state of diminished motivation to discern what's going on around us. The conclusion of this unnatural state is that, it makes us think and act exactly as the Elite want, as we suffer from a type of Abulia – the loss of will, power and initiative.[101]

In the final analysis, we are all being lead into the 'greyed-out society' whether we like it or not, and there's not much one man can do to stand in the way of the media machine that they have created to turn back the tide to a proper functioning society.

This is also why Europe is their target since it is the cradle of modern global civilization. Once this has fallen or been reduced to

---

[101] Abulia: a concept mentioned by Michael A Hoffman in *Secret Societies and Psychological Warfare.*

disfunction it will make it easier to bring about the destruction of the rest of the world - hence the disastrous bankrupting policies of the EU.

Mass Social Engineering

We are a very studied race and think tanks such as the Tavistock group have deep roots into the Network and provide the media with the general trend in order to ensure the mythologies of the Cryptocracy are maintained. These think tanks are funded and aided to the hilt to review every aspect of modern society and to make sure they can keep control of the masses through their social engineering packages. For example, from the daily news we see on the TV, to films such as Harry Potter indoctrination on its imaginative, but evil, form of make-believe magic linked to Theosophy, and Satanism, they've got it covered, for the benefit of the Elite, and to our ruination. We are subject to many massive deceptions in the world today.

Most people today simply do not have the knowledge, and dare I say it, the imagination to understand what is going on because all their information comes from the 'indoctrination machine' that is the mainstream media. Explaining the reality of the Cryptocracy takes a long time and will probably be met with anger, unbelief and a lot of ridicule. The only people who will give you a hard time about revealing conspiracy fact, are those people living under 'the lie'. Ignorance is just lack of knowledge, and most people who follow the controlled media I'm afraid to say are truly ignorant. Ignorance is power to the Cryptocracy and anything they can do to keep you away from the correct information and away from books like this will be a win for them! The Media also subtly tells us what we should believe, what we should think and what is politically correct. It tells us what is right and in the end even determines the margins of the debate – by this I mean that people who try to expose any truths about culture or race or what is really going on are marginalized and labelled as 'conspiracy theorists' or worse. This is the 'manufactured consent' which is the overall dialogue of what is seen as being politically correct at that time. It is the filtering and marginalization of any information which may upset the political class and the corporate nexus.

We see this on a daily basis, the continual stream of propaganda on just about every subject imaginable, from the BBC, CNN, Sky, New York Times and all media outlets with their little spins on the events of the day.

The problem for those who know about this indoctrination is that what they see as truth and fact, the mind control masses see as fiction! They think that people explaining this information suffer from an inability to distinguish fiction from reality. It is therefore very difficult to break through this controlled conditioning which is being instilled into peoples' minds from a very young age. In fact, there are 'slides' which the mainstream media have built into peoples' minds which shut down critical thinking when it comes to certain controversial information. The CIA and their think tanks spent years studying these psychological techniques to create a conditioned individual whereby rational thinking processes are terminated, and any debate is short-circuited at the mention of the word 'conspiracy'. After all there's no such thing as a conspiracy, is there?[102]

This is why it is quite difficult to talk to people who do not even understand or know about the basic apparatus of the Cryptocracy which was explained in Chapter 3. They just can't see it!

Others don't want to see it because they instinctively know that it will affect their world view too much and cause them to have to re-assess their entire life and even possibly get in contact with people whom they have told incorrect information. But my comment to these people is that if you are a person of truth you have nothing to fear, just make the study and reach your own conclusions.

Smoke and Mirrors of the Master Illusionists

When the media tell us there is a leak or whistle blower who is revealing some amazing piece of information, we should be suspicious about why they are revealing this supposed 'secret information'. If there is a leak of information, it's basically been done

---

[102] Micha-el J Hayes, *The Culling of Man*, Kindle location 370.

to control the situation and the opposition. This is how the Cryptocracy work - they set up, for example, the political party they want, and then they set up the opposition to the party they want, and in this way, they control both sides of any debate or situation, and therefore they control the outcome.

It's all completely contrived, politics is all smoke and mirrors and theatre, since it's the same actors on both sides in the same secret societies under control of the same master illusionists - the Cryptocracy. They control everything we see, and the history of the people involved corroborates this extraordinary picture whereby both sides of every political situation is already controlled to a conclusion they have set up years or even decades before. This is where a lot of people studying this at the outset go wrong! They think that believing this puts you in a world where controllers say - 'you are now my puppet and you will vote for this motion or else', as the logical conclusion of any controller's attempts. But it's far subtler than this, and far more a question of recruiting the correct people who can be controlled because they are fundamentally flawed, and who can be used without them being aware that they are being used. Idealists of any description are great for this!

Just to make a point, and please forgive me if I make it a little contrived. You may have a job and your boss tells you do something, (in a good way I hope), this doesn't mean you're a puppet, does it? You do the job, sometimes reluctantly because it's a chore, and other times happily. This is exactly how the Cryptocracy works. They employ people and run the governments of the world from behind the scenes with suggestions, manipulations, use of secret society meetings, money, power, prestige and titles amongst many other strategies mentioned in this book. The Cryptocracy simply request politicians to do things – they pay them a salary and they have to toe the line of the Whip and others around them asking them to do something - they are unaware that they are being controlled and just how contrived the entire event is. They just do it. Some of them know and go along with it, others just can't see it. **Most of the politicians know there is a higher group above them and just accept it.** They don't go around saying they have been made to do anything because that's not the way it works. The fact that, for example, the law they are signing into motion is hundreds of pages long and was written and published by the Government (hiding as the Cryptocracy) only a few days before, is something they don't even question. They still turn up and vote for that massive law as directed. None of them read it, and what's worse, if they did, they would see that the enactment of that law causes harm to the populace and is a further power consolidation for the Cryptocracy. Most of them know or have their suspicions, but they go along with it because, if they don't, they will fall out of the crowd and will not be popular. Or they will lose their job, or even worse. No-one dares to step outside that 'establishment view' or 'window', because if they did it would be to their ruination. The Cryptocracy runs the world's governments like a business and they remain hidden, since this way they maintain their power and no-one can take a swipe at them! All of this is made possible by incorrect information and therefore any information disseminating source has to be in their hands, and this is what we see today. As David Rockefeller, one of the most important figures of the last one hundred years to understanding all this said, in an address to a meeting of The Trilateral Commission, in June 1991.

"We are grateful to The Washington Post, The New York Times, Time Magazine and other great publications whose directors have attended our meetings and respected their promises of discretion for almost forty years. It would have been impossible for us to develop OUR PLAN for the world if we had been subject to the bright lights of publicity during those years. But, the world is now much more sophisticated and prepared to march towards a world government. The supranational sovereignty of an intellectual elite and world bankers is surely preferable to the national auto-determination practiced in past centuries."

There we have if from the horse's mouth! Without the media telling us their lies, they, (the intellectual elite and world bankers) would not have been able to make their power grabs.

Conclusion

So, to conclude if an individual or organization is able to influence and define what is seen as socially right or wrong behavior in a society, it can gain enormous power. This is great for the controllers since if people lack discernment, wisdom, and knowledge it doesn't enable them to break through into any kind of truth, and so most people can't even begin to make the simplest realizations necessary to understand what's really going on. The 'buzzing confusion' as Richard Gardner said in relation to National Sovereignty. **'In short, the 'house of world order' will have to be built from the bottom up rather than from the top down. It will look like a great 'booming, *buzzing* CONFUSION,' to use William James' famous description of reality, but an end run around national sovereignty, eroding it piece by piece, will accomplish much more than the old-fashioned frontal assault.'**[103]

This is not only a reference to the destruction of National Sovereignty, but it gives us an idea of how they are going to achieve this. The 'buzzing confusion' we see in the world today. The confusing mismatch of information and politically correct agenda is aimed to put everyone off balance, and make us scared to divulge any comments, in case we have not been updated with the new politically correct version of what we are supposed to be saying. We live in a world where our morality and thoughts are being undermined to such an extent that we don't have any moral compass left. This is how to control us.

This is what they want, the dumbing down of society to the lowest possible common denominator and to make everyone think they are as ignorant as the next person, or the celebrities they love to tout in the tabloids and papers as the norm. Then we won't make a stand against anything which we think is right because the majority, 'media driven view' dictates how and what we are to think. Step outside of this crazy boundary and get shot down! Unfortunately, the politically correct have won the argument, but they don't seem to have studied deeply enough or discerned sharply enough, and so we are all like turkeys voting for Christmas! They are unaware that they are being indoctrinated, and therefore that they are being controlled. This is the reason why people are not aware of the frightening reality of the New World Order. The masterminds behind this conspiracy have absolute control of our mass communications media and have used their subtle methods to 'hoodwink' us so we remain blind to reality. We are unaware we are indoctrinated, and this is how they are bringing total brainwashing into effect. We have become so conditioned that

---

[103] Richard Gardner, Rhodes scholar and CFR member Richard Gardner, writing in the April 1974 issue of the CFR's journal, Foreign Affairs.

the Elite can make us think 'snow is black', or 'war is peace', or 'ignorance is strength', exactly as George Orwell and Bertrand Russell wrote, both of whom were Fabianists and insiders from the left.[104] Orwell was both warning us about the totalitarian state, but also preparing us for its arrival.

Eventually these psychological-indoctrination-systems will probably be replaced by a new technology which will allow us to survive *only* if we jack into the transhumanists neural hive network central computer. A possible interpretation of 'the beast' system of Revelation.

All this Media manipulation and indoctrination, via disinformation and lies is being compounded to lead us to a new type of society. A 'managed society' in which the Cryptocracy can make us believe whatever they want, and that will lead us to their goal of a compliant humanity as a type of collective, where the rights, thoughts and beliefs of an individual are to be subservient to the rights of the collective. A society in which the individual is seen as an eccentric, and the views of the collective are higher and more important. This is a classic deception since it only puts the Elite in the driving seat of mankind as the masses cower and are lead into a type of 'glazed deadened humanity'. This is the direction we are heading in, and in order to back up this conclusion, we need to dissect one of the most seminal events of the accelerated plans of the New World Order – 9/11. But before we come to 9/11, and this new type of fakery, (which isn't so new) we just need to look at one of the beliefs of the Elite to help make sense of 9/11 and hence expose the roll out of the New World Religion.

---

[104] George Orwell, '1984', and Bertrand Russell, *Impact on Society*, page 30.

CHAPTER 6

NUMBERS AND NUMEROLOGY

Incredible as it may seem, but numbers are extremely important to the Elite and the Secret Services who work for them. If they can choose an auspicious day with a significant number for their magical mind control techniques they will go out of their way to do this. They are heavily into the occult and astrology and believe that once a symbol is created, it acquires a power of its own. Even more power is generated when such symbols can't be read by the 'profane or uninitiated' since they don't know or understand the meaning. In this manner, they gain power over the masses. It's an occult technique which goes back to Pythagoras and even to Babylon.

Freemasonry Lodges have a picture of Pythagoras in their lodges and next to him is the 'divine triangle' with the squares, all said to be part of the Mason's building techniques.[105] The famous Pythagorean theorem was that "the area of the square on the hypotenuse (the side opposite the right angle) is equal to the sum of the areas of the squares of the other two sides". This all relates to the mathematical calculations that need to be made for stone masonry and building in general, and this is the supposed exoteric meaning for the lower level Masons. But the esoteric hidden meaning of numbers relates to the power contained in the number and its ability to affect magical procedures.

Pythagoras is one of the most important Greek philosophers and he started a type of Mystery Religion which Freemasons and the

---

[105] See ceiling at Freemason's Lodge, 60 Queen Charlotte Street, London.

Super Elite believe is important to their world view. To them he **possessed a special knowledge and power**, part of which is the **special significance of numbers**. Although our knowledge of him was written down centuries later, typically by Plato and others, he was a cultic figure who was thought of as being the 'Hyperborean Apollo'. And so there you have the link of Hyperborea which is said to be the pre-diluvian Utopian kingdom of Atlantis. It takes us straight back to the Mystery Religions again. It was Pythagoras who said: **"All is number."** This is referring to the placement of numbers as being interchangeable with words which is Gematria. e.g. A being 1, and B being 2 etc, so if the word is present then the number can manifest the word and magicians use magic words like Abracadabra to affect their subject. Words turned into numbers is a magical way of affecting the world are a secret way of conveying a message to others. In other words, for the Mason, numbers can manifest a result or affect an event. This is the study of Numerology which the Elite are seriously into and use as a method to hide their symbolatry amongst the everyday. Science also teaches us that practically everything can be distilled to numbers, but it doesn't say that about words. For example, geometry, astronomy and music are dependant and can be reduced to maths on a fundamental level, but maths is not dependant on geometry, astronomy or music. Thus Maths is a primary and 'fundamental Science'.[106]

In the Kabbalah (Kbl in Hebrew means 'received') the belief in sacred numbers and names were said to be contained in the Old Testament. They would place several verses alongside each other, or one over the other and from this they might manage to find new words or hidden meanings which were running vertically or backwards. Or they placed the words in squares and reduced them to numbers.

Christianity has placed more interest in words as Jesus was 'the **Word** made flesh' (John 1:1) – Jesus was not made a number! Logos is the Greek for 'Word' and so Jesus was 'the Word or Logos' and said "heaven and earth will pass away but **my words** will never pass away" (Mark 13:31). Therefore He was placing his 'word' even above the physical universe and heaven itself. God said let there be light... God spoke the Word, and creation happened from nothing, ex nihilo. As in most things the Bible has the true version but the occult

---

[106] Manly P Hall, *The Secret Teachings of All Ages*, page 198.

has the fake version. The words of life from Jesus have been subverted and used to convey magic which has been further obscured by using numbers.

In Theosophy Alice Bailey and others speak of Jesus as being the 'Planetary Logos' which is basically their earthly Christ or Maitreya they are waiting for - but this is the Anti-Christ.

Numbers **hidden in plain sight** thrill Freemasons who think they are the only ones capable of reading their signs. Magic words are important and convey meaning, exactly the same as numbers.

Magic Numbers

The Elite, and their secret armies, like the following numbers, 9, 11, 13 and 33 and some permutations and multiples of these. The permutations, for example, are 22 which is double 11, or 39 which is triple 13, or 66 which is double 33. The Master Numbers in Gematria are 11, 22 and 33, and some include 44.[107] Words which add up to these numbers are not reduced or compressed further into single digits but remain 22 for example and not 4. Master numbers are numbers of extra special significance denoting a more powerful conjunction than other reduced numbers. They like to play their little games with these numbers, because occultists think, in their twisted way, that by using these numbers they are manifesting the power of that word, and so they believe they can gain power over us. In a way, it's about mind control, and part of some deep occult ritual and like all the worst occult ritual, it is imbued with an **evil mockery.** This is why the use of numbers in plain sight is also about 'having a laugh at us'. The message comes down from the Cryptocracy to institutions such as MI5, the CIA or Mossad, that some such decision has been made to further the Agenda and the secret services put into action the events to make these psychodramas be played out. If it can add up to 33 it will keep the powers that be happy. In other words, the date of the event when added up adds to 33; such as the official end date of the Cold War 03/12/1989, or the day the first Atomic Bomb test happened at Trinity, New Mexico on 16/07/1945, or the Wall Street crash of 29/10/1929. You simply add the numbers up as

---

[107] Faith Javane and Dusty Bunker, *Numerology and the Divine Triangle,* Whitford Press 1979.

Numerology teaches, such as the Hiroshima atomic bomb 6/8/1945 which makes 33. Other days would add up to 33 but via a slight amount of interpretation such as the First Manned Space flight 12/4/1961 (12+4+17 {1+9+6+1}) or David Rockefeller's death on 20/03/2017 which is 23 plus a 10 to make 33. Others use 11 or 22 as Master numbers. The Cryptocracy's finger prints are all over these events.

The reason why these numbers are special is that, in the beliefs of the Elite, occult numbers contain magical references and so it's a form of conducting ritual magic over their subjects. They also use numbers to inform others within the Network that this event is one of their own, it is their world, and they run everything. It's like a business; their ethos and 'corporate logo' is bound to be there. Incredible as it seems the more you understand the beliefs of the Cryptocracy the greater your understanding of this will become. Where's the fun in conducting an event of treachery if no-one knows about it? This is what we see today in our world, the occultist making their plans using these preferred numbers. Only the Initiated can supposedly understand this and no-one 'normal' notices! The magic ritual has to happen on a specific date and so they will waste millions of tax payers money to make sure it does.

The meaning of Numbers

9 is the number of Illusion since any number multiplied by 9 when you add up the digits up can be reduced back to 9. For example, take the number 210 x 9 = 1890; 1+8+9+0 = 18; 1+8 = 9. In numerology zero is always ignored. It works with any number you can think of, multiplied by 9 when the digits are added up, or reduced, the number 9 is secretly embedded within any resultant number which is why it's called the number of Illusion because it is hidden within the result.

In Numerology Master Numbers have greater special significance than other numbers since they stand together doubled; and the **Master Numbers are 11, 22 and 33.** In other words 11 is imbued with more power than the number 1.

11 is the number of magic because when you multiply any number by 11 there is a multiplying effect of the initial number which is exactly what contagious and sympathetic magic are aiming to achieve. The transference of a magical activity into the real world via a 'multiplicative activity' or by the aid of demons. The obvious example is sympathetic magic, such as voodoo when a needle is put in an effigy of the victim - the magician affects the ritual on a 'micro level' and multiplies its effect and so it comes into existence.[108]

In mathematical terms if you take any number you can think of and multiply it by 11 the numbers within are manifest and the calculation and answer is present within the number at outset. For example take the number 32 x 11 = 352. The answer's first number is 3, the last is 2 and the middle is 3+2 = 5 so all the numbers were 'manifest' at outset and so, in this manner, the magical properties of that initial number, via 11, are expanded and made larger or manifest. This works for any number and if the number goes over 10 for example you add that number into the next column. This is all simple maths, but to our occult Elite and Numerologists this is of interest!

11 is also the number of the Anti-Christ since in Daniel 7:8 he 'was considering the (10) horns, and there was another horn, a little one, coming up among them.' This is the 11th Horn and again a reason why the number 11 overall is the number of Magic.

The armistice at the end of World War I in 1918 was enacted on the "eleventh hour of the eleventh day of the eleventh month." It was a reference to 11, the number of magic, but also there were 3 elevens (hour, day and month) and 3 x 11 = 33 the number of Freemasonry. A special day for all the Masons on both sides of the War.[109]

11 is the Elites' special number representing the Devil and Magic. If they can incorporate this number in their Psychodramas they certainly will. This is because, either they really are Satanists, or they are fraudsters using this camouflage to hide behind, but bearing in mind many of the Elite network are Masons and members of secret groups with religious connotations, it seems much more likely that they really are working for the dark side. They are no match for Satan's deceptions!

---

[108] Gordon Frazer, *The Golden Bough,* page 11 and Chapter 3 on Sympathetic Magic.

[109] The armistice was signed at 5 am in the morning so only 6 hours before, which was enough time to get the message to all units, but people were killed right up until the last minutes of the war.

So we have 9 as the number of Illusion or Deception, and 11 which is the number of Magic or the Anti-Christ (the 11th horn). Combined together these numbers might stand for evil magic. It's strange also that the horrific attack was labelled a number, 9/11, rather than for example the 'World Trade Center Disaster.' But where's the magic in the 'World Trade Center Disaster'? Unless you worked in the World Trade Center the terror and processing would probably remain localised, but using a telephone number, 911, which is used for the emergency services in the US and many other countries, means that the entire global population can be psychologically processed into the subliminal panic and fear mode which the Cryptocracy want. However subtle and subconscious their programming -- it is still there present, and this is why 9/11 is called 9/11 and not some other name.

13 is the number of Death to the Elite and it is represents Death on the Tarot cards. It can also merely represent a change, or transformation of a situation, but generally it is an unlucky number. Jesus had 12 Disciples, plus himself 13. The Old Testament represents it as the number of rebellion. Genesis 14:4 'For twelve years they had served Kedorlaomer, but in the thirteenth year they rebelled.' Nimrod was the 13th generation from Adam, which is an evil aggregation. The date of the death of the Knight Templar, Jacque De Molay was October, Friday 13th 1307 and this is an auspicious day to Freemasons who don't like Friday 13th. Covens always have 13 people in them. The Bilderberg have a core of 3 sets of 13 which is 39, and the Order of the Garter is similar.[110] Perhaps this is related to the fact the solar year has 12 months whilst the lunar has 13. Or it relates to the 13 Titans of Greek mythology. The Tarot Death card of Arthur Edward Waite is the 13th card: in the background is a drawing of two towers which synchronistically refers to the mega death ritual of 9/11.

22 is another Master number which means it is imbued with more significance than merely a 2 or the number 4. It is the number of the Master Builder in Freemasonry and of special significance to Skull and Bones (322). There are 22 Letters in the Hebrew alphabet, 22

---

[110] Bilderberg number 13. See
https://www.bibliotecapleyades.net/sociopolitica/atlantean_conspiracy/atlantean_conspiracy39.htm

Cards on the Major Arcana of the Tarot, and 22 pathways or channels on the Kabbalistic Sephirothic tree. It is also the ancient numerical symbol of a circle which co-incidentally (or maybe not) is the symbol of the United Religions Initiative (URI). In the Tarot, it is the card of The Fool with the Key 0 as the circle, and so stands alone as a representation of the God force. Again, if the Secret Services can get a 22 in their Psychodramas they will.[111] Recently there have been a spate of events on March 22nd a totally obvious date since it's 3/22 which is their special number. The Brussels bombing in 2016 and exactly a year later, Westminster Bridge in 2017.

33 is the number which thrills the Elite since their Religion of Freemasonry has 33 Degrees and so they love to get this special number into any political event or activity to show they are in control and as coded messages to others who are Initiates, and to mock their victims. 33 is also special because the number of Demons who fell to Earth during Satan's rebellion was a third of the host of heaven, and 33 is a third - Revelation 12:4.

Jesus was said to be 33 years old when he was crucified but since no-ones knows exactly what date he was born it is open to conjecture because it depends on what date you take as his birth. Luke 3:23 states that Jesus was about 30 years old when he started his ministry. It is from John who mentions three Passovers that we believe Jesus's amazing Ministry lasted only 3 years.

Water freezes at 32 Degrees Fahrenheit but at 33 degrees it is as cold as it can be without actually freezing. This is one contributing factor why we have the Fahrenheit system.

The number 3 is also important since it is the number of the Trinity being the Father, Son and Holy Spirit, but of course they're referring to Satan, the False Prophet and the Anti-Christ. It's also a reference to the Third Eye which if opened twice would be 33. The Letter G is also the 33rd letter of the Alphabet when you go around a second time, so you count 26 plus 7 which is the letter G which makes 33. G is obviously the Letter in the middle of the Freemasonry compass and square.

---

[111] Faith Javane and Dusty Bunker, *Numerology and the Divine Triangle,* Whitford Press 1979 page 176. Or see Annemarie Schimmel's book, *The Mystery of Numbers.*

Numbers are far more important than you might realise. Overall this is why 2033 maybe an important year for the occultists who run our planet, or 2031 which is also a 33, (2 + 31). It is probably one of the nearest years to their twisted perverse beliefs and so they could unleash a major change in these years, also being 2000 years after Christ.

66 is double 33 and can also crop up as a coded message. (Many people believe the Bible has 66 books but it doesn't. The Psalms are divided into 5 books and so the Bible has 70 books.)

The number which Satanists think it special is 93 according to the religion of Thelema set up by Aleister Crowley. In Greek Gematria, (isopsephy), the words Thelema which means 'will' and the word agape meaning 'love' add up to 93. So instead of writing 'Do what thou wilt shall be the whole of the law' they just put 93. It's their calling card!

Folk Islam has the belief that 99 is special since there are 99 names of Allah. The number is written on the palms of the hand. On the left hand creases of the palm we have Λl which in Arabic is the number 81 and on the right hand we have the figure lΛ which is 18 in Arabic numerals. So these numbers are 18 and 81, which equal 99. Unfortunately, 18 is made up of three 6s so it only eludes to the devil, and obviously 99 upside down is 66 so it doesn't seem that likely to fulfil any true divine mathematics! It's palmistry for some Muslims.[112]

Numerology is obviously a totally fake belief and superstitious occultism, but the Elite, Rosicrucians and Freemasons put a lot of special significance in all this, and as mentioned if you want to check if some event is real with an esoteric meaning or hidden allusion, then adding up some numbers and having some knowledge of this subject will help. Christianity does NOT have any Numerology or Gematria within its writings except possibly with the famous number 666 of Revelation 13:18, but this is only because it's referring to another religion, the religion of the Cryptocracy, and anyway this is only an explanation or commentary. Since Revelations has not been fulfilled yet, we don't know precisely what this relates to. When the time comes it's likely the thinking will be obvious. Cern has its symbol of 666 and is a possible candidate for the computerised one language beast system

---

[112] Bill Musk, *The Unseen Face of Islam*, page 208.

we might be entering into. Explanations from the past have been that the spelling of 'Neron Caesar' in Hebrew Gematria adds up to 666.[113] Leaving out the letter N at the end of Neron, to give Nero, in Hebrew, (omitting the Hebrew letter nun) gives a figure of 616 which perhaps is an explanation for why some Greek versions of Revelation have 616 and others have 666. Trajan Hadrianus also adds up to 666 and is said to be a possible candidate, but it dates Revelation far too late and therefore seems highly unlikely.

Numbers are of some significance and there are some allusions within the Bible which help to make sense of various stories. For example, the Feeding of the 5,000 in Mark 6:30-44 refers to the Israelites in which the crowd are the Jews and there were 12 baskets left over, one for each of the tribes of Israel. At the Feeding of the 4,000 in Mark Chapter 8, the crowd are the Gentiles and there are 7 baskets left over (Mark 8:8) implying a symbol of the universal nature of the Gentiles. This is not the same as Numerology. God does not do Numerology or Gematria, but in order to understand what is going on you need to have some working knowledge of this so you can make some decisions if an event is real or not. If the number is of significance, and all the other evidence points to a hoax, then you have a hoax, and you should not be surprised. It's going to happen, and the frequency seems alarmingly to be increasing with every passing year. Fake news for a fake generation!

So with this you should have the 'keys' to make sense of the unusual situation that many events are planned and controlled in the world today. So now you can start laughing at them and turning the tables on their infantile games. You simply add up those numbers and see if they are any special combinations. You have to be fairly inventive sometimes to get to their number but it will be there in most of their macabre plays, or Statecraft events. If you stick to 11, 13, 22 and 33, possibly 26 (twice 13) and 39 (thrice 13), you will be able to spot the fingerprints of Cyrptocrats fairly easily just with this information.

---

[113] Interpreters Bible Encyclopaedia entry under 666.

9/11

The most obvious example of number magic is 9/11 which is riddled from top to bottom with special numbers and **this is not because conspiracy theorists have written numbers into it**, but because the perpetrators of the atrocity have used these numbers as part of their occult mind control program. They had to put the entire world under their spell, literally, and to a large extent they succeeded. 9/11 was the most important event since World War II in furthering the Networks causes, but it also exposed some of the machinations of the future New World Order, and so is a brilliant starting point to make these realisations that there is a secret cabal behind what is happening in the world today. It is quite a complex situation which needs to be put together like an enormous jigsaw puzzle to gain the entire picture.

9/11 is the birth pang of the New civilisation, the manifestation of which we will in due course be entering into, and 9/11 was the beginning *of the end* of the current economic, political and social structure we currently live under.

9/11 was when the 2 becomes the 1. In other words the two Towers representing Duality, light and dark, sun and moon and Male and Female aspects, disappeared to be replaced by the One World Trade Center representing the synthesis into the one global Unity. This Allegory for the Elite and their Luciferian Religion is their highest essence of their Deity - when the perfect union of opposites is replaced with unity. This is when their occult Equilibrium is restored.

This is their view of what happened on 9/11. The two aspects of Humanity at their most basic being represented by the two Towers of male and female were brought together to form the One, androgynous One World Trade Center also called Freedom Tower. Added to which in order to enlighten Man into the next phase of his supposed 'evolution' they have to ALLEGORICALLY bring man to a place of complete darkness and, from this deliberate place, Man can then become Enlightened. It is a type of poisonous duality that they believe in, that in order to progress to the next level they have to bring Mankind to a place of despair and destruction from which he will find his moral fibre and break free into the next paradigm.

Exactly as what happened at 9/11. The next paradigm being the roll out of several new psychological mythologies which are the 'war on terror' and the increase of Islamic terrorism to justify the surveillance state. This concept of unity being formed by the clash of opposites goes back to Hegel who discovered it from the Kabbalist school of Isaac Luria. The concept of two opposing concepts uniting to form a conclusion. This is Kabbalism and Hegelianism, which is one of the methods the Cryptocracy employ to advance their causes.

The two becoming the one was codified in the film, Back to the Future (Part1) in 1985, where the Twin Pines became the Lone Pine. Coupled with the knowledge of Back to the Future Part II where the pine trees morph into the World Trade Towers the 'programming' is undeniable. They knew about 9/11 from even 1985 a full 16 years before the event.

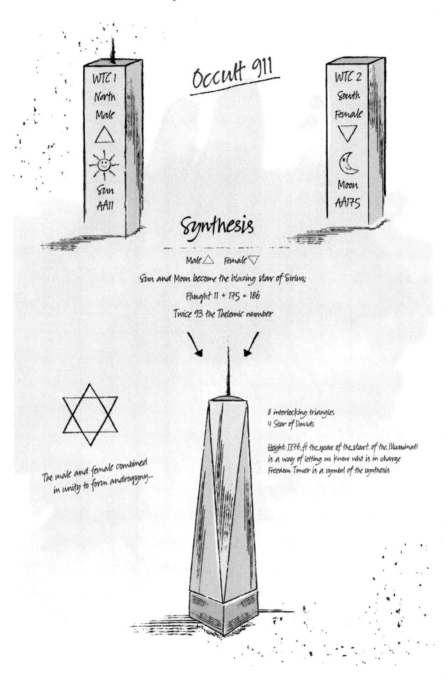

Occult 911

WTC 1
North
Male
△
☀
Sun
AA11

WTC 2
South
Female
▽
☾
Moon
AA175

Synthesis

Male △ Female ▽

Sun and Moon become the blazing star of Sirius;

Flinght 11 + 175 = 186

Twice 93 the Thelemic number

8 interlocking triangles
4 Star of Davids

Height: 1776 ft the year of the start of the Illuminati is a way of letting us know who is in charge Freedom Tower is a symbol of the synthesis

The male and female combined in unity to form androgyny...

September 11th was the first day of the New Year in the Coptic calendar which was based on the Egyptian calendar.[114] It is the 1st day of the month of Thoth, and of course Thoth is the 'illuminati' God of Wisdom and one of the most-high ranking Egyptian gods, so it was the perfect day for the furtherance of the New World Order. A New Year for the New World Order, the day in ancient Egypt when the Star Sirius could be seen rising for the first time in the year over the horizon - the helical rising of Sirius. Thoth became Hermes in the Greek pantheon and Hermes became the Roman God Janus, and this is the god of the Illuminati - Janus, the two-headed god of the gateway, the messenger of the Gods.[115] Thoth was worshipped by the Egyptians as the god of magic, science, religion and philosophy and has the personification of the Moon. On top of Thoth's head was a crescent moon.[116] What better day to start the New World Order end game? Of course, September is the 7th Month and not the 9th in this explanation. Thoth was the left eye of the sky God Horus represented by the Moon, and the right eye was the Sun God Ra. Notice here that there is a link between the Moon God of Thoth and Islam, something which will be explained further on.

The date of 11th September 2001 was also significant since it represented the end of the old system. In the film The Matrix, made in 1999, the main character Neo, was a type of archetypal new man, a new Adam Kadmon for the New Order. Neo means New in Greek and Neo is also an anagram for One, and he was also called 'The One' in the film since he was going to bring in the New Order as a type of Saviour or Messiah. His Passport is shown in the film and has an Expiry date of 9/11/2001.[117] The overall theme therefore is that the old order was finishing or expiring as the Passport showed, and a type of New Age Saviour, the One, was to bring in the New Order - a destroyed totalitarian state.

It isn't the aim of this book to explain 9/11 in full, but in order to try to make sense of how far Mankind has fallen under the 'spell' of the master illusionists, and as a starting point to delve into the themes

---

[114] See Coptic Calendar – Wikipedia.

[115] Thoth see E A Wallis Budge, *The Book of the Dead*, page 20.

[116] Ibid page 78. Or http://compilation11.com/thoth-egyptian-god-mythology.

[117] Web search, image: Neo's (Thomas Anderson) Passport.

of the New World Religion and show the dark heart of the conspirators, it is necessary to explain in outline what happened on 9/11 and to dispel the magic which surrounds it. Most people are still under its spell so my aim is to break this spell, so you can see the truth.

Disinformation

First of all, it is necessary to strip away a huge amount of disinformation. The disinformation in short is 1. That there were planes, whilst **there were no planes.** 2. That there were Islamic fundamentalists, when there weren't any. 3. That the World Trade Center buildings 'pancake collapsed' as a result of structural failure cause by the burning of kerosene fuel, when in fact it was caused by a high-tech weapon the world **still** does not know about.

For those who dig deeper the disinformation was also that, 1. Mossad, Israel, or Saudi Arabia were responsible. 2. That the US Government were involved or at least complicit in the Military stand down on the day and that it wasn't the Cryptocracy. 3. Lastly, one of the most important pieces of the deeper disinformation programming is that those '9/11 Truthers' who believe there were No Planes are 'crazy'. This is significant because the difference between understanding the planes story and the no planes story is the crux of the entire mythology of 9/11. In that the entire premise that Muslims did 9/11 is based on the story of the planes holding together, whereas, of course, it doesn't. Therefore, the story of the planes needs very careful analysis.

The Media has led us all astray on ALL of these points.

No Planes

There were no Planes. **This can be a real 'deal breaker' for most people** since we have been told incessantly that there were planes, but if you research and watch the videos you will see that every testimony about the imaginary planes is flawed, and every video of any imaginary plane is photoshopped or CGI'd. As long as you are thinking about planes you can't see the truth. It is not possible for a plane to go into a building since it would crumple up like a car hitting railings. In the World Trade Center 2 crash the plane goes all the way through the building and emerges on the other side with the **airplane cone INTACT**- a ridiculous concept! It's a plane not a missile! The nose cone is made of hard plastic or carbon fibre and is not as strong as the combined resistance of the glass and steel girders which it had to go through twice to emerge intact the other side (not to mention the central columns which make it 3 sets of steel girders). The hole that the plane was supposed to have made wasn't even there anyway if you see the photos. Planes cannot penetrate buildings!

The 9/11 'nose out' picture looks like the thumb of Satan to me (the reverse being the finger of God!)

After much research into the videos on You Tube and elsewhere you should be able to understand this, but **you have to do the research in order to arrive at this conclusion. Please do not dismiss this off hand until you have viewed as many of the imaginary photoshopped 9/11 plane crashes as you can!**[118] You don't need to read lots of books on 9/11 all you have to do is watch the plane go into the building and ask yourself the obvious question if this is real or not. Also, you could ask yourself if the pixels of the plane were deleted as it entered the building, or if the plane did indeed enter the building (like a knife through butter) through the steel and glass, defying physics!

---

[118] Search, You Tube for '9/11 nose out' or '9/11 no planes; such as https://www.youtube.com/watch?v=9cvWwIxMbmE

CGI plane 'disappears' into WTC 2 and comes out the other side intact.

- CGI plane goes through 3 sets of steel beams and comes out the other side. Obviously it is not a real plane!

WOW!! we made it to the other side!

*CGI - Computer Generated Imagery (special visual effects created using computer software)

The first **imaginary, bogus, fake, non-existent plane** that hit World Trade Center 1 was American Airlines 11. In other words, AA11 where A is 1 which means 11/11 and the significance of this that the number 11 is the number of magic according to Thelema and Aleister Crowley as mentioned previously.

The second **fantasy, non-existent plane** that hit WTC 2 was flight 175. This is the plane which went all the way through the building and out of the other side.[119]

Then there is the **non-existent, bogus plane** 93. Having just looked at numbers you can spot that, with or without flight number 93, these numbers when added up and divided by 3 equal 93.

Flight Number 11 + Flight Number 175 = 186 Divided by 2 since 2 planes = 93.

Or

Flight Number 11 + Flight Number 175 + Flight no. 93 = 279 Divided by 3 = 93.

93 is the special number of Thelema which is the Religion developed by Aleister Crowley, and this is how they sign their letters and books to each other. They put the number 93 as a signature, and here we have the most important event in recent human History signed with the number 93 - obviously no coincidence there! It's Satan's number! 39 in reverse and 39 is 3 times 13. It's the ultimate inversion of Religion which is why they like it and put it in all sorts of situations as their calling card and because love and will add up to 93 in Greek Gematria. The word Thelema comes from Koine Greek and means 'will' which is why their law is: "Do what thou wilt shall be the whole of the Law. Love is the law, love under will." Crowley received this evil, masonic filled religion from Aiwass whom he channelled and was said to be his Holy Guardian Angel, or Horus. Incidentally Aiwass looked like an alien grey - the first time the world saw one in 1904.[120] The perpetrators of 9/11 wanted us to know about these numbers and are interested in these connections since it is part of their mind control technique to put a sort of 'glaze' over the people so they can't believe the truth of 9/11. People can't see that their own Government with the help of secret agencies blew up their

---

[119] It has been argued (in my view completely unsuccessfully) that this was an explosion which was the shape of a plane, but this is planted shill disinformation.

[120] See Aiwass, Wikipedia entry.

own building killing their own people. It's just too much for most people to handle!

The two Towers also went up in a pile of smoke with a vast pyroclastic cloud. It was nothing like anything the world has ever seen before or since, and it was nothing to do with a 'pancake' collapse. Neither was it a normal demolition with conventional explosions. Nano thermite is a highly crushed form of iron oxide and aluminium which when mixed together with various other reducing agents burns at a very high temperature, typically around 4000 Degrees Celsius and if placed correctly it can cut steel beams. This is not the answer since the problem with this compound is that it burns extremely brightly and would have lit the WTC buildings up like a Christmas tree, and so should be discounted. Nano thermite is not used in conventional demolition anyway. Thousands of massively heavy steel beams **disappeared in a matter of seconds**, literally vanished into thin air, along with millions of tons of concrete - dematerialised. This cannot be explained by air planes and a few thousand gallons of kerosene which doesn't burn hot enough to melt steel anyway. Neither can this be explained by conventional explosives.

Judy Wood in her well annotated book, "Where did the Towers Go?" answers these questions and brilliantly and un-conspiratorially comes up with the answer that an Energy Directed type of weapon would explain the unusual situation better than any other known device. Certainly, Governments have been conducting research into all sorts of areas we don't even know about. After much research you will be drawn to the yet unproven conclusion that an energy directed weapon was used to reduce the towers to dust in a matter of seconds. The Hutchison effect is when a combination of radio waves along with threshold high voltage and electrostatic waves overlap to form unusual phenomenon.[121] Unfortunately, the person of John Hutchison doesn't seem that reliable a lead, and therefore the question should be asked if he is not indeed a planted shill to whom all enquiries of an energy directed devices can be aimed at. In this manner they are hiding the truth of what really happened and controlling the flow of information. How come that a man who is not even a qualified scientist, or has massive government grants

---

[121] Judy Wood, *Where did the Towers Go?* page 445.

managed to discover this powerful science?[122] Whereas the government funded research agencies, such as DARPA, with their massive budgets failed to create this! It stinks, to me, of being another control method as a gate keeper to keep people away from the facts of an energy directed device.[123]

Metal and concrete turned to dust instantly using a new weapon nobody knows about sounds like the perfect weapon for the perfect murder. And the planes, the military stand down, and the Muslim hijackers were all smoke screens - completely fabricated stories - illusions again used to hide what really happened and provide the Muslims as the patsy. **The problem with 9/11 is that so much disinformation** was propagated, that once you have done all the research, you have to decide, (using discernment and intelligence) what you are going to throw out and what you are going to keep. Even the so-called testimony of Norman Mineta that the planes were 50, then 30, and 10 miles out with Dick Cheney should be discounted - why would he reveal this information?[124] It was tantamount to declaring who did 9/11, and to what possible advantage would Norman Mineta gain from welching on his work colleague Dick Cheney, and divulging this information? Furthermore, the very idea that the 9/11 Operation was conducted from deep within the White House makes no sense - why would they suddenly be conducting operations from this location? The simple answer is that it was a false statement to continue to advertise the idea that there were planes involved. As long you keep thinking there are planes you can never completely break out from the occult mind control mechanism that is 9/11.

---

[122] John Hutchison website http://www.hutchisoneffect.com/

[123] A type of thermo-nuclear bomb, or several mini-nukes perhaps of a Plutonium Bomb type has also been suggested as a possible explanation. Every 5 floors an apple-sized Plutonium bomb could have been placed. This is also an unlikely explanation because the sound of explosions would have been heard and radiation detected. Secret since the information on what type of weapon this is still has not leaked out. (Compare DARPA and the weapons they allow us to know about.)

[124] Norman Mineta, disinformation on planes.
https://www.youtube.com/watch?v=bDfdOwt2v3Y 21. 'Kite steel hit plane must', video see https://www.youtube.com/watch?v=lEqeELMXsyo

Why did the School children at Sarassossa on that day chant 'kite hit steel plane must'. **It was to subconsciously implant the idea that there were planes involved!** That's how important the message of the planes was to the Cryptocracy since without the planes being hijacked by Muslims the entire subsequent War on Terror falls apart. At the correct moment the children picked up their books (having read the Pet Goat / Satan book) **from under their chairs,** in other words bowing down. They were bowing to George Bush in acceptance. It was occult theatre of the highest magnitude.

There were no planes. The planes were just numbers. Consider this:-

Flight 11= 11 (as a Master number it is not reduced or compressed.)

Flight 93 = 9+3 = 12

Flight 175 = 1+7+5 = 13

Flight 77 = 7+7 = 14

Total = 50

The planes were just operational numbers, their total adding to 50. What's the significance of 50?

In the Kabbalah there are 50 Gates of Wisdom. It represents the journey of man from earth to the Ain Soph or Divine Light, to Heaven. The total of these numbers was used to represent the journey of humanity into the New World Order heaven, the new paradigm (or pyramid), the Promised Land. In the book of Exodus Moses lead the Israelites to the Promised Land. This is reflected as the 50 days between the first day of Pesach and the receiving of the Torah by Moses on Mount Sinai / Horeb- this is the Shavuot - 50 days. It is also called Pentecost which in Greek means 50, and is when the Holy Spirit descended to the Apostles in Acts 2. It represents therefore the global cosmic transformation. The evolutionary processes that are taught in New Age beliefs and Theosophy about bringing humanity into the Aquarian Age by a type of cosmic transformation. Remember that this may seem all quite theoretical but 9/11 was a thoroughly and carefully concocted ritual in which every element of it had to be put into place as part of their technique to put mankind under a spell. They were making it known to their members within the Network, and the few who can read their symbols, which now includes you, (and hopefully many more) that the deeper meaning of 9/11 was that it was the start of the New Global era of transformation.

Lastly 50 also represents the Jubilee Year. In ancient Israel debts were cancelled on the 7th year and 7 times 7 is 49 the 50th year being the Golden Jubilee. (See Leviticus 25:8 following.)

This is what the number represents and a short expose of what it means. There were no flights, the entire story about planes and messages from them is a complete smoke screen - and what a brilliant one it's been, because so few people have managed to work it out!

Equally the 'Dancing Israelis story' about the young team of removal men making a video of the 9/11 imaginary plane event, makes a nice conclusion for some, but this also should be dismissed as disinformation.[125] More patsies and a good one for the conspiracy theorists to get into, but somehow it's too convenient and it's yet more disinformation and a distraction to who the perpetrators really were. There were no planes! Hard to believe I know, but it's the truth.

Flight 77 was the supposed imaginary plane which hit the Pentagon and just happened to go where the Accountants and Auditors unhappily were searching for the missing US$ 2.3 Trillion which just happened to disappear the day before. Another pointer to who did it.[126]

The question to ask oneself about all this is Cui Bono which is Latin for who benefits? The Israelis benefited through the invasion of Iraq and Afghanistan and the American Elite benefited through the roll out of the Patriot Act which was prepared months before and ready for the big event of 9/11. It was also for more spending on weapons for the military and all the allied industries related to this, more pointers to who do it. The Elite could have brought about these benefits without having to conduct 9/11, so is it possible that the reason for 9/11 goes even deeper than this? Could it be about putting Mankind into a type of torpor, where we become so spoon fed by the Cryptocracy's indoctrination and propaganda that we will

---

[125] Dancing Israelis see https://wikispooks.com/wiki/9-11/Israel_did_it/Dancing_Israelis

[126] Pentagon US $2.3 Trillion goes missing see https://www.youtube.com/watch?v=xU4GdHLUHwU

believe whatever we are told? I suggest it is - it is the moment when the Globalists knew they were on the home straight to the one world government.

Conclusion of 9/11

The burning question that everyone wants answered is, who did it? The answer to this is that the people who did it must have been: -

i) Above or in control of the FBI since the 'dancing Israelis' were released on orders from high up within the FBI.[127]

ii) Above Mossad since the trail of crumbs was made to look as if it was them.

iii) Above the most secret top weapons development agencies in the US since an unknown and previously never seen 'Energy Directed weapon' was used to pulverize and dematerialise the WTC buildings into nothing.

iv) Above the Environmental Protection Agency since they released the information that the World Trade Center site was safe and dealt with the clean-up.[128]

v) Above FEMA since the clear up operation was instigated by them and it was a cover up from the top.

vi) Above the Media since the entire coverage of the event was skewed and photoshopped to provide us with the ridiculous notion that the WTC collapsed as a result of fire, and that the culprits were Muslims with tiny knives.

vii) Above the highest members of the Bush administration since Dick Cheney was made the fall guy by Norman Mineta with the testimony that the imaginary planes were about to hit and that the order still stood.

---

[127] FBI report see
https://ia601301.us.archive.org/1/items/DancingIsraelisFBIReport/fbi%20report%20section%205.pdf or web-search 'FBI release Dancing Israelis'.

[128] For more on 9/11 site clearance see
https://en.wikipedia.org/wiki/United_States_Environmental_Protection_Agency_September_11_attacks_pollution_controversy

viii) Above the Military since the message that went through to Air Force One was that 'Angel is next'. When Bush was whisked away from Sarasota to Washington on Airforce One, a very mysterious message came through they were being tagged by another plane and that 'they were next'. [129]

ix) Above the Air Traffic controllers and the Air Force since they colluded with the covering up of the 'no plane' story and the military exercises which were happening that day. [130]

x) And above the Trilateral Commission since the official 9/11 Commission book was written by Philip Zelikow who is a CFR and Trilateral member and his team of 'cover up experts'. (The Commission leader was originally meant to be Henry Kissinger.)

So, who is above all of these? Above the Government, the Military, the Trilateral Commission, and everything else in ALL these respects and has ALL the power necessary to affect the right events and changes in ALL these areas? The answer is the Super Elite Inner Circle of the Secret Shadow Government, the Cryptocracy, which we've been exposing throughout this book. They are the only culprits who had the power to pull off such a coup. It is the higher members within the Elite Network made up of the unelected parallel government, their aristocracy and their families. It points to the top leaders of the hidden network, the visible part of which we know are the Rockefellers and the Rothschilds. Who else would have the ability to effect events at this high level? Nelson and David Rockefeller originally owned the buildings. They were even to be called the Rockefeller Towers, but then they changed their minds on the name. The PNAC writers and Neo Cons were obviously manhandled towards their obscure and outlandish political theories and beliefs which have supposedly caused so much harm. It's disinformation compounded on disinformation from the top. The Neo Cons were willing and able to 'take the hit' for 9/11. Disinformation such as the CIA's 'Operation Northwoods' was a much-leaked story just so you would think there were planes involved, and they might do this again.

---

[129] Angel is next see http://www.9/11myths.com/html/angel_is_next.html

[130] There were 28 Air Force bases within close range of the four hijacked flights and not one plane was sent up to investigate. Another indicator that there were no planes, and the testimonies, and phone calls were made up to fit

The CIA were also willing to be implicated with this story so by default therefore the perpetrators must be above the CIA and the US government, or else they would not want to be implicated.

You can just about see the hand of the Cryptocracy from behind the curtain as the perpetrators whose concealment is revealed by the truth once you have peeled away the disinformation. This is why 9/11 is important. Most people who study 9/11 instinctively know that this was a vitally important moment but can't quite put these far-reaching conclusions into overall context. The overall context will only make sense when you know their Ultimate Plan, and this is the roll-out of the New World Order as a Technocratic Police State with the New World Religion as a control mechanism, in what will become a vastly reduced population. **9/11 was the start of the accelerated plans of the Elite** and the start of the end game into the global police state and the post-capitalist world we are heading into. As Richard Haas, Director of the CFR said, in 2001, that it was the start of the '30 Year War' which would therefore make 2031 the possible start of a new set of mythologies.

Comparison of Life Before 9/11 and After

Before 9/11 there was no real Terrorism threat. People lived in a freer and better world where there was a lot less fear, conflict and worry. No-one really knew about the 'terror threat.' But now everyone knows about terrorism and everyone is on the lookout for it. We are constantly reminded to report anything we see as suspicious and to be on our guard and worried and concerned and upset and angry and frustrated - you get the picture! Our 'old fashioned' child-like **freedoms have been severely eroded for no benefit at all** other than to enhance the State's authority over us.

False Flags

False flags are when secret services conduct events which are then blamed on other people or groups. 9/11 was a false flag since the people who were made the culprits were Muslims, even though, as we know, they didn't get on any planes or have anything to do with 9/11 - that is all disinformation which makes the entire War on Terror completely false and bogus. You see, you can't build a Police State without mass State sponsored violence. So the deep State has made up a group of people who precisely fit their aim of massive violence. The Muslims are the perfect victim since their ideology can be easily perverted and linked to violence. The Cryptocracy can make us believe that they kill for no apparent reason, and with no apparent agenda, other than to make an Islamic State, which isn't going to happen because the Cryptocracy aren't going to give anything up and they are in control anyway. So you end up with the perfect enemy. Which makes the Muslims, and their religion, completely innocent and the patsy made to be the enemy, when they are not – it is the Cryptocracy which is the enemy of humanity. The media can easily sell the people that the Muslims are to blame since everyone has been conditioned to believe that they are naturally prone to violence. In the past the 'Arab Terrorists' wanted freedom for Palestine, but we never see this now - not in the western media. In this respect the Muslims have been made victims of False Flag attacks and 9/11 was the start of ANOTHER fake war - the War on Terror. The previous fake war being the Cold War since it is now well documented that at the top the Cryptocracy were not so cold towards each other and funded and aided Russia from 1917 all the way through to its break up in 1990.[131]

---

[131] Anthony Sutton, see Western Technology and Soviet Economic Development.

Hoaxes

9/11 was an awful cowardly act, completely unnecessary, but they had to instill that horror in us all and produce that festering mental cut which they could open to put new grit into the wound as and when needed. As an extension from 9/11, and as a result of the magical 'glaze' that has embedded man to his deceived unresponsiveness, the Cryptocracy use the Hegelian dialect of problem, reaction, solution to affect their changes via Hoaxes. This is when events are reported as happening when they did not in fact happen at all. The culprits are then made the patsy or fall guy for something which was completely and utterly false. Normally those patsies are the Muslims used to pump the War on Terror 'fear porn'.

They HAVE to make the people afraid of something, or against someone in order to supply the conflict into which they can provide the solution, which is greater State authority and the steady roll out of the complete Surveillance State. These macabre plays are conducted in order to keep the people in fear and looking to the State for help and protection - exactly as they want.

It's also the case that the State does not view the killing of some of its own people as a tragedy but as a necessary price to pay in order to keep people fearful, in control, and looking to the State for answers. This cost, in human life and suffering, in their twisted view, is a worthwhile price and for a worthwhile cause so they can slowly roll out their Agenda.

The Police and Secret Services have entire teams of fake 'crisis actors' and personnel willing and able to lie in front of the cameras and conduct the 'Psyop-Warfare play', so the only people they really have to fool is the media, who are in their pocket anyway, and they in turn, will fool the rest of us! They use Photoshopped or CGI'd images and made up aliases to provide a legend for the characters in the 'play'. The photos normally come from an 'in vogue, agenda friendly, in-house illuminati camera man' who just happened to be passing by, or they provide the TV Networks with grainy videos shot at a low angle, or on a slant for example to give it a crisis setting. All of these photoshopped fake images are made to make it seem like the event really happened but many did not happen at all. You will have seen them on the TV and in the Newspaper but you did not notice, **not** because you are stupid, but because no-one has ever pointed this out to you before![132]

Then there are the Defence Lawyers and Prosecutors, no doubt high level Masons, with the same dodgy Judges we have seen before passing sentences on the supposed 'play actor' lawbreakers who offer no defence for their alleged crimes and **don't even secure any eye witnesses to testify.** The Judge passes judgment on the supposed perpetrator who either just walks out the back after the trial, or spends a night or two in prison only to be released by 'special branch' the next morning and no-one is any the wiser. This could be part of the reason why there are no cameras allowed in law courts, it would be too obvious to spot the fake trials.

You may be asking yourself if this is for real and why they would be bothering with these regular hoaxes and not actually carrying through on what was supposed to happen. **The reason for this, is control,** and to make sure the **precise outcome** is arrived at. But why don't they do these events for real? The reason why they don't blow people up or kill them, as they are supposed to have done in the official version, is because the 'blow back' caused from such events is too large and **can be difficult to control** - it's not worth it! If the act really had happened and someone really had been killed the relatives of the people involved would be writing letters and demanding justice and they would keep on and on until they had some satisfaction. But if the event was stage managed from the outset with fake reports of bombs going off for example, and then fake media coverage, with fake eye-witness accounts then the whole things works brilliantly, they control every aspect of the story. No-one asks the obvious questions such as, where's the blood and body parts from the bomb which killed 13 people on the bus of 7/7? There's nothing there! Or how can a plane made of aluminium smash through reinforced glass and 3 sets of steel beams **and come out the other side intact!** We've answered that one - it can't! The Controllers get what they want, and because **it's all a hoax and didn't happen they can control the events perfectly,** with a fake family making fake statements and disappearing in the background once the news is forgotten. In this manner they don't have some grieving mother

---

[132] For more on hoaxes see Chris Spivey's website http://chrisspivey.org/

demanding justice for her murdered son, or writing letters to the Prime Minister, (who doesn't *normally* have a clue) and everyone she can think of trying to find out what happened and why.

A lot of what is going on is completely contrived, completely untrue, and never happened - it's all a hoax!

The big problem is proving it!

Hoaxes are very difficult to prove because you are going against the documentation which has been put into the public domain and so we can never be 100% certain that what was a hoax is indeed a hoax. Although in several circumstances using intelligence and discernment you can be very sure that it was a hoax, but can you prove this to others? It seems being on the other side of this conversation is a cause for complete and utter disbelief!

Muddying the Waters

The official story is convoluted and **confused on purpose**. For example, they report something which they know didn't happen or is untrue, and in this manner provide an even more convoluted story for those people who desire to investigate more deeply. Once the official story starts to unravel because it doesn't make sense, they can then either release some more information on the 'back story', which has suddenly come to light, or stick to what's already available. The main thing is that the official story becomes untenable, impossible to decipher and ridiculous. It ends up being one person's word against another, and you can guess who's word the people will listen to - the people making the most noise with the most authority, which is the media of course! Practically every hoax event in the end has about 3 versions to the story if not more. In simple terms you've got, 'the TV Story' which most people buy, 'the Journalists Story' for those who dig a bit deeper but can't draw a conclusion because it's become so convoluted, and the gifted amateur deep state researcher, 'the conspiracy theorist' who has the 'keys' to make sense of it all and when he or she does, no-one believes them! It's a brilliant strategy, since once again the Elite have controlled the Agenda. Only a tiny minority of people actually know what's going on or what really happened, and even then, they can't prove it. The official mythology wins the day! The people have been diverted away from the truth simply by lies and bluff, **although the trauma on the populace is incalculable since they've scared the entire population, but what does that matter, they have achieved their result and managed to dictate the agenda! It's a success!**

To the Cryptocracy, the **credulous masses can, and deserve to be controlled** by their mythologies and symbols, it is their world after all. This gives the Elite the controlled environment they desire. If you can cast the mythology aside, the real knowledge will be revealed. If you can read the symbols you will be able to get to the truth however uncomfortable that may make you feel. The Secret Services have deep roots into the Occult and Satanism and recruit from people who can keep secrets and don't mind doing offensive things as part of State-craft. Their aim is make you feel it's alright to lose your freedom for greater State security. **And so, eventually we will ALL be Slaves to the Authoritarian Surveillance Police State.**

Conclusion of Hoaxes

Once you have made this important and earth-shattering realisation you will have the 'keys to truth' and, hopefully, the maturity and discernment to see what is real and what is completely fake, and so you will have broken through the illusion. That regular Hoaxes are happening all the time and that the information from the media is often entirely absurd, and ridiculous and only to further the agenda of the secret services, Politicians and the New World Order Cyrptocrats. Once you have the 'keys' to this and understand how they are altering things, you will understand that the Deep State does all sorts of unusual things, a lot of the time in fact and they're having a laugh at us every day! They love mockery and **covering their tracks, hiding in broad daylight**. It's not just for false flag events, or part of some deep state activity to do with terrorism, then it might make more sense, but it's for all sorts of mundane activities as well. Could it be that these people are Psychopaths as will be explained later?

It's not always the case that everything is a hoax and you have to be very careful who you discuss this type of fraud with or else you will lose all your friends! Some people just can't see it and never will because they can't break through the propaganda which has been instilled in them from birth. Even with the 'keys' and a good knowledge of the Cryptocracy and all the photos at their disposal this is still a struggle for many, and this includes the 'conspiracy experts' such as David Icke and Alex Jones who seldom mention hoaxes - they still believe, for example, that planes were used on 9/11. It seems they could be in a compromised position providing some truth in amongst all the garbage. The Elite even seek to influence the Alternative Media - the precise people they are supposed to be exposing, are the actual people they are working for! David Icke's beliefs are basically Theosophy, with his alien-reptile-agenda which completely takes the serious enquirer away from the truth and Jesus Christ. Alex Jones of Prison Planet often provides a lot of good information, although it could also be the case that he allows himself to be used to provide information as a 'leak.'

My challenge to you is to research these deep state activities in depth, looking at the photos, the timelines and feasibility of the official story and the numerology, and to check and see if this is correct, or if you can buy the official version of events. In my view, **the default position** from which to start any research from, should be that these events did NOT happen and that you have to prove they did, rather than swallow the official story with all it's crazy machinations and disinformation and disentangle and dismantle the story to find it was another hoax. It's faster and less hassle to come at it from the opposite direction and **ask the obvious questions first** using this type of 'deprogramming disinformation technique'. Although, for many, it's a sad fact that to question the official version is seen as bad form, and not something that 'proper' researchers do. This default start position should be applied to practically all 'deep state events' and this includes the JKF assassination, the Moon Landings, the death of Princess Diana, and 7/7 amongst many others.

As mentioned, they think it's a type of game and only right and proper that we, the masses, deserve to be defrauded and duped since we are the profane, who don't belong to the top Ivy League secret clubs or have a few billion in the Bank - we deserve NOT to know the Truth! **They find it amusing that we can't figure it out, and so they are having a laugh at us mockingly - that we believe everything they tell us without question. Their Satanic doctrine**

is so twisted that they have to tell us they 'Kontrol' us in order to free themselves from any culpability. Our exposure to these violent open air Masonic rituals via the News makes an impact because we gullibly trust our media outlets and allow ourselves as spectators to become exposed to the occult symbols, cyphers, words and esoteric meanings which are encoded within these psychodramas and hoaxes. It's not our fault that without our knowledge this information is pushed into our subconscious enabling them to process us into a type of 'global occult initiation' which produces a state of putrefaction and complete indifference to our lives - exactly as they want from us.[133] As we seek greater titillation from the horrific exposes of the news, we end up succumbing more and more to their mythologies which over time become creeds which unfortunately seem very hard to break. This cycle of psychological exposure or 'magical download' is actually quite addictive and enables the Cryptocracy to have greater and greater power over what we believe and say. It makes our reality a falsehood.

But now you know the truth, you will have to be far more discerning and far less trusting, continuously seeking the reality and asking questions about the most obvious facts.

As it says in Matthew Chapter 7:7-8. "Ask and it will be given to you; seek and you will find; knock and the door will be opened to you. For everyone who asks receives; he who seeks finds; and to him who knocks, the door will be opened."

Everyone who asks will receive wisdom and discernment, but this is only from God. If you don't believe in Jesus Christ, and believe you have this discernment purely from your mind, you will be disappointed and go wrong at some stage, because the ultimate point of truth and reality is God. Without this anchor and belief, you will eventually become unstuck and loosened from the truth, like seaweed pulled from the sea; however strong you think you are, the tide is always stronger. (Ephesians 4:13 &14.)

---

[133] M A Hoffman, *Secret Societies and Psychological Warfare*, page 92.

CHAPTER 7

FREEMASONRY: FATAL IN THE FIRST DEGREE!

At the bottom of the Pyramid we have the Freemasons. Most of these individuals are clueless to the reality of the Cryptocracy and the deeper meanings we have been looking at. Freemasons are part of the control mechanism which enables the Elite to maintain power, but Freemasonry itself has very little effect at the Political level. Freemasonry is therefore a method by which the status quo of the Establishment can be maintained, with the Queen and Duke of Kent as the Grand Master at the top of the visible iceberg that is the Cryptocracy control network. Everyone below them in the Lodge from Worshipful Master to the Entered Apprentice has his 'position'. This can be used by their peers to steer the course of events in the direction to which they wish. In other words, Freemasonry is an 'insurance policy' which the Elite can use to reduce 'fall out' of information hurtful to the Network. It is also a method of subtle control with nepotism and self-promotion similar to the old school boy network of the past. In the Protocols (Number 4) it says: *'Gentile masonry blindly serves as a screen for us and our objects, but the plan of action of our force, even its very abiding place, remains for the whole people an unknown mystery.'* The Protocols concur that Freemasonry itself is not the seat of power but is a screen which enables the Cryptocracy to hide behind. The institution of Freemasonry is therefore yet another 'ring' for the hidden government, to empower themselves at the centre, which makes it a control mechanism for the divulgence of power.

Since Freemasonry is all about Secrets, and they'd better not divulge this information for fear of exposure or death, this is a control mechanism by which the top echelons of the Secret Society can keep control of everything that is going on below them. Freemasons take multiple oaths to keep the secrets of their religion away from the 'Profane' and do as they are told. It's a delusion and once adopted into the Satanic family of Freemasonry you are open to manipulation. According to Albert Pike, they deserve to be lied to, misled and deluded. Often, of course, Masons will tell you what I've written above is not true - and everything is 'above board' and that Masonry is about 'making good men better' and that they are men of honour, but there's a lot more going on that just this. They are Satan's foot soldiers and a great evil, and here's why - it's Spiritual.

The Great Architect of the Universe

Freemasonry is all about gaining 'Light' from The Great Architect of the Universe or TGAOTU. The exact God who Masons serve is actually shrouded in obscurity and is a Secret only for the top Elite Initiates, but it is a generic god with whom everyone can be at home with. Masonic writers have also described god and the god-force, as being far above humanity and unknowable. For the Mason god is not a personal god like Jesus Christ, for them he is neither just, nor merciful, neither has he any qualities of personality and he is really far beyond human understanding. The idea that God loves us and wants to bring us to Himself is completely devoid. **The god of Masonry is therefore a non-personal god** which is actually close to the beliefs of both the New Age god and also the Islamic god Allah.[134] And this is part of the reason why the Elite have a special affinity to Islam as will be explained later.

The god of Freemasonry is a 'label' upon which you could put God the Father, Allah, Krishna, Lucifer, or Buddha. In this respect their god is 'the big man upstairs' with a bit of this god mixed in with a bit of that one. As Manly P Hall wrote: -

---

[134] Masonry: Beyond the Light, Bill Schnoebelen, page 45.

The true Mason is not creed-bound. He realizes with the divine illumination of his lodge that as a Mason his religion must be universal: Christ, Buddha or Mohammed, the name means little, for he recognizes only the light and not the bearer. He worships at every shrine, bows before every altar, whether in temple, mosque or cathedral, realizing with his truer understanding, the oneness of all spiritual truth.[135]

Albert Pike wrote a similar thing in 'Morals and Dogma' on page 226: -

Masonry, around whose altars the Christian, the Hebrew, the Moslem, the Brahmin, the followers of Confucius and Zoroaster, can assemble as brethren and unite in prayer to the one God who is above all the Baalim, must needs leave it to each of the initiates to look for the foundation of his faith and the hope to the written scriptures of his own religion.

Pike then says his god of Freemasonry is above all of the Baalim which means false gods, which in this quote therefore means he puts the God of the Bible below the Masonic god.

The real problem is that Freemasonry subtly teaches that all paths lead to God which makes Christ's atonement obsolete. Furthermore, in order to usher in the One World Government, with them at the top, they need to destroy all religions, especially Christianity. Atheists and Humanists today fight the exoteric or outer religions without knowing that they are helping the enemies of Christianity - Freemasonry.

The Religion of Freemasonry is not Christianity, it has its own beliefs, rites and ethics. On its surface and exoterically it looks like just a club-about-secrets, and they mean no harm and they don't worship Lucifer or are engaged in the occult, but esoterically and beyond the obvious, Freemasonry is a complicated web of Satan's deception. As we shall see later their view of creation is a type of **Hermetic Emanationism** in which the godhead creates from a higher level to a lesser level.

They believe the soul is Immortal and will be **judged by god according to what labours they have done**. Whereas Christianity teaches that we are brought to God by Him and are justified by his Grace as we believe, not through knowledge. Ephesians 2:8 & 9: - For it is by grace you have been saved through faith, and this not

---

[135] Manly P Hall, *The Lost Keys of Freemasonry'* Chapter 5, p65.

from yourselves; it is the gift of God, not by works, so that no one can boast.

It is not us who chose God, but God who choses us. Although you may have made a step towards God. This is explained in John 15:16: You did not choose me, but I chose you and appointed you to go and bear fruit - fruit that will last.

Keeping infantile secrets

They must keep the secrets, often infantile, ignorant, revolting pieces of completely inane trivia and incorrect theology such as Jah-bul-on, which is the name of their god at the lower degrees. Jah stands for Yahweh, Bul for Baal, or Bel, the bull god, (see 1 Kings 16:29-33), and On is the name of Osiris, the Egyptian sun god. If they divulge the secrets, (which aren't worth knowing anyway) then they are breaking their oaths most of which contain blood curdling vows, such as *'having my body severed in two and my bowels taken from thence and burned to ashes, the ashes scattered before the four winds of heaven, that no more remembrance might be had of so vile and wicked a wretch as I would be, should I ever, knowingly, violate this my Master Mason's obligation.'* [136]

Yet many high Politicians in high offices in the UK, the US and elsewhere, all over the world, are Masons going about their daily tasks without anyone making any comment.

First Degree- Entered Apprentice

When you become a Freemason the first level is 'Entered Apprentice' the candidate is lead into the Lodge blind folded and with a 'cable tow' put around their neck. They then swear allegiance to the Lodge and the Worshipful Master over an open Bible with the symbols of the Compass and the Set Square, themselves representing the act of copulation.

As usual there is the exoteric which is the outer meaning and the esoteric, the inner meaning. In simple terms the exoteric is the good reason and the esoteric the real reason.

---

[136] Duncan's Masonic Ritual and Monitor.

The cable tow represents the umbilical cord and being born of the Queen of Heaven of the Babylonian Mysteries to become spiritually adopted into Satan's family. The Queen of Heaven is Nimrod's Mother Semiramis who gave birth to Dammuzi in Babylon (in Hebrew, Tammuz, Ezekiel 8:14-15). Of course, the initiate thinks this a gentleman's club and there's nothing sinister going on but on the contrary, they are being born into the Mystery Religion. Jesus said, 'Do not swear an Oath.' Matthew 5:33-37. Yet Masons swear allegiance to the Worshipful Master not to divulge secrets about which they know nothing. If they took it all as a joke and somehow meaningless then they would be breaking the 2nd Commandment, 'Take not the name of the Lord your God in vain.' Exodus 20:7 and Deuteronomy 5:11. And if they took it seriously then they would be breaking the First Commandment to have no other God besides Yahweh, -- Exodus 20:3. Freemasonry is fatal even in the first degree since the connection to Lucifer has already been made and can't easily be un-done, but by the blood of Jesus.[137]

Prince Philip got this far as a Freemason, First Degree, on December 5th 1952 at Navy Lodge 2612 but afterwards he thought it was all 'silly' and apparently didn't go any further, but we don't know because it's a secret society about secrets, for all we know he could be a 33rd Degree Mason. The Royal Family are steeped in Masonry and it's all part of the Chivalric orders such as the Order of Bath or the Order of the Garter which is the highest order. These Establishment societies and Knights (with their Knighthoods) are intermingled and closely related to Freemasonry and even trace their origins back to the Christian military organisations of the Crusades.

Second Degree Freemasonry is Fellow Craft and the cable tow is placed around the right arm, under the shoulder and is basically about receiving more 'Light'.

---

[137] Masonry: Beyond the Light, Bill Schnoebelen, page 88.

Third Degree – the Myth of Hiram Abiff

At the Third Degree, proceedings get even more scary! This time the initiate is role playing in a 'play' as Hiram Abiff who is mentioned in 1 Kings 7:13- 51 and 2 Chronicles 2:13-16 and 2 Chronicles 4:16 as the main builder of King Solomon's Temple.[138] He is the Masonic Messiah and replaces Jesus in most of their liturgy. His Father was from the Tribe of Naphtali and his Mother from the tribe of Dan which makes him Jewish.

The Initiate who plays Hiram Abiff is sworn to not reveal the password, since in Medieval Europe the Masons used to provide a password to enter the building site. Hiram refuses to divulge the password to the three ruffians, Jubela, Jubelo and Jubelum, and is killed. In the ritual the initiate is struck on the head with the felted mallet or maul, and falls into a blanket or canvas. This supposedly happens in King Solomon's Temple and he is hurriedly buried there amongst the rubbish. Fearing exposure later, his body is moved and buried elsewhere within Jerusalem. The three ruffians are found out and enlist the help of King Solomon who uses the special grip of the Lion of the Tribe of Judah to bring Hiram back to life. The special grip is a bit like a hand shake on the wrist but with two fingers splayed either side of the wrist, and at this Hiram comes back to life.

What's going on with this extraordinary mock ritual killing?

---

[138] Abi in Hebrew means my Father, Ab meaning Father (compare Abba Father in Aramaic) and the suffix 'i meaning my. But how this ending up Abiff with the double ff is a mystery. It has been suggested Abiff is Old French from the mid 17th Century when Freemasonry in its modern form approximately started.

Satanic Baptism

This is a Mystery school initiation which harks back to the old religions in Greece and has a direct parallel with Egyptian religion. The only other character who was buried three times, as Hiram Abiff, is Osiris, god of the afterlife. Hiram was buried once within the Temple grounds, once outside the Temple, and then having been resurrected he spent the rest of his life, and was buried a third time. The Osiris cult has a similar story, in that Osiris is buried in a coffin, then comes alive to impregnate Isis, his mother and sister, and is buried again in a tamarisk tree. Later on, Osiris dies and is buried in the desert. (Osiris is called On in the Bible where Joseph marries the daughter of one of the High Priests of On, Genesis 41:45. This is the only direct mention of Osiris in the Bible.) So, in the ritual play, you are hit on the head and die, which is dying to yourself as Hiram Abiff, and then you are raised up from the dead as a new creation under the Mystery Religion. The concept of being raised up as a new being has parallels in Christianity where the new believer dies to self in Baptism and is raised up as a new creation with the seal of God's approval as a Saint. But in Freemasonry you are raised up via the Lion's Paw which is said to be a reference to the birth of lions who were thought to be born dead and were brought to life by the roar of a lion. It is also said to be a reference to the Lion of Judah which Jesus is called. The only problem with this is that the Bible also refers to Satan as a Lion. 1 Peter 5:8 'Be alert and of sober mind. Your enemy the devil prowls around like a roaring lion looking for someone to devour.' The candidate is raised up as a member of the Mystery Religion Cult via the lion's grip, and this is from Lucifer. They are born again into Satan's kingdom which makes this Satanic Baptism. This is serious news for any Freemason and the damage it does is extremely hard to shake. Only by full repentance and completely turning away from Freemasonry is it possible to escape from this evil.

The upper degrees of Freemasonry are about receiving more and more Light, but this, in reality is spirit possession or 'selling your Soul to the devil', although this is a misunderstood concept. Yet many Masons are God fearing men and some are even Lay Preachers, but how discerning of the spiritual realm are they? Anyone with just a little bit of discernment can see that what's going on is wrong. They may say it's a play with allegorical meaning, and therefore it's a moral teaching, but they fundamentally don't understand how the Spiritual realm works; there's much more going on here. **The Spiritual realm works by invitation** - if you are doing rituals opposed to God's order you invite the Devil. Just because the characters and words are from the Bible doesn't mean the real deep meaning is good. If you are studying the occult for years on end and practicing it, you will believe odd things, and evil unusual occurrences will occur!

Freemasonry is the religion of the Elite and high-level Freemasonry from about the 19th Degree of Grand Pontiff and above, is Luciferianism. From the writings of Albert Pike and others we gain this truth that the god of Freemasonry is indeed Lucifer. And what is it that Freemasons seek – more light? The light bearer is Lucifer who is Satan.

Here is a helpful analogy to ponder on and cut through all the hocus pocus. Freemasonry itself can be compared to a 'computer' which is the hardware of the Temple, the rituals and the paraphernalia, into which the 'software' of the Kabbalah,

Rosicrucianism, Gnosticism (literally hidden Knowledge of religion), and Occultism can be loaded and performed and played out. This is how Freemasonry works, it is an amalgamation of many threads from ancient religions, played out in the Lodges as part of their witchcraft.

Anyone who is a mason and wants to break free from this evil should write a letter declaring they have found Jesus Christ as their personal Saviour and wish to leave the lodge and have their name removed from the register, since Satan will have a claim over them until their name is removed. Satan or Lucifer are legalistic in the extreme. If your name is still in the official register you will still be under the bondage of Freemasonry to some level. This will make a true walk with Jesus Christ difficult. I pity the Freemason. It's a pathetic shadow of reality and a disgusting perverted Satanic evil. Politicians should not be allowed to be members of this group.

Orientation of King Solomon's Temple

The original Temple had the Holy of Holies in the West. The Congregation entered the building from the East and faced West during services.The Freemasons Lodge is said to be a type of King Solomon's Temple but the orientation of the building is facing East. This is the opposite direction to the original Temple. The Worshipful Master sits in the East and the entrance is in the West. And anyway Jesus forbade his Disciples from calling anyone 'Master' yet alone Worshipful Master, Matthew 23:8-10. The Congregation actually face one another, but the orientation is towards the East - to the rising Sun (Apollo) and is more than just a nod to Sun worship, like all the Mystery religions.

Floor Plan Of Solomon's Temple

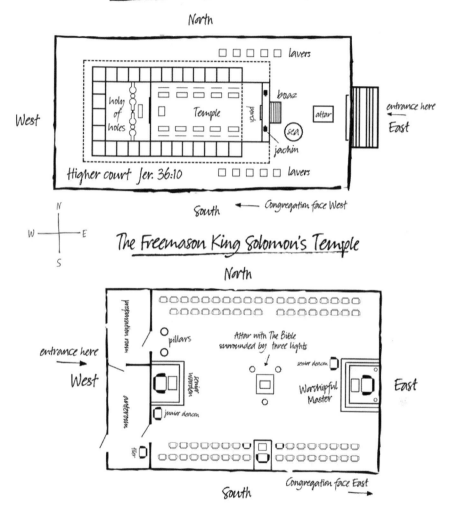

The Biblical King Solomon's Temple

North

lavers

holy
of
holes

Temple

porch

boaz

altar

sea

jachin

West

East

entrance here

Higher court Jer. 36:10   lavers

South   ← Congregation face West

The Freemason King Solomon's Temple

North

preparation room

pillars

Altar with The Bible
surrounded by three lights

senior deacon

entrance here

West

junior
warden

Worshipful
Master

East

junior deacon

South   Congregation face East →

In the original King Solomon's Temple the Congregation face WEST, but in the Freemason's King Solomon's Temple the Congregation face EAST towards the rising Sun.

See Ezekiel 8:15-18

It is worth noting that although many Churches face East with the Altar in the East, **they don't pretend to be a type of King Solomon's Temple, whereas Masonic Temples do**. So here again we see Satan's deception that whilst the charade is that there's some special activity going on to reveal the true meaning of life, it simply contravenes the Creators scheme of worship! And we all know about things being done backwards and the wrong way around, this is pure Satanism. Initiates on the left-hand path are always doing things backwards. The approach to God is from east to west. The children of Israel approached the promised land from the east to the west as they came across from Jordan. The other way is the reverse: God drove Adam and Eve out of the Garden of Eden from the west to the east, Genesis 3:24, and Cain also was driven out from west to east - Genesis 4:16, as was Jacob.

Freemasonry a Secret, but Why?

Now that we have established that Freemasonry is from the Devil and that its members can be easily manipulated, what does it say about the many politicians who are Masons? Firstly it says that their actions will probably go against humanity since their beliefs are contrary to Christ. For example, they are into mock ritual killing and doing things the wrong way around. Secondly, it says that **Freemasons cannot be trusted because they can be so easily manipulated by others above them in the structure.** Furthermore, Freemasonry is an important part of the Globalist Agenda: building the New World Order although only at a certain level are members aware of this. Often they have become so deluded and hoodwinked into the 'Establishment' world view that they can't break free from their special treatment in Society they are afforded. They have become so dependent upon its benefits that they can never break free or be told what they believe is wrong. Only a true conversion to Spirit-filled Christianity and a total rejection of their former lives will work.

Many 'builders' of the New World Order are people higher up the hierarchy and often belonging to more fearsome groups such as the

Skull and Bones, the CFR and Bohemian Grove. Then there are other political organisation's such as the Trilateral Commission, Council on Foreign Relations and Bilderbergers. The Royal Institute of International Affairs which is part of the UK arm of the Cecil Rhodes and Milner group, and the Club of Rome which is their think tank. Practically all of the people in these groups are Freemasons or belong to closely allied religious organisations.

CHAPTER 8

SPIRITUAL DISCERNMENT

But solid food is for the mature, who by constant use have trained themselves to distinguish good from evil. Hebrews 5:14.

The Religion of the Super Elite

We have an idea that the 'lower establishment' believe in Freemasonry, and that most of them are not a threat to our way of life, but what about the Cryptocracy? What do they believe in? Those people higher up the pyramid, as mentioned before, the Skull and Bones, the CFR, Bohemian Grove, Bilderbergers, Trilateral Commission members etc, what do they all have in common?

These people are working in the political arena and they do know what is going on. On the mundane level they pretend to be working for our causes and passing laws to help the average man, but in reality, they are ushering in a totally different type of Government than you might imagine. A Government with them at the top and you and I at the bottom. They intend to have total control over what you do, say and even think. It is their will which will be imposed on us. They intend to use indoctrination, propaganda and a myriad of subtle psychological methods to keep and gain control so they can feel secure and rule over us.

It's their beliefs which are important since once you know what they believe, you will be a position to second guess what they are going to do next and therefore how they might accomplish their long-range goals. We don't know what the future holds, but we can see glimpses of the future they want for us from their beliefs, writings, publications and via the laws they pass.

The Luciferian Philosophy

What beliefs do they all have in common? If I had to sum it up in a few words, what they have in common is that they adhere to the **Luciferian Philosophy.**

The Luciferian Philosophy is the belief than Man can conquer the world and nature to become a god through Lucifer.

Lucifer- the Light Bearer

Isaiah Chapter 14:12 King James Bible version.

How art thou fallen from heaven, O Lucifer, son of the morning! *how* art thou cut down to the ground, which didst weaken the nations!

The Hebrew is 'Heylel' הֵילֵל which means 'Shining' from the Hebrew root he shines הָלַל.[139]

'Ben' בֶּן־ in the Construct form i.e. Genitive, which means Son of.

'Shahar' with guttural haith, שַׁחַר means the dawn, or the morning, but early morning just as the sun comes up.[140] (Boqer also means morning in Hebrew.)

Heylel ben Shahar, "shining one, son of the morning" which was translated by the Septuagint as ἑωσφόρος *(heōsphoros)* which the Latin Vulgate in turn translated as **lucifer.** This comes from the Latin 'luci'

---

[139] Strong's Hebrew Concordance: heylel 1984 and halal 1966

[140] Strong's: shahar 7837 dawn.

meaning 'light', and 'fer' meaning 'carry' – hence this is translated as, Light Carrier.[141]

It has to be said that the King James translation of this word lucifer with a small l is a bit dubious since it comes directly from the Latin word and it is not translated this way in other versions.[142] What is true, is that this name became the focus of an entire system of beliefs, with Lucifer being a different agent to Satan.

Satan

The word Satan comes from the Hebrew Satan שָׂטָן and has the tri-root from shin, taith, noon and this means Adversary. Ha Satan means, the Adversary.[143]

For everyday people on the street, these two are the same, Satan and Lucifer, and they are right they are the same! But for the Freemasons, Palladium 34, Theosophists, Rosicrucian's, and New Agers etc they are different. This is the god which the Cryptocracy worship and revere and to whom they ultimately pledge their allegiance. Within the upper Degrees of Freemasonry they know and worship Lucifer - their lord and master!

Satan was in heaven but then fell like Lightening (Luke 10:18), and in Revelation 12:4 we read of the dragon's tail taking a third of the 'stars'. These are the fallen angels which became demons and fell down to earth. A third is 33 which is why 33 is a special number to them, it represents the hosts of Satan. The earth and the nations of the earth, as already explained, are in the hands of Satan, since he is the ruler of this earth, although everything ultimately is in the total control of God.

---

[141] Septuagint was the Greek translation of the Hebrew Old Testament written in 3rd century BC. The Vulgate was the Latin translation of the Septuagint translated by Jerome in 382 AD.

[142] King James translation was 1611.

[143] satan: Strong's 7854.

The Luciferian Philosophy comes from a twisted commentary on Genesis

It is important to understand the source of the Luciferian philosophy.

When Adam and Eve were in the Garden of Eden the Serpent said to Eve:

Genesis 3:5 (NKJV) [5] For God knows that in the day you eat of it (The Tree of Knowledge of good and evil) your eyes will be opened, and you will be like God, knowing good and evil.

The Luciferian Philosophy is that Lucifer did mankind a favour by enabling Man to know right from wrong and therefore that it was Lucifer who provided Man with knowledge. This is a different person to Satan and so Lucifer is actually, in their twisted view, someone to be revered and looked up to as mankind's Saviour. To them Lucifer is the hero who broke free from God and the bondage imposed on him by God. Obviously, this is completely untrue. It was Lucifer who fell from heaven because he thought he could be god. The Morning Star referred to in Isaiah 14:12 is indeed Satan. It is true that Jesus is also referred to as the Bright Morning Star (Revelation 22:16) but this is referring to Jesus in the Post Millennial kingdom.

"In the day you eat of it (The Tree of Knowledge of good and evil) your eyes will be opened, and you will be like God, knowing good and evil." Why is it that knowing the difference between good and evil makes you like God? The reason is that you have the choice and ability to choose right from wrong just as God does. **Before the Fall,** Adam / mankind did not know what was right and wrong because he was living like an animal or living like a child, immature of ethics and the discernment between good and evil. But at the Fall, as man emerged from his child-like state, he could see right from wrong, (animals can't see this, they just exist).

Then the Serpent said, "did God really say that if you eat from the Tree of Knowledge you would die!"

But Adam and Eve did not die physically, but they died spiritually, being unable to communicate properly with God. The reason for this is that God is 100% perfect and good, and they had evil in them, so the relationship had become broken. The reason they had evil is because they had disobeyed God. It wasn't exactly a difficult thing to do - you can eat of anything you want, but not this tree here! "The LORD God commanded the man, saying, "From any tree of the garden you may eat freely; but from the tree of the knowledge of good and evil you shall not eat, for in the day that you eat from it you will surely die." Genesis 2:16-17. The test was a reasonable one! But since they failed the test they became cut off from God, and so to restore mankind back to God Jesus became the Saviour. Why would a good God create evil? If Man had evil in him then God and Man were separate; it's as simple as that.

Atheistic or Metaphorical Luciferianism

The mystery Religions believe and teach the Story of Mankind's Fall and Lucifer as a Metaphor. It's worth just quickly going over what a metaphor means. It is a figure of speech which is a thing regarded as representative or symbolic of something else. So for example, 'the mind is an ocean', or 'the city is a jungle' are both metaphors. Lucifer is seen as a metaphor in which he saves mankind from an unjust God and gives man the Gift of Intellect. In their twisted view God held Adam and Eve as prisoners in the Garden of Eden and stopped Eve from eating of the Tree of Knowledge; it was the 'Shining Light' of the 'good god' Lucifer who enabled mankind's eyes to be opened and illuminated by eating from the tree. So, in the Fall, God is seen as evil, imprisoning Man keeping him away from the knowledge whilst the devil becomes the good god. A complete inversion of the truth. This is Metaphorical or Atheistic Luciferianism, the belief that the shining light is providing man with the intellect as a type of Promethean fire giver, but as a metaphor. For them it didn't really happen - it's an interesting story of intellectual significance. Lucifer the light bearer brought the Light, which is why Freemasons are always aiming to gain more Light.[144]

---

[144] Wikipedia entry Luciferianism.

Other groups have this light and wish to gain even more to become 'illuminated' as thousand points of light.

By extension from this they also teach **that there isn't a god besides man himself and that if you can perfect yourself as a temple within, <u>via the god within you</u>, you can become 'Christed' and so you can become god.** In other words, they believe that via the Metaphor of Lucifer, humankind can perfect itself and through interaction with Lucifer's intellect they will conquer everything and become all powerful like a God. This is precisely what most of the Elite believe, and, by extension, their illuminated knowledge enables them to be gods over us, and rule over us - the normal man in the street. They believe they have been born with that god given right to dictate to the masses what they think is the right thing to do, think and say.

It's not as you might imagine that these people have gone to Oxford, Cambridge or the Ivy League, and become successful and entered into Politics and been elected into their constituency. They have to be Luciferians to gain entry into the Club. There is always a higher motive involved in those who reach the upper echelons of the Establishment and are recruited into the Cryptocracy. If they are not in the club, which is the Outer Circle, they do not get to the top it's as simple as that. And unless they have given their allegiance to the Inner Circle they will not gain high office.

Theistic Luciferianism

This is closer to Satanism and some have said it is 'watered down Satanism.' The Luciferian believes there is a God, but choses to rebel against Jesus and the Holy Spirit. They may not worship Lucifer but revere him as a friend, a rescuer, or guiding spirit to help mankind towards overcoming suffering and nature. They could be heavily into ceremonial magic and followers of the Left Hand Path, which was a term originally coined by Madame Blavatsky, but comes from Matthew 25:32-33. They seek power for themselves via Lucifer as an expression of a better god and a higher god than Jesus. They may study Thelema, which is the religion of Aleister Crowley, or study

Gnosticism, Kabbalah and New Age religions. Of course, these believers are heavily into the occult. Once you are into the occult, you become demon possessed which is what traditional Christianity teaches, and you are for sure severely deluded.

Although Lucifer may come across as some kindly helper for mankind, he is Satan, the Devil. It is from Lucifer that the Super Elite draw their strength, earthly wisdom and power. They are directly plugged into him – this is 'The Secret'. They know something which the man in the street doesn't. They know that the world is in the control of Lucifer and so they worship and derive their earthly power from him. Lucifer doesn't ask for any rules, there are no requirements; it's "Do what thou wilt shall be the whole law." This is the difference - if you serve the one true God, Jesus Christ, you must at least try to be obedient to the teachings of Christ, try not to commit adultery, cheat or lie, or be dishonest with the truth. But if you are a Luciferian, the end always justifies the means, because you can do what you want, there's no payback in terms of Sin, or Judgement and no real rules. 'You can do what you want as long as it doesn't hurt other people'. This is the ethos of our age! In the post Christian era the need for God in the mindset of the masses has evaporated, and as long as no-one is harmed, you can do what you want. This was somewhat sufficient for society for a while and this sort of nominalism was perhaps acceptable. The people didn't perish because they still, at heart, believed in God. But now we are slowly entering into a **new post Christian era** where the watered down Luciferian philosophy and ethos is slowly turning society to become more and more twisted to the point where it is Satanic, and the inversion of Christianity. We are slowly seeing this emerging philosophy today as it becomes the new accepted norm. This is no coincidence, since it is the deliberate policy of the Cryptocracy to bring us to a place of openly accepting and enjoying Lucifer as our god.

Luciferians wish to Become Gods

They wish **to become gods**. Their view is that in Genesis it was the Serpent who enabled mankind to progress from being a 'slave' to

God and so it will be Lucifer who will usher in the new dawn of Man's Oneness to a new world. Aleister Crowley wrote about Lucifer or Satan in the 'Book of the Law' which expounded his religion called Thelema. 'I am the Snake that giveth knowledge. To worship me take wine and strange drugs whereof I will tell my prophet.'

The Snake tells man that he can become like a God, that reality is essentially an illusion, and that there is no Sin. Man is, and should be free to do his own thing and not acknowledge his Creator, but look to the one (Satan) who freed him from the clutches of nasty, petty, God in their perverted view.

'I am' blasphemy

Other evidence that the Super Elite wish to become gods is that in Theosophy and some other New Age variations they keep on referring to themselves as being 'I am'. I AM is the special name given to Yahweh (YHWH) and is in fact a play on words between the Hebrew for 'I am' which is 'Eh'ye' (AHYH), and the Hebrew for Yahweh (YHWH) which is similar and from the same root, spelt in the Qal form HYH meaning the one who is, the absolute unchangeable one.[145] God's name comes from the same word, to be, so it's a bit like saying 'I am the being'. The Hebrew and English is below.

Exodus 3:14:

וַיֹּאמֶר אֱלֹהִים אֶל-מֹשֶׁה אֶהְיֶה אֲשֶׁר אֶהְיֶה

And God said to Moses, "I am who I am."

And yet the New Agers and Freemasons insist of having a vast literature in which the Initiate declares himself to be 'I AM'. The significance of this is that 'I am' is closely associated with the Divine name Yahweh and so when Jesus said about himself 'I am' the people knew the connection that Jesus was making, when he said that before Abraham existed he was in existence and was God, as 'I am.'

---

[145] Strong's 3068.

John 8:56 – 59. Your father Abraham was overjoyed to see My day. He saw it and was glad. Then the Jews said to Him, You are not yet fifty years old, and You have seen Abraham? Truly, truly, I tell you, Jesus declared, **before Abraham was born, I am**! At this, they picked up stones to throw at Him. But Jesus hid Himself and slipped away from the temple area.

He was declaring Himself to be God, but that was acceptable because He is, and was God. This is an amazing statement because Jesus declared Himself to be God which of course He is.

The phrase 'I am' has become so special to Theosophists that there was even a denomination of Theosophy called 'I Am Activity'. This 'I AM Activity' was started by Guy Ballard in the 1930s and had some effect on Alice Bailey who had influence on the United Nations. It is admonition to godhood and a total blasphemy of Christianity. In the Gospel of John between Chapters 6 to 15 we have many occurrences of the term 'I am'. Jesus said, I am the bread of Life, the Light of the World, the Gate, the Good Shepherd, the Resurrection and the Life: I am the Way, the truth and the Life, and the Vine.

Lucifer as the Elite's Saviour

The belief in Lucifer takes the Elite to some unusual conclusions as they become completely deluded that Lucifer is a **guiding light or spiritual teacher** who will lead them into Enlightenment. They believe in rationalism and Science as being the only way to obtain knowledge and they shun dogma, the doctrines the Bible and the need for Salvation. They also believe that mankind should be able to discern right from wrong without the intervention of God or any book, and that there is no need for Hell or Heaven, and that the Bible is full of fairy tales. Many people today hold these types of views, and it does make some sense in the Secular Humanistic society in which we live today, since this is what we have become indoctrinated into. However, this moral code will eventually lead to serious problems, and it does not explain the reality of life. Believing this doesn't necessarily make you a Luciferian, but the vacuum created by the lack of moral code ultimately leads to the State filling it with its own Luciferian, Masonic version of reality. Ever since the Fall, man has utilised technology to his benefit, but the time is fast approaching in which electronic technology will render civilisation impossible on a human scale, as we enter the New World Order. It will be a false paradigm that sets the stage for the Anti-Christ in which man becomes more and more attuned to the demonic and less in touch with his Creator. This will lead to the false Prophet and the emergence of a new type of religion replacing God with Man. As mentioned before, this is what Nimrod had in mind 'to create a tower which will reach into Heaven' - Genesis 11:4. For him to have God like status, to be a ruler of men, and to have dominion over man; this is the aim of the hidden government. These beliefs are at the heart of Freemasonry and Theosophy. It is no accident that Freemasonry traces its true founder and originator all the way back to Nimrod. In fact, in the First Degree there is the Oath of Nimrod who they believe is good. Whilst the Bible says he was against God and therefore bad.

They want to bring man into recognition of his own divinity which is a very dangerous concept. As Illuminated members of the cult this is why George Bush spoke about a 'thousand points of light' and called David Rockefeller one of the 'brightest points of light' which is a reference to him being an Illuminated Initiate of the same 'Illuminati Cult' he is a member of.[146] The illuminati considered themselves to be more enlightened since they have gained more light. It is all the same evil cult.

How do we become Gods? Understanding this belief will help us make sense of many of the areas the Cryptocracy are promoting in the research and development of Science and Technology, in particular Life Sciences, Artificial Intelligence, Transhumanism and Robotics.

The Super Elite have become so warped and deluded they have no idea how dangerous it is to 'play god' with Bio-Sciences. They wish to become gods anyway and so cloning a human being for life sciences or for military applications to make a better fighter is

---

[146] George Bush Snr, Rockefeller brightest points of light see http://www.bbc.co.uk/news/world-us-canada-39333416 For a thousand points of light see Inaugural Speech 1989. Bush even started the 'Points of Light' foundation.

permitted and fully endorsed. They believe that they are on the verge of **becoming gods** themselves and immortality and convergence with machines will make them like gods. We are approaching the Age of Aquarius and so this is a deep held belief that at this juncture some transforming event will occur. This could be **Transhumanism** as the next Evolutionary step for mankind. Theosophy's goal is that Man will evolve from his current state to a further technological advancement. According to this belief, it seems there will be the merging of man with advanced robotics and computer intelligence which will bring in an age of unparalleled sophistication and knowledge, but it will also render humanity obsolete as he becomes plugged into the web of neural hive network of linkages and interfaces – an interpretation for the beast system.

The people who are pushing this agenda cannot be trusted and have shown time and time again that they are not able to make the right judgments on where the line should be drawn between what is right and what is wrong. In general, they are too trusting of technology, and their beliefs are too subversive and duplicitous for them to make the right decisions for humanity with these new extremely powerful technologies. Because they believe in this Luciferian agenda everything that ends up in their hands turns to evil (as stated in Genesis 6:5). Nano technology and Bio Sciences will be weaponised and used against us - the normal people who inhabit the earth - it is only a matter of time.

Technological Eternal Life

"Then the LORD God said, "Behold, the man has become like one of Us, knowing good and evil; and now, he might stretch out his hand, and take also from the tree of life, and eat, and live forever " Genesis 3:22.

The concept that man would live forever was spoke by the serpent to Eve in the Garden. It almost seems as if Satan has enabled Mankind to be on the verge of being able to achieve this via Science. It's as if the Knowledge gained from knowing good and evil has worked its way through to effecting eternal life. This verse is becoming more and more important as the amazing leaps that Science has made in the storing of memories, robotics and transhumanism which are just becoming realities. This will almost certainly take mankind on a very dangerous and destructive path. It seems as if nothing can stop this, which begs the question: are we in control of Science?

Going back to the Scripture for a moment, it is likely that God was going to give Adam and Eve the knowledge of good and evil anyway. As a result of this disobedience, Man was demoted from living for many years, such as the Patriarchs in Genesis e.g. Methuselah who lived 969 years, to becoming a being living only 120 years. The themes of knowing good and evil, and living forever are linked.

The Androgynous Agenda

The Luciferian doctrine also teaches that Man should eventually be **Androgynous**. I.e. that Man and Woman would become the same sex as one. Various Gods from the past were said to be Androgynous, the most obvious being the Sphinx, Serapis, Adonis and Baphomet. All of these were male and female or merged into one androgynous mass. The reason why the ancient deities were depicted as having both male and female attributes is to imbue them with power. (*In the far future the Elite also desire to make a human with two spines.)

The reason for this is that one's Gender as a Man or Woman is a crucial part of our Identity. If you remove a person's Gender, then you remove a major part of their identity. In a world in which the Elite are the masters and rulers, and the Masses are their slaves, removing one's sexuality reduces the people to Drones without identity - slaves to the State, exactly as they want. This is the direction the human race will unfortunately go in as soon as Transhumanism and Bio-Engineering make Androgyny a viable option.

In Genesis before Eve is born from the rib (or side) of Adam, there is only Adam present, but because God can't find a helper from the animals, He created a woman, from Adam. In other words, Adam which means Mankind, gave birth to the first Woman, Eve, which means 'Living Source'. In the Hebrew, 'ish' meaning man, gave birth to 'ish-ah' the woman, which is the adding of the Feminine ending ah in the Hebrew. But it is the rather dubious mistranslation of this verse which really gives rise to this Luciferian belief. Genesis 1:27. **NKJV:** 'So God created man in His own image; in the image of God He created him; male and female He created **them**.' The 'them' being the concept of an androgynous being.

Gnosticism teaches that materialism is bad and spirituality is good, and it is from this that they taught that being Androgynous was a type of salvific union, an escape from the material. The upper Degrees of Freemasonry have similar concepts. Baphomet was depicted as being both male and female. In the ceremonies of Bohemian Grove they talk of the male God Moloch, and the female aspect as the Owl. It all relates back to the concept of Man becoming Androgynous as some type of evolved salvific free race.[147]

Escaping the Judgement

Luciferians have become so deceived and deluded that they believe their god runs everything. As a result of this, they believe that they can escape the Judgement. For people who have done a lot of bad things in their life and committed a lot of sins, it becomes a very attractive proposition to believe that somehow they will escape Judgement. They probably know, deep down, that this is real since they have been dealing with these themes as Freemasons or Theosophists for years. But they chose to believe that Lucifer has a special place for them and as such that they cannot be Judged by God at all.

Whereas we know from the Bible that everyone will be judged and no-one will escape the Great White Throne Judgement. Revelation 20: 10-12: 'For we will all stand before God's judgement seat.' Romans 14:10c. Matt 25:31-46: As such there is no escape from the Judgement!

---

[147] Androgyny: Saint Simon and Manly P Hall write about this.

They also believe that it is better to reign in Hell than to serve in Heaven since they think Lucifer runs hell. The only problem for them is that he doesn't! God reigns and rules over Hell, in fact God rules over everywhere, and Satan will be in hell receiving torment for the thousand years when he is then released for the last time at the Battle of Magog. Revelation 20:7,8: 'When the thousand years are over, Satan will be released from his prison and will go out to deceive the nations in the four corners of the earth – Gog and Magog – and to gather them for battle.'

Regimented, Centralised and Standardised

As soon as you start to understand their beliefs, the globalist agenda unfolds. For example, the Luciferian ideology is that Man should be **Regimented**: the belief that all races should be melded into one. Black and white, yellow or red become merged into one vast conglomeration of people without distinguishing features. Theosophy has a similar concept that 'root races' will evolve into the sixth root race. The Elite have promoted the deliberate policy of mass immigration everywhere. This is why the prevailing attitude of people in the UK and Western Countries is that immigration is a good thing and that it brings diversity. Immigration is not necessarily a disastrous policy, and does have many benefits, but because it is promoted and controlled by the Cryptocracy, they can use the friction that they can cause at any stage by agitating the different groups. It's an easy method for them to gain more power and keep the people diverted from them, and looking to the State for all the answers. This is part of their consolidation of power. The greying out of society is one of the many methods they use as 'divide and conquer' to stop a grass roots movement from making any in roads into diminishing their power. If people come from completely different backgrounds, it makes standing up for what it is right or wrong that much more difficult. But in a society where everyone is the same it should be easier to gain support for any mass action. Divide them up and marginalise them, segregate and agitate the different groups, and you have no threat to your power base. The obvious example the Cryptocracy is using, is Islam, where the hidden government seeks to develop their surveillance state by creating the dialectic between Islam and western society. They agitate Islam, and then have their agents conduct false flags and events blaming the Muslims for terrorist events. They then impose more CCTV cameras and laws to consolidate the Cryptocracy's power over the people so that everyone can feel safe.

If only we could get this message out to people it could help the world settle down, but the reality is, it's too complicated and people have become too aggressively indoctrinated into the Elite's programmed mind set to even attempt this.

They also believe that everything should be **Centralised**. In order to have Centralisation and have complete control they have to have information which is in one place, centralised. Hence the gathering of all data, phone calls, emails, web searches, purchase history, photos and videos as part of the technocratic belief that data is power, which in a way it is. Not much thought has been given by the Elite about the loss of personal freedoms, but then again, if you're hell bent on power what do you care if everyone's information is stolen from them?

Everything must also be **Standardised**. If you think about it the only way to control an object or institution, or a good or service, is to have that thing the same, i.e. standardised. On the one hand this might seem like a good idea, such as computer systems being standardised, or production standards being kept to the same level rules across a geographical area, but on the other hand, it's just another way to gain and keep control so that eventually those goods and services may be under their control. You cannot control things that are different. This is another reason for the trade agreements and reason for the trading blocs such as the EU. The best way to make sure everything is the same is to pass laws cross-nationally on production methods and procedures and enforce them to make sure countries are adhering to them. Sounds good on the one side, but it's another power grab from the Elite. It's too difficult to control a section of the populace if they aren't standardised in every way, but once they are, it's easy to take them over.

Psychopaths and Sociopaths

The Elite are Luciferians belonging to groups such as Freemasonry and trying to forward the Agenda of the One World under their rulership, but they are also Psychopaths. The definition of Psychopath is 'a person with a psychopathic personality, which manifests as amoral and antisocial behaviour, lack of ability to love or establish meaningful personal relationships, extreme egocentricity, failure to learn from experience, etc.' Sounds a lot like the Elite, such as Henry Kissinger, Madeleine Albright, or Hillary Clinton, Tony Blair and Donald Trump. Psychopaths at this Elite level do not show anti-social behaviour, if they did they will have been 'weeded' out long before they reached high office, but the other tendencies don't leave them, and every now and again we can see their evil intents. Such as Henry Kissinger saying that Soldiers are worthless grunts, or Madeleine Albright saying the death of a million Iraqi children is worth it, or hearing Hillary Clinton saying 'they came, they saw, they killed' about the death of Saddam Hussein. These tendencies should be expected, our leaders are not saints, they are under Lucifer, so we shouldn't be surprised by their gross statements of their twisted beliefs since they are Luciferians forwarding the Great Plan. Satan rules through his followers who he seeks to deceive and ensnare into his political schemes. He presents himself as a friend but in the end, it always ends in death and destruction.

The Cryptocracy's Psychopathic leaders are duplicitous in the extreme - they can say one thing whilst meaning completely the opposite. This makes them brilliant Politicians who are paid liars at the best of times. Although they lack compassion, empathy and conscience, they only feel embarrassment if they are caught. This is the only thing that holds them back. This ethos of 'do what you want, but don't get caught' has infected the entire population, but in particular our Politicians and corporate leaders at the top of the food chain. They only thing they fear is being caught, and more fool them if they are!

Hitler, Churchill, Stalin and Franklin Roosevelt were all Luciferians as have been hundreds of other world leaders. Their agenda was death and destruction and hardship; certainly Churchill and Roosevelt were Freemasons and this is a fact. Hitler was a member of the Thule Secret Society which was a group with links further back to the Germanorden and again further back linked to the Bavarian Illuminati. Their victims were the untold millions of people who were forced to go along with the war policies of their 'dear Leaders' as they sold the people their political lies for the benefit of the elite few. The taking of sides in any war is completely contrived since the Cryptocracy control both sides of any conflict, but they have to have front men who can follow through on their schemes. War on all fronts and *no amount* of death and destruction will stop the Luciferians, because they wish to return Mankind back to the **'Pre-Adamic state'** where there is no Mankind left on earth, and as such no need for God and the Devil. Before the Fall of Man in Genesis there was perfect harmony on earth. If you want to get back to this situation of harmony, they believe they have to kill Mankind, all of Humanity, in order to return Man to the perfect state with God. This is what Luciferians believe, and this is a contributory reason why **depopulation is always on their agenda.**

This is a possible explanation why Hitler said about the war effort, 'Our losses never seem to be high enough.' The madness that is Luciferianism had gripped him and, for example, instead of retreating when he invaded Russia during the winter months of 1942 he kept advancing against his Generals advice, believing the fire from his occult covenant with Lucifer would keep his army warm and safe. As could be expected of Satan he didn't come through and his army perished.[148]

At the end of World War II, it was Churchill who was insistent that the occultism of Hitler and the Nazi Party should not be revealed under any circumstances to the general public.[149] Perhaps this is because Churchill was worried that the public may make the connection that practically all the Elite are into the occult. After all he was an alleged 33 Degree Freemason himself from 1901 until he resigned in 1912, although he did have dealings with Freemasonry after this date.[150] He was also a Druid, being a member of the Ancient

---

[148] Bob Rosio, Hitler & The New Age, Huntington House, 1993, p.176.

[149] Jim Marrs, 'Rule by Secrecy' p.145.

[150] Churchill freemason
http://freemasonry.bcy.ca/biography/churchill_w/churchill_w.html

Order of Druids from 1908 presumably until he died.[151] This order is Witchcraft. He didn't want the masses to know about occultism in high places. And this is the issue - that **all of these people have the same ideology**, the only reason why they are battling it out in the international arena is about who has dominance. But there is no difference in their ideology, and who controls them ultimately. That is why they all pull together in the same direction toward the New World Order and the creed of the New World Religion which is their ultimate conclusion. They don't need to converse and discuss it all the time, they know automatically to take the opposite side of the Helgian dialect to progress the Great Plan. We see this with Skull and Bones members as discussed by Anthony Sutton.[152]

This is what we see today amongst our Politicians, in the EU and UN, a steady stream of occultists running our affairs and conducting world politics with an agenda that no-one properly understands, or that doesn't make any sense, because we are not involved in this mindset. Only people who understand these issues can make sense of their agenda: the eventual enslavement of mankind and the establishment of the New World Order and Religion.

What could possibly be more controlling, than to dictate the beliefs of the people via a socially engineered false religion? The Bible talks about a false Religion that would emerge at the end of History in which all Mankind will worship the Beast. Many religions also allude to this point in History at which point there will be a battle between the forces of good and evil. Our leaders are being affected and influenced by powers beyond their control and understanding, for the benefit of powers and personalities few people even know about, or even believe exist. Ultimately this is for the Devil who controls the hidden government to bring about his purposes which are against God.

So you are either under God or the Devil, so, by extension if you are NOT under God you are acting to bring Satan's Kingdom forward: the Great Plan. This is what our power-hungry rulers are

---

[151] Churchill druid http://www.druidicdawn.org/node/1889 and Wikipedia https://en.wikipedia.org/wiki/Ancient_Order_of_Druids

[152] Anthony Sutton, Skull and Bones. kindle loc 1675 following.

doing. There is no middle ground, you are either under the influence of God or the Devil.

Quotes from some famous Luciferians

Here are some quotes to back this up although this is not categorical evidence for this, at the final analysis it has to be a Spiritual discernment because it is about a Spiritual issue. (It's not to do with the mechanism of government...)

"The person without the Spirit does not accept the things that come from the Spirit of God but considers them foolishness, and cannot understand them because they are discerned only through the Spirit." 1 Corinthians 2:14.

Hitler:-

- His beliefs: The heaviest blow that ever struck humanity was the coming of Christianity.
- Bolshevism is Christianity's illegitimate child. Both are inventions of the Jew.
- On himself: I believe that it was God's will to send a youth from here into the Reich, to let him grow up, to raise him to be the leader of the nation so as to enable him to lead back his homeland into the Reich.
- On being called by God: I believe today that my conduct is in accordance with the will of the Almighty Creator.
- On Social Engineering: How fortunate for leaders that men do not think.
- On Lying to Men: The great masses of the people will more easily fall victims to a big lie than to a small one.
- The greater the lie, the greater the chance that it will be believed.
- On Propaganda: By the skillful and sustained use of propaganda, one can make a people see even heaven as hell or an extremely wretched life as paradise.
- On war: A single blow must destroy the enemy... without regard of losses... a gigantic all-destroying blow.

- We will not capitulate - no, never! We may be destroyed, but if we are, we shall drag a world with us - a world in flames.
- On Power: Success is the sole earthly judge of right and wrong.
- On Government: The great strength of the totalitarian state is that it forces those who fear it to imitate it.
- On Jews: The personification of the devil as the symbol of all evil assumes the living shape of the Jew.

Stalin:-

- The death of one man is a tragedy. The death of millions is a statistic.
- Death is the solution to all problems. No man – no problem. (They wished to sort out the problem of Mankind by taking man back to a Pre-Adamic state before the Garden of Eden.)

Churchill on 12/10/1950 at a speech in Denmark told us all about the goal of humanity.

"Of course we do not have the illusion that a united Europe is the final and complete solution to all international problems. The ultimate goal, however, is **the institution of an authoritative and omnipotent government at a global level,** and that is what we will strive for. When we are unable in the short term to institute a **workable super-government at a global level**, the prospects for peace and prosperity for mankind will remain dubious and uncertain. But we are pleased with the start: without a united Europe there is no chance of a world government."[153] Emphasis added.

These statements could have been made by any of these leaders – they are Luciferians!

---

[153] Churchill quote, webpage: http://trove.nla.gov.au/newspaper/article/2803089.

CHAPTER 9

OTHER BELIEFS AFFECTING LUCIFERIANS

The Dividing Principle of the World's Religions and Faiths

The overriding criteria for judging the beliefs of any religion is what it says about Jesus, who He was, and what He did. Every sect and false religion will always deny the divinity of Jesus Christ. He is always portrayed as anything but the Son of God and as being fully divine and fully human. For Freemasons, he is an example of the ideal man, something which the Queen echoed in one of her Queen speeches - that He was 'an example' to us all. She might have meant more but she didn't say it.[154]

For other religions Jesus might be an angel (Jehovah's Witnesses), or a prophet (Islam), an Avatar (Hindu's) or as one of the ascended masters (New Agers) or not even said to have existed (Illuminism). He is never portrayed as being fully divine and fully human. Christianity has been expounding this position right from the start, for example in John 1:14, 'The Word (God) became flesh (human) and dwelt among us.' In Colossians 1:16c it states, 'all things were

---

[154] Queen says: 'Yet billions of people now follow his teaching and find in him the guiding light for their lives. I am one of them because Christ's example helps me to see the value of doing small things with great love whoever does them and whatever they themselves believe.'
https://www.christiantoday.com/article/queens-speech-i-take-strength-from-unsung-heroes/103339.htm

created by Him (Jesus) and for Him' which therefore implies that Jesus was Divine.[155]

Gnosticism

The Beliefs of the Elite do not include the fact that Jesus is both Divine and Human. Their Religion is a mixture of Egyptian and Greek religions mixed with Gnostic secret societies and occult beliefs from the past. Luciferianism is the more modern expression of these older religions. Most of these sects believe in reincarnation and so believing this does away with God's Judgement and the hence the need for redemption and repentance.

Above all, the Elite or Cryptocracy believe in knowing god via knowledge, which makes this Gnosticism. Gnosticism traces its beliefs back to Plato (3rd Century) and Pythagoras (6th Century) and is the belief that by Knowledge man can be saved, whereas Christianity teaches that it is by Grace through Faith. The Demiurge, as a type of false god, created the physical universe but the Demiurge is not necessarily the creator but an Emanation of the creator God. In their view, the Demiurge is the God which Christians and Judaism preach. He is the malevolent impostor who keeps mankind imprisoned in the material world of allusion and suffering. The Demiurge does not correspond to the creator but is more like the fashioner or maker of the heavens and the earth, but he is not *the* creator. The material world was seen by them as being evil, and since the demiurge created the material world, he was seen as malevolent; whereas the spiritual world is above, and created by 'the One.' The god above the Demiurge they call the Monad, or the 'One' and from this emanated the Nous or Consciousness of the Demiurge. The only means of escaping our earthly existence is by Knowledge, (Gr. Gnosis), and rising up through the material world to reject the Demiurge and enter the higher world of the spirit.

---

[155] The Council of Chalcedon in 451AD stated that Jesus was fully divine and fully human in *hypostasis or hypostatic union*, which meant that Jesus was and is fully Man and also fully God. (Any other Christology is flawed because Jesus also had to be the perfect sacrifice which is only possible if both elements are together in union.)

However, everyone has fallen short of God's standards which is why God is far above and holy, separated from man. You can't be accepted by God because of your 'special' knowledge - God is too far above and beyond this. God comes down to us, not we go up to Him, and this is the brilliance of true Christianity - that God came down to earth to the material, to reconcile man to God and this makes us Justified. Whereas Gnosticism teaches that once you have received the 'special secret knowledge' you too can be a Christ. It teaches that there is an element of the divine within and that this element wants to return back to God, which is a Platonic belief. Before birth the soul which encircles the 'warmth' of the godhood then 'falls' to earth and the material, as the soul 'cools' away from the god to be incarnated. This is called *psychesthai*. At death the soul returns to God to be reincarnated.[156]

This, in many respects, is what Freemasonry teaches. That there is a secret doctrine and that via initiations and special teachings you can break through the false God of Christianity and into proper union with the true God. It is via the secret knowledge that you can return back to God. The Elite are far more likely to believe this Luciferian belief system than Christianity, since this is what they are taught as Masons within their Greek-gnostic-based secret societies.

The symbol of the Monad, which in Gnosticism is the true God, is a Circle with a dot in the middle.[157] It could be the case that this is where Freemasonry gets the letter G from. It's too tricky to draw a Circle with a dot in, and so a G will suffice. Other interpretations are that G stands for God or Geometry amongst others.

Kabbalah

The Elite also look at the Kabbalah as the true interpretation and commentary on the Hebrew Bible, the Old Testament. They believe in some hidden deeper knowledge which makes the 'Ayn Soph' knowable as the Divine Spark which energises the Sephiroths or

---

[156] For more see Walter Burkert's book 'Greek Religion; Archaic and Classical.'

[157] Monad symbol: see Wikipedia entry - monad.

emanations which are attributes of the Godhead.[158] It is therefore another type of Gnostic based religion in which the Divine is known through a series of 'knowledge based realisations' to gain a better understanding of God. It is a Jewish based occult type of Mysticism which grew into Freemasonry both of which teach that it is by knowledge that you are saved. Whereas the Bible teaches that it is by **Grace through Faith** that you are saved, justified and made at one with God, not by Knowledge. (Ephesians 2:8-9.)

The Music Industry

Linked to the Kabbalah is the Music industry which is filled with Satanic imagery, their videos are explicit to the extreme. If you can read the symbols in these videos you would agree with this, that the symbols are unmistakably linked to these types of beliefs, but if you can't read the signs you won't be able to fully understand what they are trying to say, and so when people say, 'it's Satanic' most mainstream people think they are being over the top! They are not over the top if you know about Luciferianism and what the Kabbalah teaches, and can make a clear distinction between what that religion says, and what Christianity says. It's only by holding up 'the ruler or plumb line' of the Bible to other beliefs that you can differentiate between the two. That's why we continually come back to the Bible, not to use as evidence of something being the Truth (although it is for those who believe in Jesus Christ), but in order to make a clear distinction between what is going on.

---

[158] Ayn Soph is Hebrew for 'infinite' or 'never ending' as a reference to the unknowable element of God. The divine spark of the Ayn Soph is said to energise the Sephiroth which again is a link to the Luciferian concept of the fire bringing enlightenment. It's the same religion expounded in another format.

The Symbols of the 'Illuminati'

The Elite believe that by permitting us to see their symbols they think we are unwittingly handing over authority to them. We unconsciously process information when it comes to symbols and they believe that via these subliminal messages they can affect us. This does, in fact, seem to be true. We are all affected by symbols on a subconscious level whether we like it or not. Over the years the term 'Illuminati' has entered the mainstream via the books and films of Dan Brown with the Da Vinci Code amongst others. It's also turned up in cartoons and on the internet as being the highly dubious and unlikely global group which runs everything in the world with their ultimate total power. Of course, this is never taken that seriously by intellectuals and other enquirers of the truth because everything is rigged against them ever finding out what really is happening. The word illuminati and conspiracy theory have been propagandised to such an extent that it's become a complete joke. By belittling and outright lies, the truth never comes out. You should congratulate yourself on getting this far since everything has been against you finding out what is going on!

But in the music industry, and in particular music videos, the symbols of the illuminati are advertised and banded about with abandon! It's almost as if by getting more and more symbols into their music they are getting more 'points'. Below are some of the main symbols we see in music videos, advertising, and in the media in general.

The All-Seeing Eye of Lucifer, or the Eye of Providence, or Horus, sees everything without fail. It is the symbol we see in all sorts of places, from the One Dollar bill, to pop stars holding a hand over one eye, to the symbol of CBS, or Tolkien's book, the Lord of the Rings. Originally the concept of the Anti-Christ having one eye comes from the Bible, Zechariah 11:17 NIV. 'Woe to the worthless shepherd, who deserts the flock! May the sword strike his arm and his right eye! May his arm be completely withered, **his right eye totally blinded!**' It is a Prophecy about the Anti-Christ and a reference to Horus who had one eye. Could this be the fatal wound in Revelation chapter 13? The eye was supposed to symbolise protection and healing since Horus went to his father Osiris to ask him to restore it. The Anti-Christ in Islam (from the Hadith), is called the 'dajjal' and he also has one eye.

The Phoenix as a symbol of re-birth. In Orthodox Christianity, the Phoenix is a symbol of Jesus' Resurrection but elsewhere this refers to the concept of re-birth in fire, as the Promethean archetype.

Pyramids or Triangles as references to Egypt and the majesty and power of the Ancient Mystery religions. It is also the physical parliament of man with 13 layers, as in the cover of this book, whilst the capstone is the religion of the All-Seeing Eye and hence the Anti-Christ.

Other symbols are the hand signal for 'OK sign' as the horned hand denoting 666.

Another 'Illuminati' symbol is the Monarch Butterfly since this butterfly refers to trauma based mind control.

Serpents, Dragons or Reptiles as representatives of Satan.

The Owl which is a Symbol of the Enlightenment and also the Illuminati as the Owl of Minerva. The owl sees in the dark, flies completely silently and can bend its head around 270 degrees. All secret operations which Secret Society members look up to.

The Goddess of the Flaming Torch, or Goddess of Wisdom is the Greek goddess Hecate who was the god of magic, the female version of Apollo. The most notable example of this old goddess being the Statue of Liberty itself, with the Greek nose and head depicting the rays of the sun. It is also the image of Columbia film studios, which has the light bearer concept which also relates to Semiramis who was Nimrod's wife. There was also the space shuttle Columbia disaster / hoax, the light bearer of the female Apollo.

Obelisks are from the old religion and represent the phallus which is from the shamanistic fertility cult of old, the remnants of which can be seen in Shintoism and Hinduism.

The Bee and the Hive. The individual as a single person, where one, becomes the many for the many - the loss of individualism in subservience to the collective hive. Napoleon took the symbol of the bee as his own from the previous Kings of France who no doubt took this from the Egyptians who revered the bee as a symbol of the sun god Ra.

All of these are bad symbols representing occult practice and so understanding these symbols will help you to understand their agenda, which makes a knowledge of this, not some dry doctrinal academic topic, but something we see every day. Being aware of this can help us identify who is involved with events going on around us, and help us know what indoctrination they are pushing as part of their programming. If you can understand the symbols and the beliefs of the elite, and are able to relate them to the events we see every day, you will be able far more able to make sense of their deep agenda.

Hermeticism

Hermeticism is another one of the core concepts in several of the belief systems we have been looking at. It is worth exploring this further to gain insight into the 'Mystery Religions' we are unearthing.

After Alexander the Great had conquered Egypt he passed his Empire to his four successors. In Egypt Ptolemy founded the Cult of Serapis which was the joining of Egyptian and Greek Religion together. The new religion was probably an outgrowth from the various sects that existed in Alexandria at the time, but it was the deliberate policy of Ptolemy to create this synthetic new religion as a mixture of Greek Religion and Philosophy, and Egyptian Religion to keep the populace unified. To all intents and purposes, it was a Hellenised secret mystery religion mixed with Egyptian beliefs in which only the Initiates were able to gain the gnosis (knowledge) of the godhead. The rest were to remain ignorant. Similar to the belief of a Masonic lodge.

Ptolemy built a Statute of the God Serapis as a Bull on one side, and a Greek man on the other as a mixture of the worship of the Egyptian gods Osiris and Apis. Osiris plus Apis were syncretized to form the name Oserapis or **Serapis**. The Statue of Serapis, without the Bull had the face of a Greek who wore the modius hat which has a jar with grain in, which represented the fecundity of the god. It was Osiris who was the god of the Afterlife, and Apis was the ancient

Bull god mentioned throughout the Old testament as Baal and which Moses and others forbade the Israelites to worship. Furthermore, the attributes of the Egyptian god of Magic, Thoth, were mixed with the Greek god of transitions and boundaries, Hermes, which later became Mercury the Divine Messenger and Janus.

As if that wasn't enough, the religion had themes also drawn from the Greek Chthonic concept of the underworld in which earthly power is derived from the god Hades. I mention all this because the Hermetic gods we are looking at all have links to the dark, and demonic. These beliefs are just one element of the hidden system that the Freemasons and allied groups study to try to make sense of their 'Prisca Theologia' (ancient religion) from which they can gain knowledge to attain godhood. For example, Serapis carried a ruler in his hand which he used to measure the flooding of the Nile which is an obvious link to the compass and ruler of Freemasonry. Hermeticism is the old religion which grew into medieval Alchemy, and it is from this that the western roots of magical thought are derived. The main 'river' of modern occultism and secret societies flows from this. This is what the Cryptocracy are into and gain their power from.

The aim of Alchemy, on the exoteric level, is to convert base metals to gold, but this is only one part of the transformative nature of Alchemy. It is also a reference to man being changed as he seeks to perfect his own nature. This is referred to by Alchemists as the 'Great Work', not a dissimilar phrase to the Great Plan of Freemasonry, Theosophy and New Age religions. The more modern interpretation of this theme is related to the eventual emergence of the utopian man living in the new utopian society. The finding of the philosopher's stone and the elixir of life which leads to immortality are also part of their beliefs.

The Magician of the Elite

The central figure of Hermeticism and Alchemy is Hermes Trismegestus, who was the 'Thrice Great Hermes'. He is said to have written the 'Corpus Hermeticum' which was re-discovered during the Renaissance. This book is said to have launched the core inspiration for most of the occult secret societies for over the last 450 years. Old Masonic constitutions from the period all refer to Hermes as one of the founders of architecture and the building trade. This influenced John Dee who had a large impact on Rosicrucianism and later on Freemasonry as well as Enochian magic. The finding and decoding of the ancient 'pre-diluvian pillars' was also a source of much mystical and incredulous magic. Although the route is circuitous and not that easy to define, the source of this later occult tradition is derived from the same Osiris, Hermetic mystery cult from Egypt.[159]

Believers in this Cult are making exactly the same mistake the Israelites made when they worshiped the Bull as they waited for Moses and the Law to be delivered at Mount Sinai in Exodus 32:8: 'They have made themselves a golden calf, and worshiped it and sacrificed to it...'. Throughout the Old Testament and in numerous scriptures we have Bull worship (e.g. Numbers 25:3, 2 Kings 10:18 following when Jehu kills all the cult members) and even to today, the supposed Initiated, the Elite, who are running our world, are worshipping at the very same altar of the Cult of Serapis which is the Hermetic Sun / Bull god that they worshiped from antiquity even in the Old Testament. It may be rebranded as Freemasonry or Skull and Bones or Bohemian Grove or Theosophy or New Age religion but to all intents the purposes it is the same! Furthermore, the Symbol of the Horns of the Bull of Apis is still found in the symbol of the Islamic Crescent today. This is part of the reason why the Elite are promoting 'Good' Islam since it is close to their own twisted occult belief. Behind the worship of the Bull is Satan and so next time you are reading the Old Testament about Baal worship, and perhaps thinking how barbaric, old fashioned and irrelevant it might be - please remember that the same Cult which the Old Testament was against over 3,000 years ago is still in existence today! This Cult has taken over the world and still holds almost complete power.

---

[159] Hermeticism: a good book on this is, 'The Hermetica: The Lost Wisdom of the Pharaohs' by Timothy Freake and Peter Gandy.

Emanationism - the origin of things!

One of the core beliefs in Hermeticism is the belief that from the godhead emerges another god like form which creates another structure. The term Emanationism[160] comes from the Latin *emanare* meaning "to flow from" or "to pour forth or out of". It is the concept that the creation of the Universe and the Earth slowly and gradually flowed out, from the 'first reality', who is God. This gave rise to a 'second reality' which is a lesser creation, and this gives rise to a 'third reality' and so on. Each reality is less divine than the one before. In this manner we have the fallen state we are in now, according to this belief system. At each step the created is less perfect than the step before. It teaches that reality is hierarchical or graded which means that in order to gain godhood you can slowly climb the 'planes of existence' back towards god. Like everything to do with the occult, this is a totally false belief and it is totally in opposition to Creationism which teaches that God made everything. Psalm 33:6 'By the word of the Lord were the heavens made: and all the host of them by the breath of his mouth.'

This belief of Emanationism is found in Kabbalism, Freemasonry, Theosophy and 'Dark Green Religion' and is probably one of the purest Hermetic beliefs of the Elite. In Theosophy is it explained as occurring via the Seven Rays which emanate from the Godhead.

Understanding the concept of Emanationism is important since it makes sense of a lot of these beliefs. Also in 'Dark Green Religion', which we look at later, an early proponent was Ralph (Waldo) Emerson, who linked Hermetic beliefs to those of his Green spirituality and even considered Hermes Trismegestus as a pagan prophet to be followed.

---

[160] Emanationism: see Wikipedia entry.

Hermeticism, Islam and Hermes Trismegestus link

In *some* Islamic traditions, but not all, the second most important Prophet after Muhammad is **Idris**. The list therefore goes, Muhammad, then Adam, and then Idris.[161] Traditionally Idris is equated to Enoch who 'walked with God' and was taken up rather than died in Genesis 5:24. **But in other Islamic traditions Idris is said to be Hermes Trismegestus** who was met by Muhammed during his Night Journey to heaven and back. So Hermes Trismegestus is supposedly an important figure in Islam, another nod to Hermeticism. Born in Babylon and being a Magician who started Alchemy, Astrology and all manner of occult practices, the link between the occult, Hermeticism and Islam is compelling. Certainly, Orthodox Christians in Eastern Europe consider Muslims as being adept at dark magic. Although Islam prohibits the use of magic, in many areas such as in West Africa, the form of Islam practiced is mainly about magical activities.

It is even said by some Islamic genealogists that Muhammad was descended from Hermes Trismegestus. Perhaps this is another reason why the Elite like to promote 'Good' Islam - it's the closest they have to their god - the god of Hermeticism, which is the Greek god Hermes which is linked to the Egyptian god Thoth, who became the Roman god Mercury.

Another idea mentioned by commentators is that Idris is in fact Osiris and this would fit even more closely to the Religion of the Elite. Unfortunately, neither the Quran, Hadith or other writings help us identify who Idris really is, so it is open to conjecture. The main point is that Islam has a special place to the Cryptocracy since their unknowable god is quite closely related to their belief system.

For example, Tony Blair said in an interview with Muslim News: 'There is a lot of misunderstanding about Islam. It is a deeply reflective, peaceful and very beautiful religious faith and I think it would be hugely helpful if people from other religious faiths knew

---

[161] Quran 19:56-57 and see Idris entry in, 'Holy People of the World, A Cross Cultural Encyclopaedia'.

more about it.'[162] He was promoting 'Good' Islam. As was John Kerry (Skull and Bones initiate and CFR Trilateralist) with his comment; "the real face of Islam is a peaceful religion based on the dignity of all human beings."

The Cryptocracy not only like to expose us to Islam, but also to as much programming as they can on Hermes Trismegestus as the **'Wisdom Magician archetype.'** This character crops up in many films and books where he is portrayed as Gandalf in the Lord of the Rings, or Yoda, or Obi Wan Kenobi in Star Wars, or Morpheus in The Matrix, and Albus Dumbledore and Harry Potter. The Elite love to promote these archetypes to us since that's what they're interested in, and as mentioned previously these beliefs enable them to have greater control over us whether we understand the meaning or not. It's no accident that J K Rowling has made an immense fortune from her books and the subsequent film sales, and paraphernalia since the Harry Potter programming has been pushed along and propagated by the entirety of the Elite's publishing media machine.

Islam and the Beliefs of the Elite

We don't have to use some obscure reference to make the link between occultism and magic in Islam, one only has to look at the symbol of Islam to realise where some of the underlying concepts are derived. The Islamic symbol is the **Crescent Moon** with a Star set in the foreground, which is an impossible astronomical conjunction since the star cannot be in front of the moon, and hence it therefore refers to the magical. The Moon is present at the top of their minarets but the reason why it is there is rather obscure. Some Islamic fasts, and the Islamic calendar itself, is linked to the sighting of the moon. In addition, part of the salat (5 daily prayers) are made at certain prescribed times (al waqt) and there are also certain times when prayers are not supposed to be performed. It may seem incredible to know this, but these times are set according to the Sun's

---

[162] Blair interview: Muslim News, March 2000.

path.[163] When the Sun rises there is the Fahr prayer, and when it falls there is Isha. The timing of the Midday prayer (Zuhr) coincides to *just after* the high point or zenith of the Sun. This is so Muslims don't think they are worshipping the Sun, since there is no Sun worship in Islam – this is forbidden. However, what is undeniable, is that the whole system is linked to the motion of the Sun, the timings of the Moon and hence Astronomy.

The Crescent Moon is probably more than just a nod to the female god of the Moon, and the word Allah itself is a feminine word in Arabic similar to the Hebrew word for God, Eloha. It is either as a vestigial throw back from previous religions in the Arabia peninsular, or it really is part of the religion. Historically speaking, the pagan Arabs said they believed in the one god (Allah) but that there were also partner gods. This was the practice that Islam abolished with the fundamental epithet: There is only One God and Muhammad is his messenger. When Mohammed entered Mecca, one of the 360 gods they worshipped there was Ilah the Moon god, and by adding the Arabic the, which is Al, you have Al-Ilah.[164] Later on this, became protracted to Allah who Mohammed proclaimed was the same God worshipped by the Jews and Christians. But when have Jews and Christians worshiped a Moon god? Never, and so Allah cannot, and is not, the same god as Yahweh and Jesus.

The moon and the lunatic obsession are also related, 'luna' meaning moon in Latin. Another activity of the moon goddesses is that it seems to cause violence. In the book of Acts, Luke writes about the Temple of Artemis, who is Diana, which is another moon god, where the same violent temperament seemed to be present. Its followers shouted: 'Great is Artemis of the Ephesians!' Acts 19:33 and 34. This is exactly the same as the Muslims do. Allah is Great! In ancient Ephesus, not only is there this link, but, additionally a black stone was worshipped there, and is depicted on the Greek coins from the period.[165] Acts 19:35 ESV version, has 'stone' as the translation

---

[163] See Salah times: see Wikipedia entry.

[164] The etymology of the word Allah is uncertain. But the moon link is undeniable, and according to Quran 54:1 the moon will be split into two; or some interpret this as a miracle Mohamed performed.

[165] Web search Artemis Black stone coin. Also see Wylie and Naiden's 1936 article, 'The Image which Fell Down from Jupiter.'

whilst other versions translate as 'image'. 'Men of Ephesus, who is there who does not know that the city of the Ephesians is temple keeper of the great Artemis, and of the sacred stone that fell from the sky?' Also, incredibly, on Artemis' head there is a crescent moon which unassailably concludes the link.[166]

The Crescent also represents the two horns of the Cow which makes it a representation of Baal from the Old Testament. Furthermore if you compare the Egyptian Bull Statues, such as Apis, with the Crescent Moon and the Star you will see another similarity. The Crescent moon and Star are a veiled and redacted symbol of this religion from the distant past and the position of the Star is similar, but not exactly the same, to the position of the Snake, which was the symbol of wisdom in ancient Egypt. Later on, this became more a symbol of the Serpent and Satan, but these themes are all present to a greater or lesser extent with the occult symbol of the Crescent Moon and Star.

Islamic religion is, in some deep way, linked to the movement of the stars, planets, sun and moon, and this is evident on their minarets which have the moon, and the timings they place for their prayers. This is all linked to the religion of the Cryptocracy who are interested in the Astronomical, the phases of the moon, Egyptian religion and the Apis bull.

Tawaf - the Circumambulation of the Kabaa

In addition, the seven stations around the Kabaa represent the orbital plains of the seven planets known at that time. When followers of Islam walk around the Kabaa anti-clockwise seven times (Tawaf) starting at the north-eastern corner (the darkest aspect) of the Kabaa, where the black stone is situated, they walk 3 times hurriedly and 4 times leisurely. This mirrors the 'Seven Classical Planets' of the past - the Moon, Mercury, and Venus, the Sun, Mars, Jupiter, and Saturn. They are falling from heaven like Satan who's stone they kiss as the

---

[166] Diana-Artemis statue, Chiaramonti Museum, Vatican, Rome. (Search: Google / Startpage, Images).

head corner stone on the Kaaba on the final rotation. The Muslims do this anti-clockwise since this more closely represents the movement of the stars (in the northern hemisphere). It should be Jesus taking away their sins since he is the head corner stone. But if they haven't kissed the Black Stone of Kabaa, at the end of the circumambulation, their Sins will not have been forgiven and their whole Haj will have been wasted. Jesus is the 'Head Corner stone' not a meteorite! Acts 4:11-12. He is the stone you builders rejected, which has become the cornerstone. Salvation exists in no one else, for there is no other name under heaven given to men by which we must be saved.

The 'Black Stone of Kabba' was the asteroid which fell to earth in the same way as Satan fell to earth like lightening. The Stone was white and shone in the sky, like lightening, and when it reached earth it became black as a type of fallen Angel. You can see the pattern which Jesus reported in Luke 10:18, I saw Satan fall like lightening...

Venus

'How art thou fallen, O Lucifer, son of the Morning Star' - which is Venus. Venus has been known as the 'jewel in the sky,' Eosphorus as the Morning Star, and Hesperus as the evening. To the Astrologers it is the opposite of the planet Mars, whilst to the Astronomers it is known as the 'sister planet' to the Earth since it is a similar size and close by. Although, in reality it is very different planet indeed. Some high-level Theosophists and Shriners will let you think that the Meteorite represents the truth and that we even came from another planet. Or in another version the Theosophists, such as Alice A Bailey, believe that their god Sanat Kumara descended from Venus 18.5 Million years ago.

To Freemasons and other 'Illuminati' it is Sirius as the 'blazing star' which is of interest but in Islam it is Venus as the female aspect which holds their attention. The alignment of the Kaaba on its longest side is towards Canopus the second brightest star in the northern hemisphere after Sirius. The minor axis is aligned to the summer and winter solstice.[167] The Black Stone is situated at the North-Eastern corner of the building probably because this is the darkest aspect there is since the Sun rises in the East and never reaches the North-East part.

All this entails praying and careful alignment to the stars in a sort of 'night magic' that had been practiced since the dawn of time and explicated since Babylonian times. In fact, the Babylonians were in a way the first civilization, we know of, to master the observation of the stars, and this in turn lead to a complicated belief system and Religion which, in short, was a type of Astrology. All of these elements refer to the astronomic religion of the past and these are still present in a reduced and vestigial version within Islam, although, of course, Islamic scholars will deny all of this.

Islam, Shriners and the Elite

My point being that the beliefs of the Elite are linked to the ancient astronomical Babylonian religion which is also linked to Islam. The Elite and Freemasons also believe in auspicious conjunctions in the heavenly realms, Astrology and also that God is unknowable. In this respect their religions are not that far apart, and this is a reason why they are seeking to make Islam a stepping stone to their New Luciferian Religion they want us all to adhere to.

The Elite like Freemasonry, and high Freemasonry leads to being a Shriner. This is another secret society, but this time they take the Quran for their 'Bible' and **swear allegiance to Allah** as the true god above Jesus or the god of Abraham, Isaac and Jacob. In the past, in order to join the Shriners, you had to be a 32 or 33 Degree Mason and to have gone through all the degrees. From 2000 they have changed the criteria that any Master Mason may now join the Shriners.[168] As with Freemasonry they do revolting acts of ignorant

---

[167] Wikipedia entry on Kaaba.

[168] Shriner criteria is now only to be a Master Mason. From their Website http://www.beashrinernow.com/About/Shriners/BecomeAShriner

stupidity,[169] but in the final analysis Freemasonry has placed the Shriner version above the 'Christian' version of Freemasonry, another pointer to why Islam holds a special place in their beliefs.

The Elite therefore like Islam since it fits in with their religion and is why on one hand **they promote Islam calling it a religion of peace**, but also on the other hand they are demoting Islam if it is of the wrong 'fundamentalist' type. They highlight the violent aspects of Islam as one side of the dialectic to bring all religions out of their traditional orthodoxy and into the 'greyed-out' cultural humanistic relative belief system they are espousing. These issues of promoting 'Good Islam' and demoting 'Bad Islam' are further covered elsewhere, in Chapter 13. This is also why the 9/11 Memorial in New York is the inverse of the Kaaba in Mecca. The square hole in the centre of the Memorial is like the reverse 'mould' of the Kaaba. Also, the original World Trade Center buildings had many Islamic references in-built within the architecture, such as the square in the centre of the buildings. In fact the architect Minoru Yamasaki even stated that it was Mecca, and the World Trade Center towers (1 and 2) were even said to be the Minarets.[170]

The question to ask yourself is why would they be doing this?

The answers are in the next few sections, and it is to do with the building of the syncretic New World Religion. It is the Elite's desire to indoctrinate us unto Islam since it is not that far from their belief system and is a method of slowly moving us into their controlled society. It's part of their Hegelian dialect to bring about a synthesis from these two opposing positions, on the one side, Christianity and the West, and Islam in opposition on the other – the 'clash of civilisations' as invented by Samuel Huntington who was a CFR member. This later on became their official programme. They agitate both sides to create their eventual contrived unity which is their desired conclusion from outset. As can be expected, the Cryptocracy have complete control of both sides of the dialectic. They have

---

[169] One of the Shriners ritual degrees is the Devil's Path Ceremony, at which they must show they are a man by showing their penis to the other members of the congregation, and sometimes they must even urinate.

[170] Minarets / Minoru Yamasaki https://www.huffingtonpost.com/todd-fine/fritz-koenigs-sphere-mich_b_5479668.html.

infiltrated Christianity with their version of the apostate Church, and control Western Society by their indoctrination, propaganda, media, false flags and hoaxes. The Elite have subverted Islam to such an extent that they have made 'Bad' Islam the religion of terrorism and hatred whilst at the same time trying to convert us all to 'Good' Islam which they promote and endorse. For those who are Muslims it is NOT the religion of hatred and violence, but those who listen to the mainstream indoctrination have been programmed to believe this is the case. As a diversion tactic they like to get us upset. This is yet another pointer to why the entire 'Islamic terrorism hoax' even exists, and why the Cryptocracy have been funding and promoting ISIS, Al Qaeda, and many other Islamic terrorist organisations as part of 'Bad Islam'. They are ALL controlled by the Cryptocracy's secret armies such as the CIA who are funded by the Western tax payers to bring about the changes the Elite desire. It's also, not only about helping Israel and the Zionists, but it is about changing Western Society and Islamic Society into their type of controlled order. They have to smash up the entire world in order to re-build it anew as they see fit. This is exactly as stated in their Masonic maxim, 'Order ab chao', which means order out of chaos. They create the chaos into which their order can be imposed.

CHAPTER 10

THEOSOPHY AND THE NEW WORLD RELIGION

"Discernment is not simply a matter of telling the difference between what is right and wrong; rather it is the difference between right and almost right." - Charles Spurgeon (19th Century Preacher).

The United Nations has been heavily influenced by Theosophy since its inception, and even before in its former creation as the League of Nations. Practically ALL its highest and most influential General Managers and Secretaries have been New Agers and Theosophists recruited from the ranks of Socialists.

What is Theosophy?

Madame Blavatsky (1831- 1891)

Madame Blavatsky founded Theosophy in 1875 as a new 'occultic' religion. Her aim was to synthesize and merge the religions of the East with those of the West and at the same time incorporate the new evolutionary and scientific beliefs from the Origin of Species which had been published only 16 years before (1859). She sought to explain the deep mysteries of the universe and the nature of God. The metaphysical components of her belief system came from a type of Pantheistic Hinduism mixed in with the current scientific beliefs of the day and eastern 'scientific' beliefs with a good helping of Freemasonry thrown in. She believed that in the past there had been a magical civilization which had a knowledge of a superior mystery religion. It was this she was trying to uncover and so tapped into the teachings were figures such as Pythagoras and Plato. To all intents and purposes the ancient wisdom she expounded was similar to the ancient Greek mystery religion, which is in itself similar to the Babylonian Mystery Religion, which Nimrod, in theory, started back at the Tower of Babel. The concept that man can become a God and be all knowing. A belief that man can gain knowledge of the godhood is a type of gnosis, which is only available to initiates who have gone through the various degrees. She is considered the Mother of the New Age Religion.

Her first book was 'Isis Unveiled' written in 1877 where she presented her own version of the Prisca Theologia, which we looked at before. This is the belief that in man's ancient past there was a truer and more accurate religion which could be unearthed and explained. She gathered many of the main concepts and beliefs of the occult tradition into an **Eastern type of universal religion** which incorporated strands from Hermeticism, with its emanationist cosmology, esoteric Christianity, the belief in the arrival of a new Messiah, (the Maitreya), and the belief in Adepts, who were the initiates and caretakers of special knowledge. She also wrote about the Ascended Masters who were controlling the world from their occult realm called Shambhala. At the same time blending in science and the newly discovered theory of Darwinian Evolution into a comprehensive and understandable cosmology.

Blavatsky writes in the preface that *Isis Unveiled* is "a plea for the recognition of the **Hermetic philosophy,** the anciently universal Wisdom-Religion, as the only possible key to the Absolute in science and theology." (Volume 1 page 7). My emphasis in bold. Again, Hermeticism is the 'key belief', as a reminder, the concepts of transformation (via alchemy) and emanationism.

In a way it was a bold attempt at the modern defiance of materialist science, which might to us today seem like a slightly old-fashioned, and racist, occult theory of everything. But in reality, and on the **esoteric level**, it was the same old Luciferian beliefs reworked using **Eastern religions as a mask for the first time**. In other words Hinduism, Buddhism and other Eastern beliefs were used to hide the Satanic.

'The Secret Doctrine' was written in 1888, which was her major work, and syncretized all the main world religions into one coherent and cohesive whole. She channelled her beliefs from Koot Hoomi who was her Spirit guide, one of the Ascended Masters who supposedly lived in Little Tibet in Ladakh, Kashmir. The book presented an immense vision in which souls, called in Theosophy, Monads, descend from the Cosmic Source and journey to earth in different evolutionary forms to eventually become free back to the Godhead. In order to pass through the human level, the souls of humanity must be reincarnated 7 times, or make the rounds or circuits of the sequence of the 7 'globes' while being reincarnated each time in each sequence. You can spot here the link to Islam and the 7 circumambulations (Tawaf) of the Kabaa. Humanity today is said to be on the fourth globe of the fourth round, although some Europeans, Indians, and other Indo-Europeans are on the 5th, or Aryan root race, whilst the rest are on the 4th or Atlantean root race. The 5th Root Race, Aryan, would be replaced by the 6th when the philosophic Christ, Maitreya would arrive. This race would in due course be replaced by the 7th race which would be the final one. If this sounds like the inspiration for Hitler's Aryan doctrine you would of course be correct although Madame Blavatsky probably picked this idea up from the writings of Edward Bulwer-Lytton the famous Victorian writer who coined phrases like, 'It was a dark and stormy night', or 'the pen is mightier than the sword'. Edward Bulwer-Lytton was a Freemason and a Rosicrucian himself. Hitler supposedly kept a copy of The Secret Doctrine by his bedside although we can't be certain about this. Hitler was a member of the Thule Secret Society, which was the Germanenordem which itself grew out of the Bavarian Illuminati when it went underground in 1791.[171] The link to the dark beliefs of the lord Lucifer is there yet again through the Thule Society.

Lucifer brought man the divine light, in her view he was the Solar Angel bringing the Light and truth to our world. The Light is the Sun

---

[171] Hitler - Germanenorden - Thule link, see Nicholas Goodrich-Clarke's book: *The Occult Roots of Nazism: Secret Aryan Cults and Their Influence on Nazi Ideology.*

and Lucifer was therefore one of the great sacrificial beings who brought Intellect to man in the distant past. He is also the 'light bearer' bringing the 'Promethean fire' of knowledge and therefore the saviour of Mankind. This is the Luciferian doctrine or Philosophy mentioned previously, but it goes completely against the teachings of Jesus and Christianity and twists it to make Satan and Lucifer good, and of course Jesus and the true God evil. It's an inversion, and it's not the Demiurge either.

She wrote in The Secret Doctrine Volume 2 page 935. "*In this case it is but natural -- even from the dead letter standpoint -- to view* Satan, *the Serpent of Genesis, as the real creator and benefactor, the Father of Spiritual mankind. For it is he who was the "Harbinger of Light," bright radiant Lucifer, who opened the eyes of the automaton created by Jehovah, as alleged; and he who was the first to whisper: "in the day ye eat thereof ye shall be as Elohim, knowing good and evil" -- can only be regarded in the light of a Saviour. An "adversary" to Jehovah the "personating spirit," he still remains in esoteric truth the ever-loving "Messenger" (the angel)…*".

Here she is saying that Satan is the real spiritual benefactor, and Lucifer, the light bearer brought Mankind into knowledge by twisting the words of God that Man would know good from evil, and hence he is the Saviour.[172]

In The Secret Doctrine Volume 2 page 234 she quotes from another writer, Dr A Kingsford in 'The Perfect Way' if you have the authentic version of The Secret Doctrine. Like everything to do with this subject there are 'blinds' and 'tests' in every nook and cranny to hide the deeper meaning.

She writes*: "It is 'Satan who is the God of our planet and the only God,'* and this without any allusive metaphor to its wickedness and depravity"*. She quotes from this other book, The Perfect Way, but she quite obviously agrees with this and goes on in the next sentence to say: *'For he is the one Logos, the first son, eldest of the gods'* again quoted from the other book. Page 234 of The Secret Doctrine. This is where Blavatsky says that Satan is really the true god of this planet, and this makes her a Satanist. There is no escaping this however you interpret

---

[172] There seems to be an enormous debate if she wrote this or not, but what she did say is that Lucifer and Satan were one and the same. *The Secret Doctrine*, Volume 2, part 1, stanza 5. … 'Satan is also Lucifer, the bright angel of Light'…

her writings, but people who adhere to Theosophy and the New Age will scream wildly if you make this comment and raise this point. They will say that Satan is a metaphor for Saturn as the final emanation for example. Or that you don't understand the deeper esoteric meaning since Christianity has made the mistake of misunderstanding the context of who Lucifer is. But it's reasonable and correct to reply that the writings of Madam Blavatsky show her philosophy as being the same reworking of the Luciferian Doctrine we have seen many times before as elucidated in Chapter 8. Helena Blavatsky hated Christianity and her writings are full of incoherent and twisted Theology which are completely perverse and untrue expositions of the Old and New Testament.

It was her teachings which then inspired Alice A Bailey, who in turn influenced Robert Muller of the UN, and the roll out of his educational World Core Curriculum, which is unashamedly based on the writings of Alice A Bailey.

Helena Petrovna Blavatsky was hailed as a spiritual leader, but, in the end, she was proven to be a fraud at one of her meetings.[173] In 1885 the Society of Physical Research concluded that she had faked some 'miracles' by replacing a broken tea saucer with a new one from the hidden cabinet of her bedroom. It was common during this time of the late 19th Century for people to conduct seances and it was a time when people were generally very curious about psychic events, miracles, and scientific religious research, but she had been caught out as a fraud. Her reputation never really quite managed to recover from this point onward. She died only 6 years later in 1891.

Annie Beasant 1847-1933

After Madame Blavatsky the 'mantle' of Theosophy passed down through the female line to Annie Beasant who was a Freemason, occultist and an insider of the Fabian Society. She was friendly with George Bernard Shaw and Bertrand Russell, two of the most

---

[173] Blavatsky fraud: see Wikipedia entry on the 1885 Psychical Research 'Hodgson Report'.

important Fabianists who must have been influenced by her beliefs. The Fabian Society, of course, is a Progressive thinking group pressing for socialist world government.

THE NEW WORLD TEACHER – KRISHNAMURTI

In 1909 another theosophist and occultist, archbishop Leadbeater[174], saw a young boy on a beach and chose him to be the new world teacher - he was Jiddu Krishnamurti. Leadbeater, who was a paedophile and satanist said he had 'the most wonderful aura he had ever seen, without a particle of selfishness in it.' Annie Beasant and Archbishop Leadbeater brought the boy up and declared him to be the world teacher for the new modern age. In 1929 Krishnamurti rejected this claim. I mention this because, in theosophy, if you can't find a messiah you create one as a world teacher! Benjamin Crème also tried this, by putting articles in newspapers saying that the world teacher or Maitreya lived in east London but no-one came forward claiming they were 'the one'.

Alice Bailey 1880 – 1949

Alice Ann Bailey is a central character to the emergence of New World Religion, since throughout her writings she mentions the New World Religion, what she thought it would be, and how it could come about and why it is important. Other than the Bible, if there were one person's writings you could use to discover what the New World Religion would be, it is hers. Tielhard de Chardin is important as well, in terms of spiritualising the evolutionary processes of 'the

---

[174] Leadbeater mentions that when you become a high-level Freemason you receive two enormous spirits which help you with whatever you want. In the book, *The Masters and the Path*, Archbishop Leadbeater, in 1925, wrote that Lord of this World was Sanat Kumara who was the King or Lord of the World, and the head of the Great White Brotherhood of Mahatmas who had revealed the principles of theosophy. He also was an Archbishop which is a way to receive the Apostolic Baptism of the laying on of hands – Satanists like to gain this accolade.

UN-god', but most aspects of the New World Religion are explained to some degree in her writings. Obviously from the opposite point of view to the Bible because Satan's words will be counterfeited to Christ's writings.

The beliefs of the United Nations are based on the beliefs of Alice A. Bailey and many of the Elite within the UN have been heavily influenced by the Luciferian writings espousing a utopian type of future. They have openly admitted this but few have managed to convincingly point out the Luciferian nature of the belief and 'the Plan' they espouse. It is from Alice A. Bailey's writing and Mme Blavatsky that we have phrases such as, the New Age, the Age of Aquarius, the Ascended Masters, and the Hierarchy. There are many other concepts common to other types of occult beliefs and they draw from this central religion of Theosophy, which has spawned approximately 140 other different religions and cults.

Alice A. Bailey (AAB) was born in Manchester and received an Anglican Church upbringing in an aristocratic family, but both her parents died from Tuberculosis before she was nine years old. As an orphan, she was not a very happy girl and wrote in her autobiography that, 'life was not worth living'. She felt that life was pointless and having a certain amount of curiosity and dread about life and death she attempted to commit suicide three times before she was fifteen.[175]

In 1895, whilst her family had gone to Church, she had her first mystical encounter. While she was in the drawing room, *'a tall man, dressed in European clothes and wearing a turban'* entered her room. Understandably startled, and not being able to say a word, she wrote about this in her autobiography called 'The Unfinished Autobiography'.[176]

This was to be Alice Bailey's first contact with 'Master Koot Hoomi' who was her spirit guide. He was perhaps her 'upper' spirit guide since she also had Djwal Khul as another guide who spoke to her. *"He* (Koot Hoomi) *told me there was some work that it was planned that I could do in the world but that it would entail changing my disposition considerably; I would have to give up being such an unpleasant little girl and must*

---

[175] Alice A, Bailey, *The Unfinished Autobiography,* 1951 (Lucis Trust). Suicide reference page 12

[176] Ibid, p 18.

try to get some measure of self-control. My future usefulness to Him and to the world was dependant on how I handled myself and the changes I could manage to make. He said that if I could achieve real self-control I could then be trusted and that I would travel all over the world and visit many countries, "doing your Master's work all the time" ... He added that He would be in touch with me at intervals of several years apart."

Koot Hoomi

"I found that this visitor was the Master K. H., the Master Koot Hoomi, a Master Who is very close to the Christ, Who is on the teaching line and Who is an outstanding exponent of the love-wisdom of which the Christ is the full expression. The real value of this experience is not to be found in the fact that I, a young girl called Alice La Trobe-Bateman, had an interview with a Master but in the fact that knowing nothing whatsoever of Their existence, I met one of Them and that He talked with me. The value is to be found also in the fact that everything that He told me came true (after I had tried hard to meet requirements) and because I discovered that He was not the Master Jesus, as I had naturally supposed, but a Master of Whom I could not possibly have heard and one Who was totally unknown to me. Anyway, the Master K. H. is my Master, beloved and real. I have worked for Him ever since I was fifteen years old and I am now one of the senior disciples in His group, or—as it is called esoterically—in His Ashram." [177]

Later on, in the Unfinished Autobiography, she experienced Koot Hoomi also known as 'the Tibetan' in a different manner.

"Suddenly a broad shaft of brilliant light struck my room and the voice of the Master Who had come to me when I was fifteen spoke to me. I did not see Him this time but I stood in the middle of the room and listened to what He had to say. He told me not to be unduly troubled; that I had been under observation and was doing what He wanted me to do. He told me that things were planned and that the life work which He had earlier outlined to me would start, but in a way which I would not recognise. He offered me no solution for any of my problems

---

[177] Ibid, p 19.

and He did not tell me what to do. The Masters never do. They never tell a disciple what to do or where to go, or how to handle a situation, in spite of all the bunk talked by nice, well meaning devotees. **The Master is a busy executive and His job is world direction.***"*

A spiritual entity advertising themselves as an executive working on 'world direction' sounds to me a lot like the 'god of this world', who is Satan. The true God does not need to be busy affecting world direction, He is world direction, and His purposes can happen without any busy-ness![178]

2 Corinthians 4:4 "the god of this world hath blinded the minds of them which believe not."

Alice Bailey had these mystical experiences despite the fact that at this time she was a Christian and even a Missionary in India. In 1915 she was living in the US and unhappily married with 3 children. That year she read 'The Secret Doctrine' which had a major impact on her entire outlook as her religious horizon expanded enormously. She wrote that she transformed her thinking from the 'narrow doctrine of dry fundamentalist Christianity' she had been brought up with, to a new fuller version of how she saw reality. Many of the 'big questions' of life were answered and she began to syncretise the beliefs of Christ as a Son of God into **the** Christ as being a world teacher, who was the 'First Born in the great family of brothers' as Paul had mentioned in Romans 8:29, following.

When she was at the Shrine Room of the Theosophical Society at Krotona California she recognised the portrait of Koot Hoomi from the face to face meeting with him in 1891. She wrote: -

'It was during this year, 1918, that I discovered for the first time who it was that had come to see me in Scotland when I was a girl of fifteen. I had been admitted into the Esoteric Section (E.S.) of the Theosophical Society and was attending their meetings. The first time that I went into the Shrine Room I saw the customary pictures of the Christ and the Masters of the Wisdom, as the Theosophists call Them. To my surprise there, looking straight at me, was a picture of my visitor. There was no mistake. This was the man who had walked into my aunt's drawing room, and it was not the Master Jesus. I was

---

[178] Daniel 7:14. He was given authority, glory and sovereign power; all nations and peoples of every language worshiped him. His dominion is an everlasting dominion that will not pass away, and his kingdom is one that will never be destroyed.

inexperienced then and rushed to one of the senior people at Krotona and asked for the name of this Master. They told me that it was the Master K. H. .....' [9].

She gave up on a traditional type of Christianity she had been preaching, and converted to Theosophy. In 1919 she met Foster Bailey, her second husband who was also heavily involved with Theosophy and a 33 degree Freemason.

Her second fateful encounter with Koot Hoomi occurred in this year (1919), whilst she was having a quiet time on a hill close to her house.

"I heard what I thought was a clear note of music which sounded from the sky, through the hill and in me. Then I heard a voice which said, 'There are some books which it is desired should be written for the public. You can write them. Will you do so?' Without a moment's notice I said, 'Certainly not. I'm not a darned psychic and I don't want to be drawn into anything like that.'" [179]

The voice gave her three weeks to reconsider. Alice apparently completely forgot about the subject when the voice made its appearance as scheduled. Agreeing to give it a try for a few weeks the first chapters of *Initiation, Human and Solar* were written. This was who she later called 'The Tibetan' or Djwhal Khul. After about a month of channelling this spirit she got scared refusing to do anymore writing but the spirit guide Master Djwhal Khul told her to discuss it with her other guide, Master Koot Hoomi. Koot Hoomi confessed that it was, in fact him who told Djwhal Khul to contact her, and he gave Alice permission to proceed — after giving Mrs. Bailey the proper technique for enhanced telepathic communication.

Alice A. Bailey was therefore a sort of 'middleman' between the Hierarchy and the people' (her words) and as a result of this evil, she formed the Lucis Trust, became involved with the UN and went on to channel 24 books. *'Today, as the result of twenty-seven years work with the Tibetan I can snap into telepathic relation with Him without the slightest trouble. I can and do preserve my own mental integrity all the time and I can always argue with Him if it seems to me, at times, that—as an Occidental—I may know better than He does as regards points of presentation.'* [180]

So what's happening here?

---

[179] Alice A, Bailey, *The Unfinished Autobiography*, p 71.

[180] Ibid, p 75.

Channelling or Overshadowing

This is channelling with two different spirits - Koot Hoomi and Djwal Khul. Alice A Bailey called this 'overshadowing' and it is mediumship, and the receiving of vibrational energy or 'tuning' into a consciousness separate from yourself to receive messages. If you are a Theosophist you would say that the channelling of spirits is a much sought after harmless goal of the adept, and in fact to be encouraged. For Christians the Bible teaches that spirit communication and talking to the dead or familiar spirits is wrong. In fact, the view in the Bible is that communicating with other spirits is talking to demons.[181] It's even worse than this, though, since channelling is allowing a spiritual entity to possess the body and have free reign to conduct activities over the Self. It's a practice that goes back to Greece and beyond, when the witches of Delphi would divulge messages from the gods. Women seem to be better at it than men. Channelling or any type of mediumship is not, and cannot possibly be from God and Jesus Christ, and is an abomination.[182] This is what the Cryptocracy are into, Theosophy and the channelling of demons. The higher Freemasonry degrees have the same activity.

---

[181] Fallen angels can deceive us by appearing as good beings and even spirits of people we are familiar with.

Leviticus 19:31 Do not turn to **medium**s or seek out spiritists, for you will be defiled by them. I am the Lord your God.

[182] **Deuteronomy 18:10-13.** Let no one be found among you who practices divination or sorcery, interprets omens, engages in witchcraft, or casts spells, or who is a medium or spiritist or who consults the dead. Anyone who does these things is detestable to the LORD, and because of these detestable practices the LORD your God will drive out those nations before you. You must be blameless before the LORD your God.

Isaiah 8:19. When someone tells you to consult mediums and spiritists, who whisper and mutter, should not a people inquire of their God? Why consult the dead on behalf of the living? [20] Consult God's instruction and the testimony of warning.

David Icke

David Icke's journey has a similar pattern to Alice A Bailey's in that he heard a voice telling him to do things and he was initially told to buy a book by Betty Shine. He then had several meetings with her, after which he was able to channel spirits. "I suddenly felt like a spider's web was touching my face, and I immediately recalled reading in her book that when 'spirits' or other dimensions are trying to make contact it can feel like a spider's web touching you." He was also told that he would write books, travel the world and heal the Earth. All the usual spiritual things that many other New Agers are told, but they have no discernment whether the spirit is from God or from someone, or something else. In this instance David Icke says that Socrates was with him and that - 'They, **whoever they were** would always be there to protect me.'[183] The big problem is, 'whoever they were'. It seems that he could not tell if the messages were from good or bad entities. If you receive messages you must discern their source and in time discern their fruit as well, but in simple terms the Bible teaches that 'every spirit that does not acknowledge Jesus is not from God. This is the spirit of the antichrist, which you have heard is coming...' 1 John 4:3. It has to be this simple since Jesus said, "his sheep follow him because they know his voice. But they will never follow a stranger; in fact, they will run away from him because they do not recognize a stranger's voice." John 10:4-5.

In the writings of Madame Blavatsky and Alice Bailey, the Religion of the New World Order is a type of Theosophy which they want the masses to have, but notice that at its heart its pure Luciferianism. What is Luciferianism? The belief that via Gnosis (knowledge), they can know the true guardian spirit of mankind which is the 'fire of the intellect', in opposition to Jesus - this is what these people believe in! This is only a reworked version of a Pantheistic Luciferian occultism, and are completely devoid of any

---

[183] David Icke, *'Remember who you are'* page 8 and 10.

goodness, any kindness, and are a total inversion of everything which Christ stands for.

It is worth bearing in mind whenever looking at the beliefs of the Elite that Blavatsky's Theosophic beliefs are really a stepping stone from the ancient religions to the modern interpretation of Luciferianism mixed in with a reworked type of Hinduism and merged with a heavy dose of Occultism and Freemasonry. There is no secret doctrine of any description that is worth studying – it just leads to Satanism. The nearest thing that could be gleamed is that Satan exists, and will be overcome at the end of History by Jesus Christ.

Over the years Theosophy has become modernised to form the New Age, which is a nebulous and ever-changing set of beliefs, more about 'transcending the self', self-improvement, finding the inner voice and gaining miracles through visualisation and meditation. These sorts of self-attainment beliefs have been pushed into business courses and self-improvement books; all of which trace their base concepts back to these types of beliefs.

Blavatsky's beliefs are more cosmic, Eastern and Hindu, whereas Alice Bailey's are more Christianised and to do with the future emergence of **the** Christ. It is this more western-style-religion which seems to be the belief system that the United Nations is espousing. And herein is our problem - the United Nations is espousing a Theosophic, New Age Religion and is then using the United Religions Initiative (URI) to mesh all the religions together to the resultant effect that there will no longer be any 'traditional beliefs' remaining, but the new fabricated control mechanism of the New World Religion.

The Age of Aquarius

Other than being a notable song from the musical 'Hair' in the 1970's, Mme Blavatsky started the belief that successive Astrological Ages had some special significance that would be accompanied by a new World Teacher. She drew this belief from Astrology that it takes around 2,300 years for the Sun to move from one constellation to the next as the entire solar system orbits the galaxy. It therefore takes a total time period of about 27,600 years for one total Cosmic Cycle since there are 12 Constellations. Since there is no ancient convention on where the Constellations start or end, the Ages themselves are rather imprecise and open to interpretation.

The concept of Astrological Ages and the new Aquarian age did not exist at Jesus' time and it was mainly developed by Mme Blavatsky and later New Ager writers. Jesus was born right at the start of the Age of Pisces which is the symbol of the fish. At the start of His ministry He called Fisherman to be His Disciples. An interesting choice of profession, and a theme which has deep connections to Pisces and Aquarius which is possibly when the fish, i.e. Christians are being poured out from the water jug.

The Astrological Ages

Leonian Age 10,500 – 8000

Cancerian Age 8,600 – 6450

Geminian Age 6450 – 4300

Taurean Age 4300 – 2150	Sacrifices of Bull
Arian Age 2150 – 1	Sacrifices of Rams
Pisces Age 1 – 2150	Fishers of Men - Christianity
Aquarian Age 2150 - or New Age.	The Age of Aquarius, the future age

You may notice that the Zodiac list goes backwards from the months list. This is because the way the ages are 'calculated' is the position of the Sun against the 'backdrop' of the Constellations and hence this moves retrograde.

Picture of Aquarius with the fish being poured out into the Heavens.

The theology of the Age of Aquarius comes, in part, from the instructions Jesus gave to Peter and John for the booking of the Upper Room in Jerusalem for Jesus' Last Super. For the Passover, Jesus instructed his Disciples to enter into the house of the 'water bearer'. Luke 22 verse 8 following as below.

And He sent Peter and John, saying, "Go and prepare the Passover for us, that we may eat." So they said to Him, "Where do You want us to prepare?" And He said to them, "Behold, when you have entered the city, *a man will meet you carrying a pitcher of water; follow him into the house which he enters.* Then you shall say to the master of the house, 'The Teacher says to you, "Where is the guest room where I may eat the Passover with My disciples?"' Then he will show you a large, furnished upper room; there make ready." So they went and found it just as He had said to them, and they prepared the Passover.'

The Theosophists take this as a coded message in which the man carrying the pitcher of water refers to the Astrological sign of the Water Bearer. This is Aquarius, and that they would 'enter into the house' which he enters. They take this as a reference to the Astrological 'House'. Blavatsky thought this New Age would herald a new saviour. But making the reference in the Bible is completely fabricated. The reason why it is untrue is that, at the time the Gospels were written, which is between about 65 and 90 AD, with some sources such as 'Q' being even younger, the writers of that time had no knowledge of the DIVISION of the signs of the Zodiac.[184] Added to which their knowledge of Astrology may not have been as strong as this since Judaism does not really teach Astrology.

What was actually probably being referred to was a type of implicit message that a man carrying water would take them to his house. In those days men did not carry water, only women, and so it was unusual to see a man with a water pitcher. Some have commented that this is a reference to the Essene monastic community, just outside Jerusalem. It is always worth remembering, before you suddenly think that Jesus was an Essene, that Jesus' message was very different from the Essenes who believed in a type of fundamentalist Judaism which certainly involved strictly keeping the Sabbath, and hating your enemies, not loving them. It was totally different.

---

[184] The Q source is the hypothetic early New Testament sayings and writing of Jesus from which the similar parts of Matthew, Luke were derived. The date for the Q source is generally accepted to be the 40s and 50s AD.

The End of *the* Age

Jesus also implied that He will be with us until the end of the age, "…and lo, I am with you always, *even* to the end of *the* age. Amen" Matthew 28:20, the last verse in Matthew. Although it doesn't say the end of this Age, i.e. the Age of Pisces, it says the end of 'the age' which could equally refer to the current age we are under, which is the age of the Grace of God under the Blood Covenant of Jesus, (if you are a dispensationalist). Madam Blavatsky, Alice Bailey, and most of the Theosophists and Luciferians have made reference to this 'end of *the* age' statement in Matthew, Mark and Luke and taken great delight in the interpretation that it refers to the end of Christianity. They believe that as the Age of Pisces draws to a close, the new Age of Aquarius will usher in the New World Order with a new World Teacher, and a New World Religion. But since the Gospel writers did not know about astrological ages this is not what they are referring to anyway. Jesus specifically says the end of the Age will be the harvest and the judgment. Matthew 13:39 and 40 "The harvest is the end of the age, and the harvesters are angels. 40 As the weeds are collected and burned in the fire, so will it be at the end of **the** age." Again the New Age theology is incorrect!

Lucifer Trust to Lucis Trust

In 1920 Alice Bailey formed the Lucifer Publishing Company but in 1922 they had to change the organization's name to the Lucis Trust since people were beginning to feel uncomfortable with the obvious link to Lucifer / Satan, and the true connection to what the group is all about. Obviously, this had to remain hidden so they changed the name and tried to keep it secret, but the books were already published. The symbol of the Lucis Trust is the blue Triangle - the Triangle representing the same New World Religion on the one-dollar bill. As an equilateral triangle it has 60 degrees in each of the 3 corners – 666. Its colour is blue perhaps because this is the colour of the throat chakra, which is a method of communication. Perhaps because it is the 'bottleneck' between the body and the head.

Lucis Trust is a highly influential institution with 'Consultative Status' within the Economic and Social Council of the UN

(ECOSOC). This permits it to have a close working relationship with the UN, including a seat on the weekly sessions. Most importantly, it has influence with powerful business and national leaders throughout the world. Alice Bailey worked for the department of health and education at the United Nations stating that the aims and attitude of the United Nations was in line with the Hierarchy.[185]

Lucis Trust is a publishing house and charity which promulgates the work of the "Ascended Masters" who have been working 'through' Alice Bailey for some 40 years. The Lucis Trust Publishing Company and their many fronts and organizations worship an Externalized Hierarchy of Ascended Masters, who carry out the work of the Luciferian 'master plan' for the establishment of a permanent Age of Aquarius ruled by Sanat Kumara, the Lord of the World.

Through its founding of **World Goodwill**, Lucis Trust is aggressively involved in promoting a globalist ideology. World Goodwill promotes the belief in 'the energy' which will bring mankind into wholeness.[186] It was P Manly Hall who described Lucifer as being the ball of energy, the dynamo, which they seek to use to better themselves.[187]

The Externalisation Of The Hierarchy

Alice Bailey stated that the long-term goal of the Hierarchy is to externalise itself, that is to become physical, embodied in human form here on earth. **The UN is the spiritual institution through which the externalisation can take place**. This is how she put it: "What is referred to is the externalisation of the Hierarchy and its exoteric appearance on earth... (to) function openly and visibly on earth".[188]

---

[185] Alice A. Bailey, *The Unfinished Biography* p 116.

[186] Lucis Trust website https://www.lucistrust.org/world_goodwill/about_wg

[187] Manly P Hall, *The Lost Keys of Freemasonry* (reference to a famous quote that Lucifer is their energy.)

[188] Alice A Bailey, THE EXTERNALISATION OF THE HIERARCHY, LUCIS TRUST, P 260.

The Externalisation of the Hierarchy just sounds like the physical appearance of demons on earth, or the awakened army.[189] It's truly a sobering prospect. The similarity between Alice Bailey's 'Externalisation of the Hierarchy' and the United Nations sponsored Venus project, is striking. The Venus Project talk about the same concepts of Sustainable development in a futurist world where applied science and advanced technology can to be used to take mankind to the Utopian future. This may be good in theory, but in the hands of the Cryptocracy it will always be a disaster. In this respect the Externalisation of the Hierarchy and the goals of the Venus project are the same. The Venus project forwards the Zeitgeist films as part of the furthering of this agenda, but in reality, these videos are full of incorrect Theology and disinformation.

'The Christ' according to Alice Bailey and the Lucis Trust

She said '*the Christ*' *was 'the energy of love'* and that his "return" would usher in the awakening of the energy in human consciousness. The new Christ may be of "no particular faith at all."

"He may appear as an Englishman, a Russian, a Negro, a Latin, a Turk, a Hindu, or any other nationality. Who can say which? He may be a Christian or a Hindu by faith, a Buddhist or of no particular faith at all; He will not come as the restorer of any of the ancient religions, including Christianity, but He will come to restore man's faith in the Father's love, in the fact of the livingness of the Christ and in the close, subjective and unbreakable relationship of all men everywhere." [190]

'The Christ' is the future Buddha or Maitreya, currently living in Shambhala. *"...humanity itself must first produce the conditions in consciousness and in world affairs essential to the eventual physical appearance of the Christ. When a measure of peace has been restored on Earth, when sharing begins to govern economic affairs, and when churches and political groups have begun to clean house, the Christ will then be drawn into the arena of His work."* [191]

---

[189] The Venus Project https://www.thevenusproject.com/the-venus-project/aims-and-proposals/

[190] Alice A Bailey, *The Reappearance of the Christ*, p 10.

[191] This quote below is taken from the Lucis Trust website
https://www.lucistrust.org/world_goodwill/key_concepts/the_new_world_religion1

Their aim is the fusion of faiths

"Today, slowly, **the concept of a world religion and the need for its emergence are widely desired and worked for. The fusion of faiths is now a field of discussion.** *Workers in the field of religion will formulate the* **universal platform of the new world religion.** *It is a work of loving synthesis and will emphasise the unity and the fellowship of the spirit. This group is, in a pronounced sense, a channel for the activities of the Christ, the world Teacher. The platform of the new world religion will be built by many groups, working under the inspiration of the Christ...*

God works in many ways, through many faiths and religious agencies; this is one reason for the elimination of non-essential doctrines. By the **emphasising of the essential doctrines** *and in their union will the fullness of truth be revealed.* **This, the new world religion will do and its implementation will proceed apace, after the reappearance of the Christ.**"[192] Emphasis mine.

So here we have it directly from the Lucis Trust which the UN is linked to! The New World Religion is something they are developing, *'The fusion of faiths is now a field of discussion'.* As might be expected, the writings of Alice Bailey are belittling towards Christianity and anything to do with Jesus Christ who she demotes at most opportunities.

The New World Religion bought to us by the Ascended Masters

Sanat Kumara is the head of this Hierarchy and this is the God of Theosophy. He is supposed to have reached the 9th Ray level and as such lives in Shambhala which is a floating city on the etheric plane somewhere above the Gobi Desert. Interesting to note that Sanat is an anagram of Satan, they love to have these anagrams and plays on words.

Madame Blavatsky wrote that he belonged to a group of beings as the "Lords of the Flame" and that the Christian tradition have

---

[192] Lucis Trust website
https://www.lucistrust.org/meetings_and_events/three_major_spiritual_festivals/the_christ_s_festival/the_reappearance_the_christ1

misunderstood Lucifer as the fallen angel.[193] Sanat Kumara is sometimes portrayed as a 16-year-old boy, and sometimes as a good looking super human, as a Nordic or Aryan superman from Venus. This leads directly to the demonic UFO sightings of the so called 'Nordic aliens'. The Venus connection also being a Luciferian one since Venus is known as the 'bright morning star'. The same mentioned in Isaiah chapter 14 and the same link that exists in Islam as previously explained.

The system of governance of Theosophy runs like this. At the top we have Sanat Kumara who is Satan in his Council Chamber of Shambala surrounded by his demons. This is the equivalent 'reverse theology' of the Heavenly Council spoken of in Kings and elsewhere in the Bible.

Sanat Kumara is the creator, but not 'the ultimate creator', he is the **Lord of this World** who supposedly descended to Earth some 18 Million years ago.[194] This is the Emanationist (Hermeticism) again where the first principle as the highest 'Godhead' creates another lesser entity.[195] From Shambhala, or Shambala as Alice Bailey spelt it, the Hierarchy receive the fire of God. The power of God comes to man from another God-like agent.

Shambhala is supposedly situated in the Tibetan Himalayas or the Gobi Desert which is a dry place.

Generally Jesus spoke of evil spirits going to dry places for example in Luke 11:24 "When an unclean spirit goes out of a man, he goes through dry places, seeking rest; and finding none, he says, 'I will return to my house from which I came.' [25] And when he comes, he finds *it* swept and put in order. [26] Then he goes and takes with *him* seven other spirits more wicked than himself, and they enter and

---

[193] Madame Blavatsky, *The Secret Doctrine'* Vol 2 p 243.

[194] In Sanskrit, 'Sanat Kumara' means Eternal Youth, with Sanat meaning 'eternal', Ku meaning 'with difficulty' and mara meaning 'mortal'. In the Hindu scriptures Sanat Kumara is the Son of Krishna and also known as Pradyumna, but this is different.

[195] It's paralleled and similar in the Kabbalah where they speak of the 'Ayn Soph', the divine light of wisdom energizing the Sephiroths or Chakras from the higher planes to the lower, and so you can go back up those chakras to reach god - it's the same evil message! And from this that man will evolve to Godhood and live in Utopia!

dwell there; and the last *state* of that man is worse than the first. (Luke 11:24 and Matthew 12:43).

This is the belief in spirits living in dry places, and where does the Hierarchy live? Supposedly in the Gobi Desert or the Tibetan planes north of the Himalayas, which is one of the driest places on earth.

The Hierarchy direct world events and influence and transmit energies from Shambala to the Ascended Masters who form the Ashrams - this is the Externalisation of the Ashram.

"The work of the external lies ashrams is creating and vitalising the new world religion. The gradual reorganisation of the social order. The public inauguration of the system of initiation. The esoteric training of disciples and of humanity in the cycle." Alice Bailey, Externalisation of the Hierarchy.

The Hierarchy of the Masters of Wisdom or Ascended Master or Ascended Hosts are the world teachers of the past and the supposed most important today are Jesus and Koot Hoomi. This is not the Jesus of the Bible, but Jesus as an Ascended Master. The Theosophists never quite managed to explain who Koot Hoomi was but he seems to have lived in Tibet and have been an inspiration behind the Theosophical Society from around 1875. Madame Blavatsky, Colonel Olcott, Bishop Leadbeater and many others mention him. The Ascended Masters are also called The Great Brotherhood and are supposed to be in a different realm to ourselves. They are also supposed to have reached at least the 6th Ray and undergone the initiation into the 'Mighty I AM Presence'. I Am, being the code for the blasphemous use of the Divine name. The Ascended Masters further direct Mankind helping the Group of World Servers which are praying for the reappearance of the Christ via the Great Invocation.

Benjamin Creme

Benjamin Creme (1922-2016) started Share International in 1977 which is a New Age religion based on Theosophy and the writings of Madame Blavatsky and Alice Bailey.

Share International teaches the same belief in the Ascended Masters, and that one of the Ascended Masters in the function of Maitreya will return. At the Maitreya's return there will also be the counterfeit Star of Bethlehem, the day of Maitreya's return will be called 'The Day of Declaration', when the Maitreya presents himself to the world as The World Teacher.

'For 30 or 40 minutes the Teacher's thoughts will be heard inwardly, telepathically and everyone in the world, in their own language, will feel the warmth and love of the Maitreya. Everybody above the age of 14 will hear this - he will give a speech about humanity and how old we are, and how we have descended from a spiritual high point to our rather low position now, and how we are endangering the very future of the species, and that we need to take steps to amend this. At the same time, he will show what the future can be like. It will be based on being brothers of one humanity which will take us to the very stars. The masters will give to humanity their wisdom and age-old experience and knowledge and stimulate and galvanise humanity to make the most brilliant future. An energy and love will pervade the world and create an inner certainty that this is the Christ, and on the physical plane many healings will occur all over the planet'. This is a summary from a You Tube video of Benjamin Crème explaining the Day of Declaration.[196]

This will probably occur after some sort of global economic melt-down and is one method by which all the world's religions would unite. This could be a precursor to the One World Government.

It almost sounded as if Benjamin Creme was describing a psychotropic weapon that seems more than likely that the US, Russia and other countries have been developing. These weapons are

---

[196] Benjamin Crème video – Day of Declaration
https://www.youtube.com/watch?v=PS9BjFTn2R0

capable of delivering voices inside someone's head without them being auditory.[197]

Whatever the weapons side of this, it seems that most people with any common sense would outright reject this notion of the Maitreya, and many non-Christians would simply see this as the Anti-Christ. People don't need to have read and understood the Bible, they just can't buy into the notion of the Maitreya since in the west this is a foreign concept to most people. And so, could it be that the whole Share International concept is another false religious event? Or was Benjamin Crème onto something when he said that the Second Christ would appear on Monday 21st June 1982 (the Summer Solstice), which just happened to be the date for the induced birth of Prince William?

Share International was at one time linked to the United Nations as an NGO of the UN, but his group is no longer listed on the UN website.

The end goal of Theosophy is therefore Man becoming like a god, living in a physical Utopian society with complete access to awesome god like powers, which will to enable him to fulfill his destiny and for mankind to become god.

It is the complete inversion of Christianity which teaches that man will remain man, and God will be God at the center of the New City of Jerusalem with the New Heaven and New Earth, which God has made to replace the current dispensation. And so, this is where you can see the evil, Luciferian, nasty belief that somehow these Masters are in control of humanity from a place which is not heaven, but on earth somewhere. It's plain Satanism because it's saying that Spiritual beings other than God are running mankind and 'evolving humankind' to a greater purpose and that mankind's ultimate destiny of 'oneness and brother-hood' is in their hands, not God's. This is what the UN believes.

---

[197] Psychotropic weapons see
https://www.bibliotecapleyades.net/ciencia/ciencia_psychotronicweapons10.htm
Russia and American development
http://cosmiclog.nbcnews.com/_news/2012/04/06/11061093-reality-check-on-russias-zombie-ray-gun-program?lite

Every belief is the reverse of Christianity and there is no goodness or kindness in any of these beliefs. Jesus referred to Satan as "the Prince of this world" in John 12:31 and 14:30, and Paul referred to him as "the God of this world" in 2 Corinthians 4, also describing the hierarchy of fallen angels as "the rulers," and "authorities" and "the powers of this dark world" (Ephesians 6:12). Although the disciples of Madam Blavatsky and Alice Bailey might not have known that Sanat Kumara was Satan, there are many indications that these two leaders knew precisely who they were espousing as they peddled this belief to others. This is the true mark of a Satanist – someone who sells other fellow beings into the hand of the devil, knowing it is Satan, but all the while pretending it's something else. Another illusion!

The Bible says that in the end times there will be many strong delusions 1 Timothy 4:1 and 2 Thessalonians 2:2-4 and that there will be a "falling away first" and then the Man of Perdition, the Antichrist will exalt himself and proclaims himself God as he leads the New Religion.

- Sanat Kumara is Satan, the fallen angel Lucifer or Prometheus.
- The Hierarchy are Fallen Angels / Demons.
- Shambhala is the dry place on Earth which is a dwelling place for evil spirits.
- The Council of Sanat Kumara is the meeting place of demons. The opposite of the Heavenly council mentioned in 1 Kings 22:19, Psalms 82:1, or Hebrews 12:22-24.[198]
- The Ascended Masters are lists of high ranking Antichrists from the past who stay behind to complete the Great Plan.
- The Externalisation of the Hierarchy could be the physical appearance of Satan's army or even spirit possession of the human race. Or even the 200 Million referred to in Revelation

---

[198] Hebrews 12:22-24. But you have come to Mount Zion and to the city of the living God, the heavenly Jerusalem, to an innumerable company of angels, [23] to the general assembly and church of the firstborn who are registered in heaven, to God the Judge of all, to the spirits of just men made perfect, [24] to Jesus the Mediator of the new covenant.

9:16 although this army in Revelation is bringing God's judgment after the four Angels are released from the Euphrates.

- The Group of World Servers are the equivalent of the Ministers of the new religion who serve humanity, the Plan, the Hierarchy, and 'the Christ'.
- Planetary Cleansing is Eugenics or the false Rapture.
- Channelling is Spirit Possession.
- The Great Invocation is the invocation of the Light of Lucifer, and 'reverse' of The Lord's Prayer.
- The New Age Messiah or the 'Christ Consciousness' is the Antichrist or the personification of the Beast system in Revelation.
- The Seven Rays of creation emanating from the Godhead are in antithesis to the Seven Days of Creation. (Again Emanationism.)
- They talk of the Master Jesus as being another World Teacher, not the Son of God.

Conclusion

Theosophists and New Agers are unashamedly keen to subvert Christianity which they see as an outdated expression of their faith. Their objective is to discredit Jesus and the Bible as much as possible. They try to portray Jesus as being another one of their Ascended Masters, or one of several World Teachers who studied in Egypt, Persia or India. In fact, there is a growing body of New Age fabricated literature covering the 18 'lost years' of Jesus' life between about age 12 and 30. According to these writers, who offer not a shred of evidence, they claim Jesus travelled to India to become a Yogi (such as Shirley MacLaine) or India, Nepal and Tibet (Elizabeth Claire Prophet) where he developed his psychic powers.[199] They often also quote the fake Gnostic Gospels written a further hundred years or so on from the true Gospel writing era which ended around 92 AD. For example, they use the Gnostic Gospels of Peter, Thomas, and Judas to prove Jesus was a Gnostic or an Essene, or they try to

---

[199] Reference: *Dark Secrets of the New Age*, by Texe Marrs p 206.

reinterpret them to gain credence about their doctrines of Reincarnation and Karma.

Their end goal is to replace Christianity and all Religions with their own version.

The fact that this New Age religion has impacted the United Nations to such a large extent is evidence that something very dark and deep is going on within our world. If there were no truth to these beliefs then the UN would be totally secular, but the fact the UN are also pushing these ideas is tantamount evidence to the dire situation we are entering into. These beliefs are something we explore in the next chapter.

CHAPTER 11

THE BELIEFS OF THE UNITED NATIONS

The United Nations was an outgrowth from the League of Nations set up by the Milner Group and Council on Foreign Relations for the benefit of the Elite Network. The posts of UN Presidents and Secretary Generals were chosen almost entirely from the Socialists of the day and practically all of them have also had leanings towards New Age beliefs of one description or another. The first General Secretary in 1945 was Paul-Henri Spaak (Socialist), followed by Trygve Lie (Socialist), Dag Hammarskjold (Socialist and New Ager), U Thant (Socialist and New Ager), and other important members such as Robert Muller, (Socialist and New Ager) and Maurice Strong, (Socialist and New Ager). The belief in Theosophy and the writings of Alice A. Bailey have had a large influence on the UN as a whole and their leaders. As mentioned before, the Lucis Trust which continues the New Age teachings of Alice Bailey, has been closely linked to the UN.

The next 'set' of Secretary's and influencers at the UN were keen to push the deliberate policy of weakening National Sovereignty at every step. Kurt Waldheim (Centre Right Austrian Politician), Javier Perez de Cuellar (Peruvian Diplomat and alleged alien abductee), Boutros Boutros-Ghali (Egyptian Socialist), Kofi Annan, Ban Ki-moon and today António Guterres. Yet another Socialist and One Worlder, in fact Guterres was President of Socialist International, a group whose policy is to establish the New International Economic and Political Order.[200]

The most influential people within the UN relevant to our study are: Dag Hammarskjold, who 'transcended' Christianity as a mystic. U Thant as a New Age 'enabler', Robert Muller who was said to be 'the Philosopher of the United Nations' and Maurice Strong, the fake New Age Moses, who also had a major impact on the UN. Pierre Teilhard de Chardin (described below) is also an influencer. They all believed in the New Age and that the United Nations was to be the vehicle and method that was to bring mankind forward to their version of Utopia. This is the spiritual motivation of the one world government and they 'spiritualise' the UN as the bringer of the new order. But as we proved in the previous Chapter, the New Age movement is based on Luciferianism - the belief that, via the false divine light, man can make a perfect future in which he is all powerful and full of knowledge and wisdom.

Dag Hammarskjold held strong Theosophical beliefs and was said to be a type of Christian mystic. Alice A Bailey in 1930's even predicted that there would be a Swedish disciple who would be working for the UN so it was engineered this way. It was Dag Hammarskjold (General Secretary to the United Nations from 1953 to 1961) who developed and designed the **Meditation Room** at the UN headquarters in New York. It was planned to be a room where all people could come and presumably pray. The room is a small rectangular shaped Interfaith area facing north in the centre of which is a huge 6 and ½ tonne stone haematite altar-- 'not because it is an altar to an unknown god, but **because it is dedicated to the God whom men worship under many names and in many forms.'** Emphasis mine: 'many names and forms' sounds like the god of Freemasonry except this time marketed as the New World Religion in the UN Headquarters. At one end of the room is a modern painting which is *in the style of* Picasso. The esoteric meaning, with a chink of light as a wavy line coming through the centre of the painting, represents the emergence of Lucifer. The Lucis Trust look after the

---

[200] http://www.socialistinternational.org/viewArticle.cfm?ArticleID=31

UN meditation room and administer it.[201] As an aside, Mondrian and Kandinsky's original paintings were inspired by Theosophy.

Sri Chinmoy was the United Nations 'priest' and New Ager who used to hold twice weekly ceremonies in the room. He was invited to do this by U Thant who was a Theravada Buddhist and the third UN Secretary General from 1961 to 1971. Needless to say, these ceremonies were not Christian, and neither were they Buddhist, but they seem to have been New Age and about 'Self transcendence'.

After Hammarskjold set up the occult UN Meditation room and U Thant had set up the New Age meetings. It was U Thant who introduced Robert Muller to the writings and beliefs of Teilard de Chardin.

Pierre Teilard de Chardin (1881-1955) was a Jesuit trained Catholic Priest and missionary in China who has had a major impact upon the beliefs of the Elite and how they see the UN developing in the future. He was also a geologist and a palaeontologist whose major book, 'The Phenomena of Man' was published after his death, although most of his teachings were known before he died. He was a most interesting mystic attempting to explain the deeper mysteries of God and life within the context of a more scientific world. He taught that all of humanity would eventually meld into one super-being through the coming of the 'Cosmic Christ'. He believed that God was acting through union with Christ, 'pulling man' to a final conclusion which was his vision of the Omega Point in the future where Man will have evolved to know God. In this respect Man's evolution is an ascent toward consciousness and becoming God. He abandoned purely Biblical notions of the creation and re-interpreted the Genesis and Salvation story as a type of evolutionary orthogenesis: that God is slowly evolving man into some definite direction via some internal mechanism or 'driving force.' Some of his Theology came from the reinterpretation of the following passages: -

1 Corinthians 15:28

---

201 UN Mediation room info
http://www.un.org/depts/dhl/dag/meditationroom.htm

Now when all things are made subject to Him, then the Son Himself will also be subject to Him who put all things under Him, that God may be all in all.

And Colossians 1:15-17. He is the image of the invisible God, the firstborn over all creation. For by Him all things were created that are in heaven and that are on earth, visible and invisible, whether thrones or dominions or principalities or powers. All things were created through Him and for Him. And He is before all things, and in Him all things consist. And He is the head of the body, the church, who is the beginning, the firstborn from the dead, that in all things He may have the pre-eminence.

Teilard de Chardin thought of Christ as, not only just the risen Saviour of the Gospels, but as a huge continually evolving Being, as big as the universe to which everything must return so that all things consist in Him. His reinterpretation of the nature of Jesus made his Christology far too cosmic and a transcendent type of Christianity, far too close to Theosophic concepts. He thought of each person existing as a living cell within the Body of Christ. And Teilard attempted to show how we can participate in, and nurture the whole of the life of the Total Christ; the end result being the return of all things to Christ – what he termed the Omega Point. This was the concluding state of God's purposes for mankind and represents the maximum level of complexity and consciousness toward which he believed the universe was evolving.

But the mistake that Teilard de Chardin made was that he went too far with this interpretation, and envisioned humanity merging into God and realising his own godhood at the Omega Point. He taught that the god to be worshipped is the one who will arise out of the evolving human race.

He wrote about religion that "...a general convergence of religions upon a **universal Christ** who satisfies them all: that seems to me the only possible conversion of the world, and the only form in which a religion of the future can be conceived.... I believe that the Messiah whom we await, whom we all without any doubt await, is the universal Christ; that is to say, the Christ of evolution."[202]

---

[202] Teilard de Chardin, *Christianity and Evolution*, p. 130

Emphasis mine. This 'universal Christ' is not Jesus Christ of the Bible, but more like a 'new age ascended master' that will lead all religions into unity. This is not what the Gospel teaches and in effect his commentary played into hands of the New Agers who jumped on it as a concept they could work with. All of which just makes Teilard de Chardin another heretical Theologian with Luciferian tendencies. But for the those at the top of the UN, this is all confirmation that their vision of the One World Government is correct, and that a deeper destiny and process will lead to the establishment of their spiritualised UN Utopian society.

Robert Muller, the so-called Philosopher and Prophet of Hope for the UN

Robert Muller (1923 – 2010) worked for the United Nations for forty years advocating world government as humanity's only hope for peace. He was heavily involved with setting up all sorts of UN organisations and his ideas about the one world government leading the world into peace with a new world spirituality led to the increased representation of religions in the UN. One of Muller's key influences was U Thant (1909-1974), whom Muller called "my spiritual master."[203]

One of his contributions was the setting up of the World Core Curriculum.

World Core Curriculum

Alice A Bailey in 1957 established the educational goals for the future which were later picked up by Robert Muller. She wrote that Freemasonry would be the new world religion and that they would work towards the Great Plan to bring this into existence. She even says how she is going to do this. *"The three main channels through which the preparation for the new age is going on might be regarded as the church, the Masonic fraternity and the educational field."*[204] For those who don't go to church or aren't members of the Masonic fraternity, it would be

---

[203] Robert Muller's website http://www.robertmuller.org/

[204] Alice A Bailey, *Externalisation of the Hierarchy*, page 271.

schools and educational establishments that would be the means by which the New World Order Religion would be brought in.

Muller's educational brain child of the World Core Curriculum was launched in 1975 and set out the principles which are to govern the worlds education programs. In the preface to the World Core Curriculum it states that, *"The underlying philosophy upon which the Robert Muller school is based will be found in the teachings set for in the books of Alice A Bailey..."* In other words, the teaching she channelled via the Tibetan Djwhal Khul, Master Morya and Koot Hoomi. We demonstrated previously that Alice A Bailey was a Luciferian and here we have the world education establishment clambering to get a bit of Lucifer into their classrooms! (This is not to be confused with the US educational 'Core Curriculum State Standards Initiative' which is a new system of national Education from 2010.)

Muller's World Curriculum framework is therefore basically shoving New Age beliefs to children since his 'curriculum' teaches "Spiritual exercises of interiority, meditation prayer, communication with the universe, eternity and God." This is pure New Age spirituality being taught to children!

According to United Nations Online, *'The scope of the curriculum will always be the same; to allow the student to see himself truly, as **an integral part of the Cosmos**...At the moment, it seems the only limitation will be the imagination of the Cosmic-minded and spiritually oriented teaching staff.'*

A comic piece of nonsense. The World Core Curriculum is a set of glossy United Nations indoctrinations for the New World Order, full of New Age dogma, as below.

"Today I can only praise the United Nations for having taught me the truth and the real facts: the Earth which is my home, humanity which is my family, our place in time and the dignity and miracle of individual human life. This is why I made these United Nations teachings into a world core curriculum which should bless every school and child on Earth. A different world, the true world, a more beautiful, miraculous, astonishing world and humanity, and not the dissected world created by nations emerge from it.

"I urge all educators and governments to have a look at this curriculum. It is not the product of my mind, but of the United Nations, the recent first universal organization which thinks for the entire planet and humanity.

*"An educator wrote to me: "Through your world core curriculum, the world's teachers can now have **access to the soul** of every man, woman and child on this planet." I hope this will be the case."*[205]

I hope that the UN will not have access to the soul of every man, woman and child on this planet, that would be to place them in the hands of the devil; since we know that the UN is the spiritual institution the conspirators are establishing for their final Kingdom.

Robert Muller also said that we should, *"steer our citizens towards global citizenship, **earth centered beliefs**, socialist values and the collective mindset which is becoming a requirement for the 21st century workforce. A world core curriculum might seem utopian today. By the end of the year 2000 it will be a down – to – earth daily reality in all the schools of the world."*

Although it seems that the implementation of this curriculum may not be filtering through as strongly as Robert Muller would have liked, the determination to implement this program has not gone away.

The literature itself is filled with phrases such as "well-being and well becoming". **The term 'well becoming' is an occult term referring to the evolution of the individual to godhood** which itself is a Luciferian concept as explained many times in this book.

So there we have it again from the United Nations themselves. The long-term goal is heavily linked to the New Age Movement which is promoting the setting up an amalgamated belief system and global culture which they would control for their benefit.

The worlds citizens will have the same world view, sanitised, standardised, and legalised. There will be no expression of individuality. As Robert Muller wrote in the World Core Curriculum: *"Assisting the child in becoming an integrated individual who can deal with personal experience while seeing himself as a part of 'the greater whole.'* In other words, promote growth of the group idea, so that group good, group understanding, group interrelations and group goodwill replace all limited, self-centered objectives, leading to group consciousness.

---

[205] World Core Curriculum
http://www.robertmuller.org/rm/R1/About_WCC.html

Mikhail Gorbachev – the man with the 'still unfulfilled ambition'

Mikhail Gorbachev is an important promoter of the New World Religion being a co-writer of the Earth Charter, which is like a religious declaration of human rights. This is the document which is in the Ark of Hope. His co-writer was Maurice Strong. After the fall of the Soviet era in 1991, he moved to the US and set up the Gorbachev Foundation and Green Cross International. He also helped set up Sustainable Development at the Rio Earth Summit in 1992.

As a hardened advocate of world Socialism, Gorbachev called for the creation of a 'new civilisation' based on Socialism. He writes *'The socialist idea is inextinguishable....'* And later on he explains how this will be achieved. *'We understand that building such a civilisation is a long-term task (although on the scale of history a task that cannot be postponed). Few people are ready for the profound, fundamental changes required for the creation of this civilisation.'* [206] The instrument to be used in this, would, of course be the United Nations, and behind the United Nations controlling everything is the Cryptocracy.

Maurice Strong

Maurice Strong (1929 – 2015) was high up within the United Nations for over 40 years. UN Secretary-General U Thant invited Maurice Strong to lead it as Secretary-General of the United Nations Conference on the Human Environment (the Stockholm Conference) in June 1972. He set up the UN Environmental Program (UNEP) creating all the various clubs and alliances to do with Global Warming. He helped push the Climate Change hoax which is one part of the argument the Cryptocracy are using to enable them to bring in the type of ordered society they are striving to reach. This a control mechanism and method whereby they can

---

[206] Quoted from Lee Penn, *False Dawn*, pages 369 and 360 from Mikhail Gorbachev's book, *On My Country and the World*, page 67 and 269.

bring the New World Order into effect. If he had started his campaign on Climate Change at outset, and not on Global Warming, then this is more likely to have been a psyop which would have fooled us all. But because global warming came first and was proven to be false they then changed this to climate change. However Maurice Strong was hailed as an environmental guru and called 'the Custodian of the Planet' in the New York Times. He also earned the nickname 'Father Earth' as Chairman of the Earth Council.

Maurice Strong was a Canadian industrialist who lucked out within the UN where he started right at the bottom. But there is some evidence that the Rockefeller's spotted him and he became one of the darlings of their cause. Why this should be the case remains a mystery - perhaps he was related to the Rockefellers and Rothschilds, or perhaps he was a Satanist of some worth they could look up to! Or perhaps, it was because one of his relatives had come to the notice of the Rockefellers. Maurice Strong's Grandmother was Anna Louise Strong who was a Journalist who sympathetically reported on the Communist regime and was a supporter of Lenin and Stalin.[207] In this respect, it seems he was an insider.

Maurice Strong was also Trustee of the Aspen Institute (linked to the Trilateral Commission) which is one of the major think tanks studying the Behaviour of Man. He was also a member of the advisory council of Planetary Citizens which is a major force within the environmental and New Age movement. He was on the board of Directors of the Lindisfarne Center which is a New Age talking shop based in the Episcopal Cathedral of St. John the Divine in New York. The group was funded by Laurence Rockefeller, the Rockefeller Brothers Fund and their Foundation.[208]

---

[207] Anna Louse Strong; see comment on Wikipedia: One of her books was even prefaced by Trotsky. She lived in Russia and died in China, just like Maurice Strong. Source: http://www.foxnews.com/story/2007/02/08/at-united-nations-curious-career-maurice-strong.html

[208] The Rockefellers are linked to the Lindisfarne Group which is a New Age group heavily influenced by the New Age and Teilard de Chardin.

The New Age Moses of the New World Religion – with his own burning bush!

Whilst out walking in the Baca Grande, Colorado, Maurice Strong bragged about how he saw a burning bush, the implication being that he was a new Moses. He was out walking with his friend Bill Moyes, a Journalist and CFR member, when according to Strong: *"We'd been walking, talking, heading back to my parked car. Suddenly, this bush – some sagebrush – erupted in flames in front of us! It just burst into flames. I was astounded. Moyers was, too. A bush bursting into flames!"*[209] So here we have the fake Moses writing the New World Order 10 Commandments which is the Earth Charter!

---

[209] Interview with Maurice Strong about the burning bush see http://nwodb.com/?e=03620

The Earth Charter History

The original blueprint for Agenda 21 went back to the Club of Rome in the 1970's and the report from Iron Mountain.[210] The 'seed concept' for the Earth Charter started in 1987 with the Bro Gruntland report which really started Sustainable Development which lead to Agenda 21.

*"The Earth Charter is an **ethical framework for building a just, sustainable, and peaceful global** society in the 21st century. It seeks to inspire in all people a new sense of **global interdependence** and shared responsibility for the **well-being** of the whole human family, the greater community of life, and future generations. It is a vision of hope and a call to action."*[211] My emphasis in bold.

Translation: The Earth Charter is the Elite's unethical plan for making you subservient to the New World Order and the collectivist society of the new earth worship religion.

The Charter was actually started by Robert Muller with the UNESCO Global Education Project, but brought to fruition by Maurice Strong and Mikhail Gorbachev. In 1995 at a UN celebration at the University of Berkeley, California, Robert Muller described the three stages in the history of the United Nations in the quote below: -

The first period took up human rights. The UN Charter was for humans, and no one thought of the earth. By 1980, suddenly climatologists warned us that climate might go berserk. The atmosphere was getting warmer and warmer because of CO2.

*This is the third period. Now Earth is number 1. **Humanity is number 2**. Now, we must deal with **rights of the planet**. There will be an <u>Earth</u>*

---

[210] Iron Mountain is in upstate New York near the Hudson River not that far from the Rockefeller's home at Pontanico Hills. Could it be a Rockefeller funded report? See Servando Gonzalez, *Psychological Warfare and the New World Order'* Chapter 10 Kindle Location: 4661

[211] http://earthcharter.org/discover/

Charter ...... *We need a* **universal declaration of ethics** *and a universal declaration of duties and responsibilities.'* Emphasis mine.

Muller went on to list what he thought were the world's ills which he saw as: large families, over-consumption, rubbish, business and religious differences etc. He admitted that the Charter must be flexible. One that can be defined or interpreted according to the world's changing needs and perceptions: 'We need ethics in time,' he said. 'What is right today may not be right tomorrow.'

It was Maurice Strong and Mikhail Gorbachev who together produced the final Earth Charter version in 2000. They both stated that they wanted the Earth Charter to become 'like the Ten Commandments' and they both targeted children to indoctrinate them into the pantheistic religion that is the UN New World Religion.

At the Rio Summit in 1992 Strong pushed his Declaration of the Sacred Earth. **'The changes in behavior and direction called for here, must be rooted in our deepest spiritual, moral, and ethical values.'**

Translation: We are going to change the spiritual, moral and ethical values of Society, to our system of values.

According to the Declaration, 'The **[ecological] crisis** transcends all national, religious, cultural, social, political and economic boundaries. The responsibility of each human being today is to choose between the **force of darkness and the force of light.** We must therefore transform our attitudes and values, and adopt a renewed respect for the **superior laws of Divine Nature.'** Emphasis mine.

Translation: The liberal environmental agenda will be the excuse for us, the Elite, to do what we want since ecology is global, not national. We will pretend to give you a choice of light and dark, but you will conform to our dark Earth Religion.

Criticism of the Earth Charter

The Earth Charter has been said to be the prototype constitution for the New World Order and is a set of obscure semi-New Age doctrines. Here are some sections of the Earth Charter,[212] with some comments, that we must:-

• 'Recognize that all beings are interdependent and every form of life has value...'

Unborn children, of course, are not included in the UN's definition of 'every form of life.' The Earth Summit II documents continue to support the UN's pro-abortion policies.

• 'Affirm faith in the inherent dignity of all human beings.' UN agencies have been shown to generally support policies of euthanasia for those determined not capable of living a 'quality' life.

• 'Adopt at all levels sustainable development plans and regulations...' This is the Agenda 21 program for the super-regulated global state.

• 'Prevent pollution of any part of the environment...' This links in with their strategy of introducing carbon taxes and usufruct licenses as an excuse to regulate small farmers out of existence and into the hands of large scale agri-businesses.

• 'Internalize the full environmental and social costs of goods and services in the selling price.' This seemingly harmless sentence would empower the state to set the price and regulate all production and consumption.

• 'Ensure universal access to health care that fosters reproductive health and responsible reproduction'. This is a thinly disguised call for socialised medicine that includes abortion and population control. One of their long range plans is to reduce the population to a figure in the region of 500 million to a billion people in total, dependant on which document you are reading.

• 'Eliminate discrimination in all its forms, such as that based on race... and sexual orientation.' This provision is aimed at criminalising those who refuse to accept same sex couples bringing up children. The reality is that same sex couples bringing up children creates an insurmountable amount of confusion for most children as they see Mummy and Mummy together, or Daddy and Daddy as a

---

[212] Earth Charter: has been translated into 50 languages and is found here: - http://earthcharter.org/ http://earthcharter.org/virtual-library2/the-earth-charter-text/

couple, when other children have a Mummy and a Daddy. It's the family and androgynous psyop agenda.

• 'Promote the equitable distribution of wealth within nations and among nations.' Exactly the same agenda as Agenda 21, where the industrialised west has to decouple its production to save the environment. Few Socialist documents have put their 'redistribution of wealth' program more blatantly.[213] But this would not be true Socialism, it would be even worse. An all-encompassing Technocracy based economy, where the production of goods and services would be calculated by the amount of energy used. Energy consumption would be the currency.

Result of the Earth Charter

This is a modern Technocratic, Fabianist document, exactly as you would expect from the UN and UN enabled institutions. Mikhail Gorbachev told us that in the future we would all succumb to World Socialism and this is the sort of document they are using to get us there. It's all about respect for the environment and the community and how we all want to live in peace and love each other without war and conflict. It's about how unfair it is that some parts of the world are poor, and others are rich. It's slightly flippant in places as well, and looks down on us as if they have the right to tell us what is the right thing to do, as if they know something we don't. It seems obvious to a degree that they intend for this Charter to become a universally adopted creed to psychologically prepare the next generation to accept the one world government and guide us into the economy of sustainable development. The excuse they are using to enable this, is again the noble banner of saving the environment. There's an unmistakeable air of pretension and New Age dogma within it, as it aims to indoctrinate the world into the UN's creed of Agenda 21, that fits in as the New World Religion. In the final analysis the Earth Charter document sounds hollow.

---

[213] Citation: Article in The New American, by William F Jasper. *The New World Religion.* https://www.thenewamerican.com/culture/faith-and-morals/item/15091-the-new-world-religion

At the end of the 4-page document there's the call to commit to the UN which will become the Global One World Government. '*In order to build a sustainable global community,* **the nations of the world must renew their commitment to the United Nations**, *fulfill their obligations under existing international agreements, and support the implementation of Earth Charter principles with an international* **legally binding** *instrument on environment and development.*' Emphasis mine...

But what if you don't want to renew any commitment or even implement their daft agreements? Did you ever get a vote in any of this? How democratic is that?

The UN is not Secular

The UN, at the top, is awash with New Agers although the vast proportion of the UNs Employees are 'westerners', from Christian backgrounds. But these New Age enablers have been promoted to positions of influence and power within the UN by the Cryptocracy to bring in their final agenda. If we just cast aside our own beliefs for a moment, surely a UN which represents all of humanity would be best if it was Secular? Religion, if we are brutally honest, is a deeply political entity and so, wouldn't it make sense that no favouritism of any belief system should be allowed? If we are to adopt a global society, surely it should be Secularism that they would be promoting, but instead we have this strange occultism that pervades the UN with hidden messages. This is because the Elite are affected by the long-range plan of Lucifer in more ways than they can tell or understand. Satan's intellect is no match for their puny brains, he outsmarts them at every step and they don't even realise!

The Ark of Hope

The New World Religion has a symbol, and this is the Ark of Hope which is modelled on Judaism's most sacred object, the Ark of the Covenant. It is housed at the UN building in New York and contains a copy of the Earth Charter, and the Temenos books. This is the first line on their website: '*The Ark of Hope, a 49"(124.5cm) x 32" (81.3cm) x*

32" (81.3cm) wooden chest was created as a place of refuge for the Earth Charter document, an international peoples treaty for building a just, sustainable, and peaceful global society in the 21st century.' [214]

This is the Religious aspect of the UN Sustainable economic agenda or New International Economic order spoke about by the Trilateralist Commission.

The Temenos Books are 'a magical sacred circle where special rules apply and extraordinary events inevitably occur, each artist made a Temenos Book: a handmade book filled with pages of visual prayers /affirmations for global healing, peace, and gratitude.' From the Ark of Hope website.

It's interesting to note that the term 'temenos' is Greek and comes from the word 'to cut' and relates to a piece of land or sacred area which was given to Kings or Priests in ancient Greece to be used for their religious ceremonies. It might have been a holy grove or precinct, for example the Acropolis of Athens was the holy temenos of Pallas. We're back again to Greek mystery religion!

On the Ark of Hope website it says '*...groups in the creation of Temenos Books and Earth Masks, believe that the artistic process can inspire people to a deeper commitment to Earth and to the Earth Charter principles.'* [215]

Sounds a bit like a new religion to me - deeper commitment to the Earth and the 'sugar coated' Earth Charter principles.

The concept of the Temenos gets even weirder if we consider what Carl Jung wrote in *'Psychology and Alchemy'* about the temenos being the place for a deep encounter or meeting with the Shadow self. It was the magical place of the mind in his occult view.

On the Ark, on each side, are oil paintings of each of the elements - Air, Water, Fire, Earth and on the top Spirit. This takes us straight back to the Pythagoreans who taught that the elements were permeated by the vitality of life which they called 'ether', which is Spirit. It's the old mystery religion again!

---

[214] Ark of Hope: http://www.arkofhope.org/

[215] Tenemos
http://www.arkofhope.org/Temenos%20Books_files/Temenos_Books.html

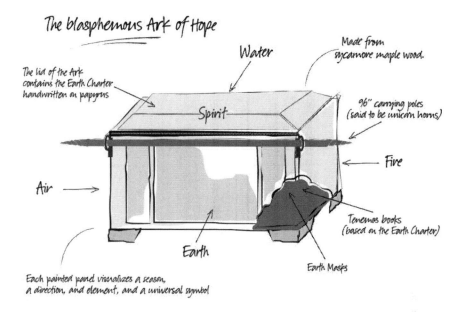

The blasphemous Ark of Hope

Water

Made from sycamore maple wood.

The lid of the Ark contains the Earth Charter handwritten on papyrus

Spirit

96" carrying poles (said to be unicorn horns)

Fire

Air

Tenemos books (based on the Earth Charter)

Earth

Earth Masks

Each painted panel visualizes a season, a direction, and element, and a universal symbol

Lao Tsu in the 6th Century BC taught something similar and categorised the phenomenon around him in terms of Water, Fire, Wood, Metal and Earth. The Spirit energy which they called Chi and could be Yin (female) or Yang (male). Perhaps the Ark builders wished to incorporate these beliefs in addition to the more outwardly Judaic ones.

The true Biblical Ark of the Covenant had the Mercy Seat, the Kipporeth in Hebrew, meaning atonement which has the same word as, 'Yom Kippor', the Day of Atonement (yom meaning day in Hebrew). It was where the sins were atoned for. Obviously, the Ark of Hope doesn't have the Kipporeth because there are no sins to be atoned for in their belief system. In fact the people who believe in this evil replica want to become gods anyway, so what do they care about sins!

The poles that hold the Ark are 96 inches and are said to be Unicorn's horns, which 'render evil ineffective'. This is an obvious reference to the New Age religion. The world Religions alluded to with the Ark are: Judaism, Christianity, New Age / Theosophy, Mystery Religions, Taoism (Lao Tsu), Indigenous Religions, Zoroastrianism (fire), Hindu (Earth), Islam (Water), and Shinto

(Wood). Steven Rockefeller described the Ark of Hope as incorporating the 'wisdom of the world's religions'. [216]

The wood used to make this fake Ark came from a Sycamore maple tree, sycamore being the same wood that Osiris's coffin was made from, and in the Egyptian mystery religions, was considered sacred.[217]

It was Steven Rockefeller who carried the Ark of Hope from Vermont to New York in 2002, in response to the 9/11 attacks. His father was Nelson Rockefeller, the older brother of David Rockefeller. In a way it's surprising it wasn't Maurice Strong who carried the Ark since he is the fake New Age Moses of the United Nations, but obviously it's the person who pays for these events who gets to choose who has the glory, and this went to Steven Rockefeller. He helped write the Earth Charter with Strong and Gorbachev, and is a Professor of Theology at Middlebury College, Vermont. From his essays we can see that he is a 'green religionist', believing in the ancient pantheistic religion.

Instead of the manna, Aaron's staff, and the two tablets with the 10 Commandments, (Hebrews 9:4 compare 2 Chronicles 5:10), we have the blasphemous Temenos books, and the Earth Charter with its 16 sugar coated agreements.

Can't they even think of a more original concept than copying something from the Bible for their One World Religion; are they so unimaginative, they just have to use what's already there and twist it to their demented agenda? A fake Ark of the Covenant for a non-existent, bogus, fake religion, peddled by fake 'prophets', funded by fake institutions made by man and not God, for the glory of the Devil and not Jesus! Why couldn't they get a big Globe with a few palm trees around it and put their plastic 16 Commandments in that, and call that their new world religion? The Ark of the Covenant was the most sacred treasure of the Old Testament, covered in gold and imbued with enormous significance and lethal power. Yet they present it to the world as a cheap model to the world's problems and

---

[216] Steven Rockefeller: from The New American
https://www.thenewamerican.com/culture/faith-and-morals/item/15091-the-new-world-religion

[217] George Fraser, *The Golden Bough*, page 72, abridged version.

a pagan-catch-all religious symbol that everyone can supposedly feel at home with. The Elite probably hope that once Jerusalem has become the New World Religious centre, this counterfeit Ark may even find its way into an international temple in the UN controlled city of the future, dedicated to a new spiritual unity and pagan peace.

CHAPTER 12

HOW THEY INTEND TO FORCE ALL
RELIGIONS TOGETHER

Ecumenism

Ecumenism is the attempt to bring all the diverse Christian traditions into one unified Church group. The adjective ecumenical is often used to refer to any inter-denominational activity that encourages greater cooperation amongst Christians and their churches. Ever since Vatican II in 1965, the Catholic Church has been one of the biggest advocates of the need for Christian unity and for the other churches to join it - the supposed first and only true version. The problem with this is that for many denominations, the doctrines of the Catholics are abhorrent as they seek the intermission of sins from Mary, the Mother of God, and the endless crucifixion of Jesus at the Mass. This runs contrary to the Bible based doctrine that the atonement was achieved via the once and for all sacrifice of Jesus on the Cross. (1 Peter 3:18). Many Church leaders have somehow exchanged the idea of Evangelism and making converts, to getting along with other Churches, and being unified. They might quote from John 17:22-23 'that they may be one as We are one: I in them, and You in Me; that they may be made perfect in one'... But whereas the world may see hundreds of denominations, God sees the one Church, the body of Christ. In 1 Corinthians Chapter 12:11-31 Paul writes that the body of Christ is one, with some to be hand, or the body, or the head, or the foot etc. This not only refers to the different activities of the body, but it refers to the body of

Christ, which is the Church itself. The Church is already one. Jesus' prayer in the upper room was already answered. You are either in the body of the Church or not and the qualifying criteria is, "For as many of you as were baptized into Christ have put on Christ. There is neither Jew nor Greek, there is neither slave nor free, there is neither male nor female; **for you are all one in Christ Jesus.**" Yes, the Churches may be different with their differing emphases, as in Revelation Chapter 2 and 3, but the important issue is that the correct doctrines and beliefs are held; not that people get together, so they can look like they are unified - that is not God's way. There's no point unifying each other! It doesn't work... if you believe the same thing then that's great, Catholic, Pentecostal and Anglican can all worship together; it's the world which somehow wants some building with 'we are Christians' on it. God has done amazing things when different denominations do come together, so ecumenical meetings can work, but it has to come from God, and not be forced from 'religious political leaders' and especially not from the CFR and UN leaders who are Luciferians.

Long-Range Strategy

Their long-term strategy for ecumenism is for the Roman Catholics to try and force the Protestants to merge with them. Perhaps each side will compromise on some of their doctrinal beliefs. The Catholics may move to being a little more Bible-based, and the Protestants may move to being more conciliatory to their history and their treatment of Mary. After 500 years since the Reformation in 1517, perhaps it will be a kind of repenting and making up between the two groups. This is the direction they will go in, and they will make it extremely appealing to everyone. Those who oppose it, will no doubt be branded as fundamentalists.

Once the Catholics and the main Protestant denominations, such as the Anglicans have merged, then they will try to forge all the other religions together. We are already seeing from the activities of the Pope, Rick Warren and Kenneth Copeland that this is the direction they are going in. To sell us the **'deep ecumenism concept'** resulting in the merger of Evangelical denominations with mainstream Protestant groups and then eventually into Catholicism. Once this is done they will try and form 'Chrislam' – the bolting together of Islam and Christianity. Other religions such as Hinduism and Buddhism will readily be forged into the mould and later on, the New Age religion and Atheism which are easy to deal with. All these beliefs will form the New Apostate One World Universal Church. They will sell it as being an attractive alternative to the violence of the past and the duty of good planetary citizens. There is plenty of evidence from New Age writings that those who stand against it will be removed forcibly.

How will they do this? **Interfaith meetings** such as United Religions Initiative (URI) will merge the religions together via the slow gradualist approach and education over the next 60 years or so. With this in mind it does seem that URI leaders are unwittingly building the foundation for a syncretic belief system. A list of these Interfaith meetings is provided in the 'Chronology of the New World Religion' in the Appendix.

United Religions Initiative (URI)- the strategy

The United Religions Initiative is a global interfaith movement seeking to find common ground between all the World's Religions. The movement was an outgrowth from the Parliament of World Religions started in 1893.

United Religions Initiative (URI) was started in 1995 by Bishop William Swing of the Episcopal church diocese of California. "The URI, in time, aspires to have the visibility and stature of the United Nations." [218] In fact, the URI was promoted by the UN in 1993 after Gillian Sorensen (CFR member) and the deputy secretary of the UN invited Bishop Swing to hold an interfaith service at Grace Cathedral in 1995 to celebrate the 50th Anniversary of the signing of the UN Charter. He then travelled all over the world via UN headquarters seeking to make relationships with religious leaders and interfaith activists. Talks with these leaders were not very successful and so it

---

[218] Quoted from the *United Religions Initiative Charter*. Lee Penn, *False Dawn*, page 35.

was concluded that the best way to initiate and influence this interfaith dialogue would <u>not</u> be to start with the leaders, but to try and make URI a 'grassroots movement'.[219] Over the years up until the turn of the millennium, Bishop Swing along with Dee Hock and 14 others put together the 'United Religions Charter' that its religious members would sign, establishing a working relationship with other interfaith organisations. From here they started to create the global network that is URI.

This is how they describe themselves from the URI.org website.

'Purpose

The purpose of the United Religions Initiative is to promote enduring, daily interfaith cooperation, to end religiously motivated violence and to create cultures of peace, justice and **healing for the Earth and all living beings.**

Vision

URI envisions a world at peace, sustained by engaged and interconnected communities committed to respect for diversity, nonviolent resolution of conflict and social, political, economic and environmental justice.

Mission

URI is a global **grassroots interfaith network** that cultivates peace and justice by engaging people to bridge religious and cultural differences and work together for the good of their communities and the world.

We implement our mission through local and global initiatives that build the capacity of our more than 883 member groups and organizations, called Cooperation Circles, to engage in community action such as conflict resolution and reconciliation, environmental sustainability, education, women's and youth programs, and advocacy for human rights.'

Emphasis mine. The comment 'healing for the Earth and all living beings' puts the purpose in line with the 'green agenda' and certainly

---

[219] Bishop William Swing, *The Coming United Religions*, CoNexus Press, page 14,15. Quote from page 15 Bishop Swing: 'The overwhelming realization for me was that if there were ever to be a United Religions, the impetus would NOT come initially from religious leaders.'

URI has also deliberately aligned itself with Sustainable Development, Climate Change and Agenda 21. In fact, they even described the 'Guidelines for Action' in the URI Charter, as a 'Spiritual Agenda 21'.

The URI is part of the effort to shape a new world order with the new world religion in anticipation of Agenda 21. How **grassroots** can this be when it's so obviously conceived, assisted, and funded by the UN? URI has also been funded by the Bill and Melinda Gates Foundation, the Soros Foundation, and the Theosophically linked groups such as the Lucis Trust, the Rudolf Steiner Foundation (founder of Anthroposophy) and the Tara Centre (of Share International and Benjamin Crème) amongst others.[220] However, since the URI is a mandated, supported movement of the United Nations it doesn't really make it grassroots does it?

In January 2001 Robert Muller told Bishop Swing that **"URI will go very, very far, even beyond the United Nations."** There are two ways of taking that comment by Robert Muller, the Under-Secretary General at the UN. It can either be taken as an overstatement that the URI is very important and he was being kind to Bishop Swing to encourage him; or it can be taken at face value, that in the future the United Religions Initiative will indeed survive and go 'beyond the United Nations'. The United Nations and may well dissolve, to be replaced by the 'Earth Trust', or some such similar New Age pseudonym, but the common ground religion of URI would remain. Certainly, Alice Bailey referred to the amalgamation of all religions to form the 'One Universal Church.'

Deep Ecumenism

The United Religions Initiative attempts to find, 'Common Ground' as a unifying principle. This is partly looking at the religions of the world and deciding which elements overlap, a bit like a Venn diagram. The obvious example is that Christianity, Judaism and Islam all meet at Abraham – he is a prophet of all of these religions, so

---

[220] Lee Penn, False Dawn, page 60 and 61.

perhaps some sort of interfaith activity could grow out of this common ground.

As Bishop Swing said: *'Everyone will be invited to bring their best, richest, deepest stories to the common ground. And there we will build.'* [221]

The main concept is one of a wider and more inclusive set of global beliefs where the emphasis will be putting the diverse religions and gods on an equal footing. *'{URI}... does not depend on reaching a consensus of vision as much as it aims to create an ever widening, more inclusive set of global visions and relationships that enliven local action on behalf of the emerging United Religions. As such, it responds to the challenge of creating a transboundary organization in the postmodern world where imposing a single vision can only lead to failure.'* [222] 'Only later would the **'more inclusive set of global visions'** evolve to what Bishop Swing calls a 'common purpose' for all religions and spiritual movements'.

To this end the movement has opened up many 'Cooperation Circles', which are decentralized networks of people who meet 'to discuss their religion and find common ground or simply meet to make friends and have some fellowship together.' The UN committee on Spiritual Values Global Concerns (CSVGV) are also aiming for the same thing, a syncretic religion which is authorised by the UN.[223] In 2007 URI was granted consultative status at the UN.

The United Religions Initiative also uses the writings of mystics to justify their concepts, such as Meister Eckhart who speaks of God as being 'a great underground river'.[224] For a more modern commentator, this is what Matthew Fox (Theosophist/ New Ager) calls 'deep ecumenism'. He writes:-

There is no such thing as a Jewish ocean and the Lutheran sun and a Buddhist River and Taoist forest and a Roman Catholic cornfield. Once you move to the level of creation, you're into an era of deep ecumenism, and I think **for mother earth to survive** *we need this awakening of wisdom from all world religions, and not just the five thousand-year-old patriarchal ones, but the*

---

[221] Bishop Swing. Message for all the People. Quoted from Lee Pen, *False Dawn*, page 190.

[222] Gurudev Khalsa, quoted in Lee Penn, ibid page 203.

[223] Spiritual Values Global Concerns (CSVGV) see http://csvgc-ny.org/

[224] Barnhart Bruno quoted in Lee Penn, *False Dawn*, page 192.

goddess religions, the religions of the native peoples of America, Africa, and Asia, and ***I think this and this alone is going to awaken the human race – this combination of mystical wisdom – to its own salvation..... God works through all religions****, and that's why we have to draw for the wisdom of all religions today,* **to recover our own divinity***.... Eckhart says God is a great underground river. So we come to the stuffy well and the Buddhist well and the Catholic and Protestant, but they sink into one deep underground river. There is only one divine source of all this wisdom, you see.'* [225]

At the heart of the New World religion is the belief, according to this statement, that the mother earth can impart some sort of salvation which will enable us to **recover our own divinity**. This is exactly the concept contained in Genesis, that Adam and Eve would have the knowledge of the tree of good and evil and **become like Gods,** recovering their own divinity. And yet here we have a well-known author and supposed Christian Episcopal Minister, explaining this belief. It's pure Luciferianism! What did the Serpent say in the garden? 'For God doth know that in the day ye eat thereof, then your eyes shall be opened, and **ye shall be as gods**, knowing good and evil.' Genesis 3:5. Not surprising therefore to see that Matthew Fox was expelled as a Roman Catholic Priest for disobedience to the Church. Later he was brought into the fold by Bishop Swing. Some call him the second Teilhard De Chardin. It's interesting to note that Adam and Eve ate the fruit of the tree - something that mother earth produced, but **something that God created.**

What they think the problem is

The problem, they think, is fundamentalism, and this is why there is so much Islamic Fundamentalism in the world today ('Bad Islam'). <u>**Very little gets through into the mainstream as a grassroots movement which is not from the Cryptocracy via Governments**</u>

---

[225] Matthew Fox expounded Creation Spirituality, Intuition Network, from 'Thinking Allowed: Conversations On The Leading Edge of Knowledge and Discovery'; book by Dr. Jeffrey Mishlove.

or the UN. In other words, if the Elite wanted something to exist in the mainstream domain, then it does. But if they do not want something to be in the mainstream domain, it isn't present. There's very little in the way of music, culture, religion, TV, films and radio etc that is disseminated to the public without having had the filter of political correctness and State sanctioned authority applied. The belief that one religion is the truth, and that a belief can be THE TRUTH is a serious problem for them. Firstly, they are concerned about the friction and 'violence' that any religious belief has, according to them. In their worldview, religions have caused all the harm, the wars of the last hundred years and divided humanity against itself. The truth is that it has not been any religion that has caused these wars it has been them – the unwanted, unjustifiable destruction by the Elite, Secret Bankers, Freemasons, the Illuminati, the Knights of Malta and the high-ranking insiders such as Skull and Bones and Bohemian Grove. You could say it is rather naïve to think that religion is uniquely prone to generate slaughter and violent persecution; whilst it is far more likely to be just one, among a number of factors, including race, political persuasion, social class, language or nationality. It was these issues and not religion that produced the wars of the last century. World War I and II were fought predominantly by Christians, against Christians. Indeed, many wars in history have had nothing to do with group hatreds or religion but have been more to do with the desire for territory, power and the theft of resources - plunder. The belief that if we removed religion we can somehow remove the main goals of human conflict is clearly incorrect. Perhaps they can't see that though because Religion has actually been calculated to be the primary cause of about 7% of the wars in recorded history, of which a high percentage involved Islam.[226]

---

[226] Day V, *The Irrational Atheist*. Dallas: Bella books Inc. page 105.

War on Terror - a State Hoax

This is why we have the deep-state movement of Islamic Fundamentalism today. 9/11 was the official starting point for the War on Terror, although, as we have seen, 9/11 was actually a False Flag conducted by the Cryptocracy to blame the Muslims and make them the new enemy. It is well documented that Al Qaeda and ISIS are US projects funded and armed by the deep state to effect the changes the Cryptocracy desire. It's also another **State hoax** to push the agenda of Religiously motivated violence, to create 'Religion against Religion' as a new Crusade – the clash of civilisations. **The Synthesis of these two sides of the Hegelian dialect will be the new earth worship Religion.** This is why they are pushing this psyop agenda of unity through the New World spirituality. On the one side we have religious violence, and on the other, a call to unity. If they are NOT highlighting the differences how can they get the synthesis? To get to this point they have to set the Religions against each other. This is why we have the concept of Islamic Fundamentalism today. They keep on exposing us to 'Bad' Islam, and if there aren't enough terrorist events going on, they make them up with their hoaxes or set ups, which is when they knowingly aid a patsy to carry out an event. In this manner eventually, it will become so bad, that 'Bad' Islam will be destroyed enabling 'Good' Islam to merge with Christianity. This would form the talked about 'Chrislam'.

Truth unknowable, orthodox beliefs not welcome

The world's citizens are therefore being exposed to the concepts that there is no knowable truth and that not one group can make that claim. In this manner the agenda, coupled with a perverted new set of immoral beliefs, will lead to the evil light of the pure doctrine of Lucifer being brought into the open.

Fundamentalism as a belief (or Orthodoxy, which is when the doctrines and dogmas of Christianity, for example, are taken seriously), is therefore something they cannot tolerate. The problem is that truth is actually absolute, and if you know something to be true you can't just brush it under the carpet. Perhaps they would be better off thinking in terms of actions which have been created by fundamentalism. Perhaps they should aim for allowing people to believe whatever they want, as long as they're not blowing people up! William Rankin, a trustee of the United Religions Initiative, in 1988 wrote, 'The United Religions initiative exists to bring people together from all the religions of the world, to create a world where no one has to die because of God, or for God, anymore.'[227]

Secondly, as mentioned earlier, the aims of the elite is to create a more general mass of pliable, ill-educated people, who don't believe anything, don't know much, and can be moulded according to their will - not putting up a fuss about their lives. In order to achieve this 'diluting' they seek to replace any belief with anything non-moral, Pantheistic or ideally Luciferian, and therefore they seek to use Education as a tool to subvert the traditions from the past. Are we not seeing this everywhere in Society today?

Education

If you are struggling to believe that there is a link between the New World Religion and education, it was Robert Muller who they used to call the Philosopher of the United Nations, who created the 'World Core Curriculum' and as a result he received the UNESCO prize for peace and education. These educational ideas were meant to be incorporated into schools throughout the world. He was a believer in the one world government and said: *'we must move as quickly as possible to a one world government; a one world religion; under a one world leader.'*[228]

He also said *'peace will be impossible without the taming of fundamentalism through United Religions that professes faithfulness only to the **global spirituality and to the health of this planet.'*** This is from a high-ranking member of the UN, Robert Muller, the belief that a One

---

[227] William Rankin made at Claremont School of Theology 9/10/89 quoted by Lee Penn, *False Dawn* page 215.

[228] Not to be confused with Republican, ex FBI Director, Robert Mueller.

World Religion should emerge with a one world government and a one world religion. Part of this also is the belief in the earth and the planet being above man, a great excuse to gain power. He went on to say *'my great personal dream is to get a tremendous alliance between all the major religions and the UN.'*

URI is not a Religion - so they claim!

Bishop Swing and others have specifically stated that URI is not creating a religion. However, there are many indications that that is precisely what they are doing via making religious ceremonies and distilling religious beliefs into a form which everyone can accept – this is a new form of religion - the religion acceptable to Agenda 21 and the New World Order. Alice Bailey called for the creation of the **One Universal Church** and so we can imagine URI becoming a sort of the coalescence of all the world's religions into a type of watered down smorgasbord in which beliefs can be picked and chosen at will.

Bishop Swing describes a new spiritual unity that will emerge via their interfaith meetings. 'In the United Religions: (a) *Silent respect would be rendered to every religion as each pursues it's sacred path.* b) *That Which Binds Us Is Beyond Us.* As each religion renders silent respect to other religions, the rising mutual sympathy will lead to the discovery of a **unifying mystery**. c) *That Which Is Beyond Us Will Bind Us.* The **unifying mystery** that will be discovered will persuade religions of an ever-increasing kinship with each other and all life.'[229]

It's not explained what the 'unifying mystery' that 'will bind us' is, but I suppose it's not unreasonable to think this might be something as basic as, 'we are human' or, 'there is a god,' but we do not know. In the next sentence but one he further writes: 'The time comes, though, when a common language and a common purpose for all religions and spiritual movements must be discerned and agreed upon.' Could this be a shared god, or the development of their version of State authorised religion? In an interview in 2004 Bishop Swing stated that '... *all of us have learned our religion in tribal settings, and*

---

[229] W Swing, *The Coming Religions*, page 63.

the day is coming quickly when we're going to have to understand our religion in global terms.... That is going to cause a radical form for every religion and in all theological thinking. ... Therefore, a lot of the work we're doing right now is pioneering for the next religious explosion.' [230]

Most of the growth of URI via the cooperation circles has actually been in the Third World and its relevance to western culture still has not permeated the mainstream. But the fact that it is a fully mandated and supported group of the UN with a Trustees of one the most important CFR members, George Shultz, just shows how vitally important they believe URI is. [231]

Criticisms of URI

There is a major flaw with this type of syncretic religion. For people to hold beliefs in religions, they need to be acceptable as being the truth. If your beliefs are not held to be the truth, but one amongst many, you are in effect being a type of spiritual adulterer. For some this may be acceptable, but for others this issue will be unsurmountable and unworkable. You can't have a multi-faith religion in which everyone has the truth, and everyone has equal say. The Truth by definition is exclusive.

The other major flaw with this 'sacred ground religion' is that it would mean that the State would effectively be above the religion. Whereas any true belief will always have the state below religion. In other words, for a true belief to flourish it has to fulfil all the higher aspects of the human condition, as well as the here and now, with life's successes and failures, suffering and disasters. Yet the New World Religion by mixing all the beliefs together would simply become another form of state enforcement. This cannot work because it is the belief in God which legitimizes the moral aspects of the social order, and not the belief in the State. **The Divine has to stand outside and above the State to be a true faith.**

---

[230] Delman Interview with Swing. PCN online Feb/March 2004 quoted from Penn page 191.

[231] George Shultz – Trustees of URI https://uri.org/books/bishops-quest

Encountering God is the truest point of existence and must be above everything else, or not be God.

But then, in the final analysis, the New World Religion will never have a fixed doctrine but be quite variable, and, as with so many things to do with the New World Order, it's really yet another complicated diversion from the even more sinister agenda they have in mind. The exoteric hidden agenda behind uniting the world's religions is to enable the people of the world to accept the UN's dictates on human rights, population control and the one world government. We are already heading in this direction. The esoteric reason for the New World Religion will be for mankind to eventually worship the Cryptocracy, and their Anti-Christ Saviour, and so worship Satan, and enjoy doing this without even knowing they are doing it. So, the New World Order is not just about the coming world police state, but the arrival of the coming spirituality.

If we are to believe the writings of Albert Pike, he said it would be the revealing of the 'pure Luciferian doctrine' in his letter to Mazzini.

Alice Bailey says the New World Religion would be a type of Freemasonry. *"The old established rhythms (religions) must give place to the newer ideas."* [232] *"A new RACE, a new culture and a new World outlook."* [233]

Madame Blavatsky said the New World Order Religion would be *'...the religion of the ancients is the religion of the future. A few centuries more, and there will linger no sectarian beliefs in either of the great religions of humanity. Brahmanism* [i.e. Hinduism] *and Buddhism, Christianity and Mahometanism* [i.e. Islam] **will all disappear before the mighty rush of FACTS.** *But this can only come to pass when the world returns to the grand religion of the past; the knowledge of those majestic systems which preceded, by far, Brahmanism, and even the primitive monotheism of the ancient Chaldeans."* [234] Emphasis in bold mine.

This is the Prisca Theologia explained in Chapter 2. The belief that in the past there was a wonderful truth which has become unknown, but as we know this really refers back to Garden of Eden and the Proto-Evangelium.

---

[232] A Bailey, *Esoteric Psychology*, The New World Religion, page 269.

[233] A Bailey, page 37, *The New Group of World Servers*.

[234] H.P. Blavatsky, *Isis Unveiled*, Vol. 1, p. 613.

It would come somehow from a Spirit of Inclusiveness whereby all people would realise all religions come from the same source. It would be a return to the ancient occult nature religion. **Robert Muller said that the UN is not a man-made creation but primarily a spiritual organization with a spiritual source.** The Bible says that any spirit which does not acknowledge that Jesus Christ is Lord is from the anti-Christ.[235] This is what anti-Christ means, instead of Christ Jesus, and so the spiritual source of the New World Religion, by definition, will be from Satan.

Conclusion

United Religions Initiative pretends that, through its activities, it is only creating dialogue leading to peaceful co-existence and unity, and not creating a world religion. But how easy would it be for the UN or another group to take it over and use it as their own organisation for their own nefarious purposes? It would not be the first time that a 'political group' had been set up, that was later distorted into another institution. For example, the European Union was originally set up as a trading block whereas all along it was intended to be political union, the evidence goes all the way back to its founding. The single European currency was also mentioned as a goal by the Bilderberg group back in the 1950s and among the Elite there was never any doubt (from their writings) even from before its inception that it would be anything but the **dictatorial super-state it is today**. In this respect, URI is almost certainly just a front waiting to be used by the Cryptocracy in order to bring in the control mechanism that will be the New World State Authorised Luciferian Religion; and from this enable the acceptance of the Anti-Christ and False Prophet.

There will firstly be a global spiritual body speaking for all the religions. United Religions Initiative will probably be that body, but this is not the only method by which the New World religion will

---

[235] 1 John 4:2 and 3. By this you will know the Spirit of God: Every spirit that confesses that Jesus Christ has come in the flesh is from God, and every spirit that does not confess Jesus is not from God. This is the spirit of the antichrist, which you have heard is coming, and is already in the world at this time.

emerge. The New Age religion itself, with its hundreds of different groups, are also helping to usher this in. It will probably emerge at a time when humanity is under terrible pressure from a regional war and general upheaval. This is what the Bible says, that when Peace is announced then we know the end is near. (1 Thessalonians 5:3.)

CHAPTER 13

WHAT WILL THE NEW RELIGION LOOK LIKE?

The Core Beliefs of the New World Religion

The central core belief of the New World religion will be a type of environmental Pantheism. In order to create their 'sustainable society', living within its ecological constraints the new religion will be grounded within an ecological-evolutionary worldview. At the moment the URI is laying the ground for the **new unified religion of the 'Sacred Earth.'** The statements made by their leaders, their rituals, and the symbols they use in their ceremonies and worship services demonstrate this undeniable syncretism in action. A non-transcendent new revelation from the earth will enable humanity to move forward in the spirit of our time. For some URI activists such as New Agers and Theosophists this is the intended result - whilst other URI leaders will deny that charge, which means they are therefore unwittingly building the foundation for this synchronistic religion. *"Everyone will be invited to bring their best, richest, deepest stories to the common ground. And there we will build."* [236]

At the core and heart of the syncretic faith will be the concept of the 'Sacred Earth.' At St John the Divine Church, James Parks

---

[236] Bishop Swing, *A message for all the people*, article. Page 190 Lee Penn, False Dawn.

Morton, a URI supporter and founder of the Interfaith Center of New York said: 'The language of the 'Sacred Earth' has to become mainline.' [237] This will be the central unifying belief, and surrounding it will be the State Authorised versions of Christianity, Islam and other faiths which will be slowly morphed over generations into the New Religion. The Cryptocrats wish to control the people by making us 'worship' the earth and treating it with due reverence. It will therefore be a type of pantheism which teaches that everything is alive and connected. The belief that the Mother Earth needs to be protected more than man, in order for man to survive. This concept has been woven into most of the larger inter-faith meetings initiatives and organisations.

This is precisely the same concept which fits in with Agenda 21, which is a political agenda masked within an environmental agenda. The conclusion of which is a New Earth control Religion which will lead eventually to open Luciferianism.

Mother Earth worship

The god at the heart of the New World religion will be the Mother Earth goddess and from this a certain 'greenness' will emanate from this fake belief. It is the opposite of the Genesis account that man should use the Earth to sustain his life, and not abuse it to his own glory. It will either be presented as a metaphor, for those who don't want to believe in a theistic manner, or as the true Spirit Goddess for those who prefer a more theistic traditional approach. This type of belief has its root in the modern interpretation of older pagan religions. It is most succinctly phrased by the term 'Dark Green Religion' which itself are the poetic expressions on the writings of Theosophists, Evolutionists and Animists.

---

[237] Quote from Lee Penn, *False Dawn*, page 38.

Background to the New World Religion's Central Core Belief: Dark Green Religion

Ever since it was decided for the Environment to be the unifying principle that the Economy, Politics and Religion can be 'bolted together' with, it has been necessary to 'beat the environmentalist drum'. The Club of Rome and later the Wilderness Conferences via their think-tanks brought this concept to the Elite's notice and so over the last few decades, since around 1980, we have had an enormous increase in the number of books and films declaring that Man is ruining his Environment and destroying the eco-system. Books such as: The Fate of the Earth (Jonathan Schell, 1982); The Dream of the Earth (Thomas Berry, 1988); The Crisis of Life on Earth (Tim Radford, 1990); Earth in the Balance (Al Gore, 1993); The Sacred Balance (David Suzuki, 1997); and Five Holocausts (Derek Wilson, 2001) all have these themes in. These books have been contributory to the Anthropomorphic Man-Made carbon emissions and global warming hoax which we have been subjected to from about 1985.

Carbon dioxide

The United Nations is behind the Climate Change scare and have used bent, corrupt, Scientists to tell us that **carbon dioxide** is affecting global temperatures. But not only is their science completely false, but the conspirators themselves have even admitted that everything they have been doing is completely false! For example, Christina Figueres admitted that climate change was not about the weather but about destroying western capitalism and creating the new economy. The International Panel on Climate Change (IPCC) have, in the end, been forced to essentially say that carbon dioxide has no affected on the climate. But that it is human activity, since CO2 has no impact on temperature. Overall the UN have created a completely false climate debate. [238]

Also there is the 'Climategate' leak, where thousands of emails were hacked and made publicly available which proved without any shadow of doubt that the message was fake and the Scientists themselves were having to doctor all the data to make it fit in with their new world controllers. [239]

---

[238] The evidence is all over the Internet but you have to look several pages into the Search Engines results. https://www.armstrongeconomics.com/world-news/climate/global-warming-is-about-destroying-capitalism/

IPCC website for research of the conspirators' bogus science is http://www.ipcc.ch/index.htm

[239] We all want to live in a pollution free world and protect the environment. It is just that this highly politicised and false meme is being used unfairly as a lever to create a bogus economy based on 'sustainable development'. Having popularised unstainable life styles this concept is being used to make us feel bad about our standard of living and even worse about questioning this scientific fraud, which is really a power grab by the Elite to bring us into their kingdom. It is not the role of this book to argue the science, this has been proven conclusively by many proper scientists who are not interested in 'consensus' but true science. As a psychological warfare counter offensive, every time you hear or read of the phrase 'Climate Change' you should replace it with the word 'Genocide' because this is what the conspirators really mean. For example, when you hear about the devastating consequences of climate change and how it will wipe out humanity you should translate that as being the devastating effects of their genocide, because this is what their agenda really is. Perverse perhaps, but you will be closer to the truth than believing their outrageous mythology on 'carbon credits' or 'carbon footprints'. This is a semantic deception anyway since Carbon Dioxide is CO_2 and not just carbon, but they make us use terms such as 'Carbon emissions' because the word carbon makes a link in the mind to something sooty and messy which is from the industrial-coal-fuelled past. And that in the future we need to do away with this - it's all part of the deception! CO_2 only makes up 0.041% of the atmosphere which makes it a trace gas – and it's not like cyanide or arsenic, but a harmless gas vital for life. (Have you ever considered the possibility that any climate change is being made by the Cryptocracy anyway? And where are the polar bears Al Gore said would be invading Canada?)

Dark Green Religion

But just to lay the ground work on the stream of beliefs at the centre of this utilitarian creed and where the modern environmental movement derives it doctrinal beliefs, we will go back a bit further still.

Ralph, (Waldo) Emmerson (1803-1882) was probably the first true exponent of nature-related spiritualties writing 'Nature' in 1836. He was perhaps the first person to recognize the ecological spiritual construct in which man and animals are connected to the earth and that via the simple undomesticated life one can see meaning imbued within a type of innate earth wisdom that can be experienced through nature and in being in nature. Beliefs that nature is alive and can somehow teach us something. Henry David Thoreau is another Transcendentalist writer who wrote very soon after the publication of the Origin of Species in 1859 and expressed the beliefs which Sociologist, Bron Taylor and others have identified as 'Dark Green Religion.' Dark, because it refers to the belief that nature has an inbuilt sacredness and is alive with the godhood. Green because it is flowing from a deep sense of belonging to the connectedness of nature. Here, Man is simply another creature belonging in nature and is a product of evolution. And so this is the new form of civic religion we are seeing today. Thoreau was really a pantheist believing that all creation is alive and connected and he also held animistic beliefs that there was a spiritual element to everything that exists.

These beliefs contributed to those of John Muir, the Scottish US, author and philosopher who advocated for the creation and preservation of National Parks and Yosemite in particular.

These concepts were further elaborated and expanded by Aldo Leopold after WWII. With his 'eye to eye conversion' when as a young man in the Sierra Nevada, he killed a wolf and whilst looking into the green eyes of the dieing animal felt an awesome sense that the wolf and mountain didn't agree with what he had done. He was another important writer of the green religion which leads into the beliefs of the central element of the New World Religion. [240]

These concepts were heavily sold to us in the film Avatar, where the local inhabitant tribe of the Navi could directly plug into Earth Mother who was called Eywa. Some decoding shows how subtle their programming is. Via the world tree 'natural' hive network, they could feel the entirety of their natural surroundings and hence feel the interconnection of all things. This is almost precisely how the future state could possibly be - interconnected to the central State hub. The obscure connections to the Bible are present. In the film Avatar, the word for their Earth Mother, is Eywa which is an anagram of the divine name Yahweh, having the same root from the Hebrew verb, to be, as explained in Chapter 8. Ewya has become the world tree in place of Jesus being on the world tree, crucified. In addition to this, their tribal name was Navi, which is the Hebrew word for prophet. So their religion was one of a centralised environmentally-connected-consciousness where they all lived as one with nature. A shadow of the future hive network?

Gaian Animism

The beliefs or themes that all these creeds have in common are that:-

Nature is alive and can somehow teach us something. Nature contains some sort of ancient wisdom which can be imparted by exposure to the great outdoors and enjoyment of the mountains, hills and forests etc. This is Animism – where everything is alive and imbued with spiritual powers. In a way it's the old science of man supposedly linked to his survival as he emerged from the forests and savannahs in the past.

Nature spirituality where nature is sacred and connected in the Circle of Life.[241] These ideas are further expanded by more modern

---

[240] For a review of Dark Green Religion a good starting point is Bron Taylor, *Dark Green Religion, Nature Spirituality and the Planetary Future.* He is a Sociologist and a promoter of this.

[241] Circle of Life song from the film, *The Lion King*, 1994.

writers such as James Lovelock with his 'Gaia Principle' where the belief in the Earth as more than just a metaphor meant that the earth was alive and able to take revenge on humanity.

'Theistic' New World Religion

Interwoven within the New World religion will be the belief that it doesn't particularly matter how strongly you hold these beliefs because the doctrines will be quite changeable, so it will allow some people to believe on a metaphorical level and enable others to believe on a purer, spiritual level. In other words it can be a non-religion to some whilst being a serious doctrinal religion to others.

The true indoctrinated hardcore new religionists will believe that the Earth is fully in control of their life and that all things that happen to them and what they do, how and where they live and what they eat, drink and breathe will be a prayer to the entity that is Gaia, the Mother Goddess. This orthodoxy will be expressed in ceremonies to do with water, soil, which is where the living and the dead meet, and the air. This will be infused with some serious 'Planetary Citizen nationalism', wild nationalism, and earth nationalism. The belief that we must live our lives to glorify the Earth since the interconnected living Earth is the generator and creator of everything that we have. This is part of how they will get rid of Nationalism, to grey out society and then make us Global Citizens.

Multi-faith Ceremonies

At the moment we have seen a number of multi-faith meetings in which various Ministers read a section out of their religion's book, or they play some music, or even do a dance. The concepts of water, soil, fire and air have been present in their meetings. Also walking the labyrinth as a type of meditational activity has been popular because anyone from any religion can do this.[242]

Christianity is drawn into the green abyss.

How are they bringing Christianity into the New World Religion?

Through the activities of URI and the plethora of other conferences and subtle manipulations they are attempting to bring all Christians into the one denomination or directly into the new world religion. The current Pope, Francis is a willing and able puppet of the New World Order although probably unwittingly. Kenneth Copeland and Rick Warren are CFR members which makes them insiders near the top of the pyramid. They would not be there if they were not working for the Elite in taking their denominations in the direction the Elite wanted them. The fact that they are members of the CFR is a give-away! They may be well meaning, but the illusionists use their skills to get what they want, even if the people involved do not understand what is really going on. This is because they cannot see the overall agenda. Their long-range plan is to bring all the Christian denominations together. Once this is completed, Interfaith groups will be coalesced further into one easy to manage group. Eventually this earth worship religion will lead to open Luciferianism, which is the true desire of the Cryptocracy.

Going Green

Christianity has recently felt the need to become more 'Green', and ecologically in line with Humanist secular beliefs. Christian leaders

---

[242] Labyrinth concept see
https://www.catholicculture.org/culture/library/view.cfm?recnum=3440.

have elevated the idea that environmental stewardship and looking after the planet go hand in hand with Christian beliefs. Pope Francis in recent years has been 'beating the environmentalist drum' and in his 2016 Encyclical even made the claim that it was the biggest threat to our existence. The emphasis that has been placed on this issue is an indication of how much the Church has succumbed to the 'green agenda.'

In the first chapter of Genesis, God says that Man is to have dominion over the Earth, but this was prior to the Fall. Later on, God says Man is to 'fill the earth' which is a euphemism to populate the Earth. The Biblical idea of stewardship is certainly there but Christianity seems to have become under attack from the Secular world that somehow it has caused, or at least exacerbated, the ecological problem with God's call that Man could and should 'dominate' his environment. "Be fruitful and multiply, and fill the earth and **subdue** it, **have dominion over** the fish of the sea, and over the birds of the air and over every living thing that moves on the earth." Genesis 1:28. The word subdue and 'have dominion over' cannot be translated in any other way - it is what the Hebrew says. This has been ammunition to the New Agers, Occultists and Humanists, that Christianity is the root cause of the environmental problems there are today, and this has given grist to the environmental movement. The mistake they make is not taking into account who, and what, really is the cause of these problems.

The belief that the Earth should foremost be viewed as being **Sacred** and not separate from God is Pantheism. The Biblical criticism of these Pantheistic beliefs is brilliantly covered by St Paul in Romans Chapter 1. Here it is explained that you should not worship the created but the creator (verse 25). They exchanged the truth about God for a lie and worshiped and served created things rather than the Creator. This succinctly covers off the Christian view point on this important issue.

For since the creation of the world God's invisible qualities—his eternal power and divine nature—have been clearly seen, being understood from what has been made, so that people are without excuse. For although they knew God, they neither glorified him as God nor gave thanks to him...

Throughout the Old Testament the Israelites were an agricultural people and many of their festivals and religious practices were related to seasonal and agricultural events. But the Cryptocracy like to promote Pantheism since it fits in better with their Emanationist beliefs. In addition, they have to get rid of Christianity since it one of the stumbling blocks to the fulfilment of their Great Plan.

Methods of bringing Islam into the New World Religion and Chrislam

Part of the dialectic will also be to bring Islam and Christianity together. The strategy here is to find the common ground and through education and subtle indoctrination pacify both religions so they can join in inter-faith meetings and not be a threat to the Cryptocracy. This is why we have the promotion of 'Good Islam' which is the mainstream version of Islam which teaches that Islam is non-violent and non-threatening, so it can be made more palatable for western society. On the other hand, we have 'Bad Islam,' which as mentioned, is part of the dialectic to highlight the problems of fundamental Islam and link this to fundamentalists of ANY religious persuasion. This enables them to subdue believers across all religions, as it makes us believe that we best not hold dear anything too strongly because we may be branded as a fundamentalist. In the end this makes everyone more pliable and willing to conform to the deep psychological programming that the Cryptocracy promote. Whenever debates on 'fundamentalism' crop up, it is mostly Islam that is used to win the argument that orthodox or traditional beliefs are bad. If traditional beliefs are bad it breaks the believer down making them more susceptible to the wiles of the Cryptocracy.

As is normal for the Cryptocracy they use a number of different methods with multiple agendas in order to create their goals. On a political level, most of the Middle East, like the rest of the world, has signed into the UN Ecological Sustainable Development Goals (SDGs). This will slowly enable them to infiltrate their ranks and make policy changes as they want. In addition to the Good / Bad Islam agenda, the green agenda is again their method.

If you are doubting whether Islam can be unified into the New World Order religion consider that Islam is far 'greener' in its cosmology than Christianity, and man's position in the world is far less anthropocentric (man centred) than Christianity. In Islam, man is **not** the centre of the creation. Quran 40:57 'The creation of the heavens and the earth is greater than the creation of mankind, but most of the people do not know.' And 'Whoever plants a tree and diligently looks after it until it matures and bears fruit is rewarded.' 'If a Muslim plants a tree or sows a field and men and beasts and birds eat from it, all of it is charity on his part.' 'Whoever brings dead land to life, that is, cultivates wasteland, for him is a reward therein.'

It is no accident that they have chosen Islam as their religion of choice for the amalgamation of all the world's faiths. Islam could well be the most difficult religion for them to subdue and 'break' into their conformity, but eventually they will succeed. It may be difficult to see that now, but the Cryptocracy always get what they want. Either by mass genocide, making laws, or social conformity programs, they always eventually succeed in their plans even if it takes them many decades and generations.

The New World Religion and Sustainable Development fit hand in glove

The realization that man owes his life and all his food, air and water to the Earth is central to the New World Religion and heavily included within the Agenda 21 writings. All of man's needs come from Her and so we should be good 'planetary citizens' since we live for the 'good of the planet'. These sorts of mantras will be used as an excuse to micro-manage every aspect of our lives, which will make it an economically and environmentally viable belief, and extremely utilitarian. In the New World Order, you will have to be a good planetary Citizen. **If you are a polluter you will be punished.** People who are 'fundamentalists' will also eventually be legislated against. In fact, URI has no room for any type of absolute belief – absolute beliefs will be discouraged. In the future, it seems likely any certainty of belief will be legislated against. It will be treated as a type of violence and probably made illegal. It will be close to thought crime and 'intent'.

Result of New World Religion

The new religion will be a means whereby the Elite enforce their laws. This is why Robert Muller said that URI would be bigger and last longer than the United Nations. When the New World Order does eventually come out from the shadows, and the technocratic economy is enforced, it will be the new global ethos and this New World Religion which will underpin the entire system. You can't create a new society without a new creed! This is why what we see happening today is happening! It is slowly being rolled out in subtle ways. It will give the Controllers the Control they desire, and the Environment will be their 'excuse' allowing them to do anything they want by citing that **the Earth needs protecting and is above Man**.

To the old and infirm they would say that they are using up the Earth's sacred resources, and since the quality of your life is significantly diminished, **you will be required to take a pill** and die for the good of humanity. The 'useless eaters' argument of Henry Kissinger. That's how they will legalise Euthanasia.

For unwanted pregnancies / abortion, and the legalisation of post birth death - they will claim that man is a bundle of evolved cells and that life is not sacred and can be terminated according to their laws. The Bible teaches that the image of God is within Man (Genesis 1:27 f, 9:6b) and that eternity has been put in Man's heart (Ecclesiastes 3:11) which makes abortion plain wrong, but these issues are trivialities to the Elite.

This then leads to population control which they can control either in the 'soft' way, by birth control, or by financial methods such as taxation. In most western countries it's just not financially viable to have lots of children. They can alternatively use the 'hard' way of war, genocide, poisoned food and water, biological cancer producing agents, or man-made viruses which suddenly decimate sections of society.

The New World Religion will underpin all these beliefs. The future religion will fundamentally be Earth worship and doing the right thing for the planet. It will be a type of communitarian State, where the needs of the many outweigh the needs of the individual. The problem with seeing a 'forest rather than a tree' is that suddenly man has ceased to be an individual and has become a commodity which can be used and abused according to the might of the global Elite. The Earth worship concept will also be linked to the use of energy and being a good global citizen, not using too much energy, not having too many children, and following the rules, laws and dictates that come with the belief that the Earth is our Mother.

It is a form of pantheism reworked for the modern mind. It is also a link to the ancient mystery religions, such as Egypt with Isis, and Roman Catholicism with Mary worship and reverence. Furthermore, ancient Canaanite religion, Asherah and Baal, and in Greece Dionysus and Artemis, are all female fecundity religions related to the new belief, which is not so new. This is the religion which is revealed in Revelation: 'Mystery Babylon the great the Mother of prostitutes and of the abominations of the Earth'. Revelation Chapter 17:5.

You see it is not enough for the elite to have control over you in terms of your daily finances, the running of your home or what you do for a living. They wish to have complete and utter control over what you believe and what you do as well. In the future you won't even be born unless the Elite have a reason and need for you. Via these beliefs they will manage to control the people, and that, at its heart, is what it's all about! The New World Religion will be a unified social amorphous creed as a type of control mechanism which will lead the masses to accept like sheep, and without complaint, the coming collectivist fascist state of the New World Order. A totalitarian dictatorship of terrifying proportions and a slave like existence which will be pure hell on earth. How are they going to get to this point? This we look at in the next chapter.

CHAPTER 14

THE EMERGENCE OF THE CRYPTOCRACY'S UTOPIAN SOCIETY

Global Convergence

Drawing it all together

How is the Global Community going to converge, or come together? Many members within the Network have spoken about the **final push** of the World's Governments into the New World Order. We know what their Agenda is, as a reminder, for example the Rhodes Scholar, Strobe Talbot, (Clinton's Deputy Secretary of State) said in Time magazine in July 1992: 'In the next century, nations as we know it will be obsolete; all states will recognize a single, global authority. National sovereignty wasn't such a great idea after all.'

It is the creation of a New World Order in which the amount of electricity used is balanced across all its users, and the one world government micro-manages everything in what is an all-powerful global surveillance police state. In this Scientific dictatorship everything will be monitored, and all people will be treated as resources, and there will be no freedom. To the Elite it will be their Utopia, but to the masses it will be hell on earth.

History is littered with examples of societies which have tried to reach a Utopian state by force. The Soviet Union, with their 'workers paradise', Hitler with the Third Reich, Mao with his Red Revolution, and Pol Pot, are all examples of leaders who have tried to make a Utopian Society by terrorising people into submission. This is the same belief as the United Nations, that they, via their occult New Age beliefs, can take Humanity to a new level of society and usher in a better world order. The inspiration of the United Nations, as explained, is directly in line with the New Age which justifies the arrival of their Utopian State in which it will be allowable to use force and kill people. In much of the New Age literature that inspires UN Leaders, we have this concept that no-one will be left behind in the New World Order. In other words, there won't be any section of society that can remain unchanged – there will be mass killings and chaos from which their global society can then be generated. As H.G. Wells, in his book, 'The New World Order', written in 1940 says, "It is the system of nationalist individualism that has to go.... We are living in the end of the sovereign states.... In the great struggle to evoke a Westernized World Socialism, contemporary governments may vanish... **Countless people... will hate the new world order.... and will die protesting against it.**"

What sort of Crisis could it be? How will the Leaders of today willingly give up their Sovereignty, and how will the New World Order which they see as the Utopian Society emerge?

It is difficult to know what precise form this chaos will take, but it will have to be enough for the leaders of the World and its populace to be convinced that a serious change in the way the Nation States are managed will have to come about. It will also have to be not devastating enough for a **true people's grass roots popular revolt** to be able to emerge. In other words, any scenario for entering the New World Order will have to be one in which the **Network manages to maintain the complete control it craves.** They will have to create enough chaos to convince the worlds' leaders and their populaces to give up whatever the Elite demands. In other words, we need the **right crisis.** As David Rockefeller said: 'We are on the verge of a **global transformation.** All we need is the right major crisis and the nations will accept the New World Order.' [243] Emphasis in bold mine.

---

[243] David Rockefeller speaking at a UN Business meeting 14th September 1994.

Henry Kissinger gives us a glimpse of how he sees it. "Today, America would be outraged if UN troops entered Los Angeles to restore order. Tomorrow they will be grateful! This is especially true if they were told that there were an outside threat from beyond, **whether real or promulgated***, that threatened our very existence. It is then that all peoples of the world will plead to deliver them from this evil. The one thing every man fears is the unknown. When presented with this scenario, individual rights will be willingly relinquished for the guarantee of their well-being **granted to them by the World Government**." [244]

*Promulgated means broadcast, so he's referring to the media broadcasting an 'outside threat' which might NOT be real but broadcast - in other words, a made-up threat. This begs the question: is the threat real, a false flag or another hoax? We're back to hoaxes again!

What sort of world calamity will shock all the Leaders to unite and create a global One World Government, a New World Order, enabling Sovereignty and the rights of billions of people to be coalesced into a central body such as the UN?

Scenarios for Entering the New World Order

The period of transition - various theories from New Age writers

New Age writers refer to a 'period of transition' which is the supposed big awakening that soon will usher in a new period of human history. They believe that in the future there will be a moral awakening, into the new age, and this will not be Secular but based on the Luciferian concept and belief than Man can and will overcome everything through knowledge. At the dawning of the New Age the whole of humanity will be Initiated into a New Religious experience. As we enter into the Age of Aquarius **a new evolutionary shift will**

---

[244] Henry Kissinger. Bilderberger Conference, France, 1992.

occur which will propel man to the next level of his existence as we are to undergo a **mass-planetary initiation that will usher us into a New Age**. So Transformative Evolution or a 'Planetary Consciousness of Transcendence' are all ways whereby man might enter into the New World Order.

Transformative Evolution

'Normal' evolution is too slow to transform the consciousness of man, so the concept of 'transformative evolution' was invented: what you could call 'fast evolution'. Not only does Man evolve into a better human, but his consciousness is somehow raised as he makes a quantum leap in ability to become 'like god', or even 'a god'. In the various New Age writings, we have all sorts of terms for this process and the end result is the same - man reaching a type of godhood under the auspices of a New One World Religion and the One Government. Here is a distillation of those concepts from across various New Age writers.

Writer	Name of Concept	Result
Helena Blavatsky	Transformation	Restored worship of the dragon and the Sun, the religion of the Ancients is the New World Religion.
Teilard de Chardin	'Omega point' (end point)	God is evolving man back to himself.
Teilard de Chardin	'Christifying'	Man is becoming Christ consciousness.
Teilard de Chardin	'Convergence (or confluence) of Religion'	One World Religion
Barbara Marx Hubbard	'Planetary Pentecost'	Birth of the New World Religion/ we are gods.
Barbara Marx Hubbard	'Quantum Transformation'	Evolutions into godhood.
Alice Bailey	'Global shift in consciousness'	Church Universal
David Spangler	'Luciferic Initiation'	To become 'Christed' / to become God.
Vera Alder	'The Great Awakening'	Leads to the new World Religion and State.
Benjamin Crème	'Day of Declaration'	The Christ – 2nd coming

All of these terms refer to approximately the same belief that suddenly somehow man will evolve from his current state of consciousness to some greater unified super being, or that an outside influence will bring in a new age. The concept that a 'mind altering' spiritual moment will emerge in which the entirety of humanity will become greater, unified and at peace with itself. In essence, therefore, we have the belief that Man can overcome the problems of the world when he becomes a 'Christ.' This will lead to him becoming a God and this will happen via an evolutionary process which is being worked out by god. "Evolution… is the response to the call of the Logos, of God. It is the purpose behind the Plan. It is God's drawing of creation back to himself." [245]

Obviously the supposed 'Christ' of the Theosophist or Luciferians, is not the same Jesus Christ of the Bible, and so any resultant appearance will be a false one. Once mankind experiences the 'New Light' they believe man would be changed and manifest a new set of world views and values which would change man for the better.

Luciferic Initiation

David Spangler in his version said: "No one will enter the New World Order unless he or she will make a pledge to worship Lucifer. No one will enter the New Age unless he will take a Luciferian Initiation."[246] He called it the "Luciferic initiation" because of its association with the experience of light. He is the Director of the Planetary Initiative, who works for the United Nations and is a New Age author who helped form the Findhorn Foundation in Scotland.

The Luciferic Initiation is some sort of face to face encounter with a being of Light who they say will lead the way into an era of peace and prosperity. It is the coming of their 'New Age kingdom' and not the Judgement spoken of in Christianity, or the Thousand Year Millennial rule of Jesus Christ. It is some other event. Could this be the mass culling of mankind leading to the conspirators dream of

---

[245] Quote of Barry McWaters, *The Rainbow Bridge,* from Texe Marrs, *Dark Secrets of the New Age,* page 20.

[246] David Spangler, *Re-imagining the World,* Spangler and Bloom.

their own utopia? This is what the United Nations seem to imply as they drive mankind into their Agenda 21.

As explained previously, the Luciferians are a group of people who believe that Lucifer is the true God of this world. They think they are smarter than the rest of humanity and seek political power to exalt themselves over the average man whatever the cost. But in the final analysis you are only under the Kingdom of Light, or the Kingdom of Darkness. You can only serve Jesus or the Devil, and you are only under God if you have submitted to God. There is no middle ground. Who do you think David Spangler, Director of the Planetary Initiative of the United Nations is serving with this comment, 'No one will enter the New World Order unless he or she will make a pledge to worship Lucifer'?

Another New Age writer, Barbara Marx Hubbard spoke of the 'Planetary Pentecost' which will be the 'new gospel of Christ' and a planetary smile' will flash across the face of all mankind as an 'uncontrollable joy' as the 'joy of the force' will 'ripple' through the one body of humanity. [247]

Benjamin Creme describes the event 'as a Pentecostal experience for all. The world will end in peace and laughter' is how he explained it. [248]

The source of the concept of 'evolutionary shifts in consciousness' was actually derived from the Hindu Upanishads, and later on expounded by Blavatsky and other Theosophists including Carl Jung.

---

[247] Barbara Marx Hubbard, THE REVELATION, p. 243.

[248] Benjamin Creme, Maitreya's Mission: Volume Two (Los Angeles: Share International Foundation, 1993), p. 239. From A Course in Miracles: Combined Volume.

Criticism of Consciousness raising awareness is the New Age 'Urban Myth'

This concept that somehow man can evolve to a greater consciousness, or become a god through gnosis or spiritual exercises is all a lie, and a sort of 'urban myth' which has led many people into the New Age movement which original broke through from the 1960s and the 'hippie movement' espoused by writers such as Timothy Leary, Joseph Campbell and Carlos Castaneda.

Once you know and understand this important concept (evolutionary shifts) you will see this cropping up amongst practically ALL the writers of the new age and allied genres, and that even includes Al Gore. Of course, it's complete nonsense, but understanding this concept makes sense of a lot of the writings of the New Age. The concept that man will suddenly wake up and reach for the stars in some evolutionary leap forward or planetary awakening. It's just another deception and a deeply occultic and Satanic belief. The biggest problem with this belief, other than the fact it is a lie, is that somehow this challenge has rendered Christianity impotent and an irrelevance, since no concept of evolving to a greater humanity is present. And herein is another issue - that the entire evolution, New Age conscious enhancing metaphysics, is almost like a drug induced trip. For our modern world, with its stark choices, this escapism seems more interesting than the morality of Christianity. There is no meaningful gnosis into a great evolutionary consciousness for humanity on a vast scale. The rate of biological evolution is far too slow anyway. There can't suddenly be a mass conscious raising event which will enable us all to have a greater sense of knowing, or to awaken and realise that we are interlinked, and all the same humanity.

Hinduism and Buddhism also teach this belief about the coming new age. Whereas in Christianity there is no utopian future, there is only the thousand-year rule of Christ. (Revelation 20). Jesus talks about the new Kingdom calling it **'The Regeneration'** in Matthew 19:28 (KJV and NKJV translations) whereby the parliament of God will exist on Earth, and mankind will come and worship in Jerusalem where Christ and his Apostles will judge.

Christianity teaches that mankind is in a 'foreign state' and that whatever he does will fall short of God. That there is no golden age as taught by New Agers, Rousseau and other writers from antiquity, such as Hesiod, Plato, or even St Augustine. We should be renewing our minds via Christ, as it says in Romans 12:1-2. **Do not be conformed to this world, but be transformed by the <u>renewal of your mind</u>, that by testing you may discern what is the will of God, what is good and acceptable and perfect.**

It is only during the Millennial rule when Christ returns and reigns from Jerusalem that there will be peace. God's rule brings peace – not man's genius, which will only bring war.

Transhumanism

But if the Elite can't transform humanity to its ugly One World Government via these spiritual methods they will try via Transhumanism, Artificial Intelligence and Robotics which is increasingly becoming a viable option. In the hands of the Cryptocracy it is likely this technology will lead to the enslavement of humanity, leading to the emergence of the precise stratified society that Plato spoke of with the Elite as the 'god class', the Police drones as 'the enforcers', and the Workers as 'the slaves'.

Transhumanism (abbreviated as **H+** or **h+**) is the application of sophisticated technology to enhance and make the human condition better. It is the overcoming of fundamental human limitations, such as the ability to jump higher, run faster, and for longer, or the ability to access information via the mind from a computer rather than reading or normal senses. There could also be the ability to live forever as our brains neurological activity, which makes up our consciousness, can be downloaded to a central cloud computer and we can live on within a robotic body. It is only a matter of time before people embrace these technologies due to their enabling abilities. The 'Luddite position' that we will not embrace this technology has been proven time and time again to be incorrect. At every advance of technology, the resistance to using the 'improvement' is too strong. But this time, with Transhumanism it will probably be irreversible, and so it will produce two types of humanity. In Biblical terms this will be those people 'made of clay' who do NOT want to take on board Transhumanistic abilities, and those who do want to enhance their abilities - people 'made of iron'.

Daniel Chapter 2:43 states that in the last kingdom; "And just as you saw the iron mixed with baked clay, **so the people will be a mixture** and will not remain united, any more than iron mixes with clay." Adam was the first man and was made from the earth (clay) or dust. Genesis 2:7. "the Lord God formed the man from the **dust of the ground** and breathed into his nostrils." The Hebrew for Man and Adam are the same, and the Hebrew for Ground comes from same tri-root, except with an h (feminine) ending - adamah is ground. (eretz is land). The interpretation could be that in the final days, some people will be 'clay', as normal humans, whilst other humans will have 'iron'. This will make them transgenic, and so this could therefore describe a trans-humanist future.

This scripture is further backed up in Revelation 20:10 where the devil, the beast, and the false prophet are all thrown into the lake of fire. They are NOT judged at the Great White Throne Judgment of Revelation 20:13, whereas, the Bible teaches that "**each person** was judged according to what he had done". Every **person** who was ever born will be Judged at the Great White Throne Judgement of Revelation 20:11. But if the beast and the false prophet were not judged, this implies that they were NOT human because they were not a person, and hence judged. They had become trans-humanly mixed with iron to such an extent that they no longer qualified for the Great White Thrown Judgement. Therefore, accepting Transhumanism could be the 'mark of the beast' which would enable man to become a super-enhanced being, and live for thousands of years, or even indefinitely but it could also lead to the spiritual death spoken of in Genesis whereby their salvation is forfeited.

The people who take this Transhumanist, AI mark will also not be able to die physically. Revelation 9:6. **During those days men will seek death, but will not find it, they will long to die, but death will elude them.** In other words they will have become so genetically altered they will not be able to kill themselves. This harks back to Satan's comment in the Garden of Eden to Eve, 'And the Serpent said unto the woman, **Ye shall not surely die**. For God doth know that in the day ye eat thereof, then your eyes shall be opened, and **ye shall be as gods**, knowing good and evil.' The Lie in the Garden of Eden was firstly that they would 'not surely die' and secondly that they would 'be as gods' knowing good and evil. It's the same commentary, the lie of Satan which has gripped mankind right from the start!

It will be a strong and powerful delusion 'so that they will believe **THE LIE**. As it says in 2 Thessalonians 2:9-12: 'The coming of the lawless one will be accompanied by the working of Satan, with every kind of power, sign, and false wonder, and with every wicked deception directed against those who are perishing, because they refused the love of the truth that would have saved them. For this reason, God will send them a powerful delusion so that they will believe **the lie** in order that judgment will come upon all who have disbelieved the truth and delighted in wickedness....'

Those who take the infamous Mark of the Beast will not be human; they become like beasts, as they take onboard the transhumanists vision of humanity. This could be the Luciferic Initiation spoken of by David Spangler.

Perhaps therefore the Mark of the Beast will be a type of Transhumanist upgrade or DNA source code which will turn man into 'a god' and able to live forever. This is 'the image' of the Anti-Christ, since the image of God, which man was made in, will have been removed. Those who refuse to worship the image of the beast will be killed.

Revelation 13:15. He was given power to **give breath to the image of the first beast**, so that it could speak and cause **all who refused to worship the image to be killed.**

This could also be the moment that the Anti-Christ declares that he is God and all who have taken the mark of the beast are declared as gods. In this manner they will be linked into the transhumanist hive network and speak one language – the language of computers. The people of clay will be killed.

At the Tower of Babel in Genesis 11, the religion of Mystery Babylon had all the people speaking the same language. 'If as **one people speaking the same language** they have begun to do this, then **nothing they plan to do will be impossible for them'**.

Genesis 11:6. The concept of speaking the same language is also part of the computer hive network one language which the Transhumanists seek for the future of Man.

This could be one of several likely scenarios. The exact situation I believe we will know when the time approaches. But the Bible says that people will not listen and will keep believing the rubbish and lies spoken to them from the mainstream media, which the Cryptocracy own and run for their benefit.

Economic Collapse

Other types of transformation into the One World Government might be through the collapse of Capitalism. George Soros in his book *The Crisis of Global Capitalism* in 1998 argued that we are already in the throes of a global bear market which will lead to a worldwide depression and the disintegration of the capitalist system. Agenda 21 is already the substitute economy waiting in the wings to be enacted. When the Cryptocracy are ready, they will be able to cause the worldwide collapse, which will lead to the invisible Government B which runs us, becoming the openly visible government, as Government A. That's how every political coup happens. The legitimate Government, which I'm calling Government A, is taken over in a coup by Government B, which eventually becomes the legitimate Government A. In order to regain prosperity and restore the world's economies back to how they were, every country would have to sign into a new set of peace treaties and agree on the formation of a New World Order centrally administered by their new One World system. All of this would probably simultaneously involve the emergence of their One World Messiah spoken about in Revelation 13:7b. 'And he (the Anti-Christ) was given **authority over every tribe, people, language and nation**.'

But this new government will be far harsher on its populace than that which has been seen in western society recently. There is talk of global eugenics and making the population as low as 500 million people. No doubt there would be enormous social unrest and the putting down of insurrections all over the globe. But with the enormous power and advanced secret weaponry of the Cryptocracy any popular uprising would soon be quelled.

After this, robots would tend the land and every whim would be ministered to the families of the Cryptocracy, who would live in an advanced society which looks to us now like a science fiction film (perhaps such as Logan's Run), whilst the masses live in a state of neo-feudal serfdom.

Alien Invasion

One other possible scenario for entering the New World Order is the 'Fake Alien Invasion'. In 1994 Serge Monast disclosed the four-stage method by which the Fake Alien Invasion would be simultaneously enacted across the planet. He claimed this came from a source who released secret documents from NASA for what they called, Project Blue Beam.[249] Using holograms from space, advanced secret technology and robots, mankind would be made to believe that aliens were invading. The 'Report from Iron Mountain' written in 1967 also mentioned that, as a substitute for war: 'Experiments have been proposed to test the credibility of an **out-of-our-world invasion threat.**' Emphasis added.[250] This is also linked to the fake Christian Rapture which would involve the disappearance of millions of people who would be herded into FEMA camps and the like to be exterminated. Using secret technologies such as telepathy weapons, the Nations would be made to believe that they were under attack from an advance alien race which would lead to the Elite being able to push whatever agenda they want to the rest of the world. The conclusion of which is the long-awaited unified New World Religion.

---

[249] Serge Monast was a Canadian Journalist who wrote about Project Blue Beam. It does seem far-fetched in places, but then again why would there be quite so much predictive programming in the area of space travel if there weren't some reason for it? For further information, see http://educate-yourself.org/cn/projectbluebeam25jul05.shtml

[250] *Report from Iron Mountain*, page 51. A free PDF of this book can be found at: - http://www.stopthecrime.net/docs/Report_from_Iron_Mountain.pdf

The overall impression of this leak is that it seems a very drastic and far-fetched version for entering the New World Order. It could be possible since we do not know what level of sophisticated weaponry and technology the deep State has at its disposal, or how clever or manipulative their mind control techniques might be.

Possibly this could be a reason for the endless amount of predictive programming about aliens, alien invasions and space travel. From Star Trek, written by illuminati-script-writer Gene Roddenberry, to Mission to Mars and allied films, such as Men in Black, this type of belief in the viability of space and the likelihood of the existence of alien species and advanced civilisations, just around the corner, could be leading to a massive space deception. Could it really be possible that the entire 'space programme' could be a hoax?

Gradualism

Gradualism is the favoured method of the British Fabianists in which small imperceptible steps are taken to create the One World Order. This is when no one step is taken to awaken the people to the conspiracy, but minute steps are made to bring Society to the place the Elite want us to be. This is probably the safest method but it takes a long time! It seems likely, and possible, that once robotics and transhumanism have become a viable option to the Elite, there will no longer be a need for vast numbers of humans to exist and so the roll out of the new system will arrive quickly. If this is correct then we are only probably about 20 or 30 years or so away from viable robotics and transhumanism, which therefore indicates that by about 2050 it is possible we will have entered into the New Order. Certainly Agenda 21 describes a plan which should be completed by 2100 and so working backwards from the end result they describe, we can get a very approximate timeline. There are a lot of pieces of the plan which still need to be put into place. One of them, for example, which seems difficult to accomplish is the destruction of personal property ownership. Surely the people will put up a massive fight against this, but perhaps through interest rate increases and the usufruct laws mentioned in the Global Biodiversity Assessment this could be accomplished faster than we might imagine.

World War III

The process of globalisation could lead to intensified hostilities and the explosion of tensions which could trigger a third world war. The Cryptocracy will probably be avoiding this confrontation since this method will be a bit drastic (even for them!) since even they would not be able to guarantee fully the complete control they crave. Due to the advances in sophisticated weaponry, even the nuclear option available to nation states, a regional conflagration, is a far more likely scenario. One of the most obvious situations, and the one which fits in with the books of Daniel and Revelation, is the invasion of Israel by a coalition of forces.

Another possible plan would be an Electro Magnetic Pulse (EMP) where a large burst of energy would knock out all the delicate electronic circuitry and even plant machinery and cause a complete crash of the system. All computers and cars would cease working properly after an EMP event. The supply and distribution of food would be severely disrupted and cause widespread panic and anarchy which only the Governments of the world joined together could sort out.

Post-Capitalist Society

In the next few decades we will see the slow roll out of automated farms in which robots and Artificial Intelligence (AI) do all the work, eventually putting millions of farmers out of work. It is likely that robots will take over the running of millions of other jobs leading to a society in which the state pays a universal basic income to placate the workers. This is the emergence of the Post-Capitalist system, and the universal income an idea even Thomas More wrote about in

Utopia. In Finland and some other countries, we are already seeing the concept of the universal state income being rolled out.[251]

But my question is, why do the Cryptocracy need humans anymore? If they can maintain their power amongst themselves why bother allowing billions of people who could overturn their power get in the way. Isn't it easier to control robots who control food production and all other processes? Of course it is. So why would they not do this? They've already written in their books, from the Club of Rome, and via their New Age 'theologians' that the long-range plan is to depopulate the planet. This plan seems to be on their agenda, and everything which has been on their agenda has eventually been enacted without fail. You can see in their writings what they wanted to do and slowly and eventually they always succeed.

For example, the reduction of freedoms and the emergence of the surveillance state and the emergence of a debt-ridden service economy, with its moral relativism and greyed out humanity - you can see that the march of the New World Order is ever in this direction. The emergence of political and economic trading blocs also indicates this, not to mention the writings of the conspirators themselves categorially stating that they are working towards a New World Order.[252] This is a real threat and one which will lead eventually to population decrease. The loss of food production, viruses which kill millions, the anti-biotic apocalypse or the vast array of secret unknown agents which their scientists have developed and

---

[251] Universal Income see article https://www.ft.com/content/3b7938e6-c569-11e7-b30e-a7c1c7c13aab

[252] See Strobe Talbot, *The Great Experiment: The Story of Ancient Empires, Modern States, and the Quest for a Global Nation*, (CFR member) justifying the roll out of the New World Order.

Or Jacques Attali, *A Brief History of the Future*, Arcade Publishing.

Or Henry Kissinger's article, '*The Chance for a New World Order*' website link: http://www.nytimes.com/2009/01/12/opinion/12iht-edkissinger.1.19281915.html

Or the video of Zbigniew Brezinski giving a talk to CFR members about the 'moral imperative' for the One World Government.

http://humansarefree.com/2016/12/brzezinski-decries-global-political.html or https://www.youtube.com/watch?v=rEw3JI35Crg.

are at their disposal, all combined to fulfill their de-population agenda.

Whatever happens, the roll out of the New World Order with the New World Religion will be happening before 2100 since this is the end date of Agenda 21. It's not some vague concept they are working towards, but a system of global governance they have envisioned from time immemorial but only made possible in the end times.

CHAPTER 15

THE CRYPTOCRACY ARE MESSING IT UP!

We have seen with good evidence that there is an all-encompassing move to create a New World Religion which fits in with the overall Agenda for the 21st Century. The making of a compliant docile population who can be made to believe and do exactly what the Elite desire. They are the creators of our society after all, and the enormous deceptions and outright lies will only get worse as we steamroll to the emergence of the one world government and the new global economic and social system this century.

One World Government

At some point the New World agenda is going to have to come into the public domain. We may be approaching this point quicker than we realise. We need to get ready and be prepared. For example, extrapolating forward the level of surveillance we have seen in the last 20 years or so, can only lead to us into a world where we are all living in a complete surveillance state. If you had told someone in the UK that there would be police cameras on every street corner (in the major Cities) 20 years ago, they probably would not have believed you. We have now entered into a situation in which everything about a person's existence is known about and stored indefinitely to be used as evidence against them should the need arise.[253]

Population Reduction

Ultimately the plan of the Cryptocracy is to create a global society which is under their total control after having eliminated in the region of 95% of the world's population. This horrific cull would mean the killing of 7 billion people from the world's current population of 7.5 billion to 500 Million. The evidence for this plan comes from many of their writings and sayings quoted below from the conspirators at the top of the system. In addition, practically all the most important writers on the New Age and Theosophy have written about the population reduction when the 'paradigm shift' occurs.

H G Wells wrote, 'countless people will hate the new world order and will die protesting against it'.[254] The Club of Rome writing in 1972 with their *Limits to Growth* publication and later on 'The First Global Revolution' pushed their neo- Malthusian doctrine to new heights. This is no co-incidence. They wrote: 'In searching for a common enemy against whom we can unite, we came up with the idea that pollution, the threat of global warming, water shortages, famine and the like, would fit the bill. In their totality and their interactions these phenomena do constitute a common threat which must be confronted by everyone together. But in **designating these dangers as the enemy**, we fall into the trap, which we have already warned readers about, namely mistaking symptoms for causes. All these dangers are caused by human intervention in natural processes, and it is only through changed attitudes and behaviour that they can

---

[253] Utah Data Center, in Bluffdale / Salt Lake City is where **the computer stores** every email, telephone conversation, tweet, transaction, in fact anything that happens online. See Wikipedia https://en.wikipedia.org/wiki/Utah_Data_Center or http://facilitiesmagazine.com/utah/buildings/nsa-utah-data-center

[254] The New World Order, H G Wells, 1940. Page 10, the full quote is: 'Countless people, from maharajas to millionaires and from pukkha sahibs to pretty ladies, will hate the new world order, be rendered unhappy by the frustration of their passions and ambitions through its advent and will die protesting against it.'

be overcome. **The real enemy then is humanity itself.**' In bold my Emphasis.[255]

In the same Club of Rome's publication, *Limits to Growth,* we gain an idea of the timeframe for these changes. From the back cover of the book we have: 'The earth's interlocking resources - the global system of nature in which we all live - probably cannot support present rates of economic and population growth much beyond the year 2100, if that long, even with advanced technology.'

And on page 184, the equilibrium they seek for humanity to last generations into the future is mentioned. **'He (mankind) has all that is physically necessary to create a totally new form of human society- one that would be built to last for generations.'**

But in order to get to this point, there will have to be a vast population decrease and they will decide the timeframe and ultimately who gets to live. Furthermore, *Limits to Growth* states:

'We suspect on the basis of present knowledge of the physical constraints of the planet that the growth phase cannot continue for another one hundred years. Again, because of the delays in the system, if the global society waits until those constraints are unmistakably apparent, it will have waited too long.'[256]

Maybe these writers overstated these comments, but we can also see these beliefs higher up the chain of command within the Cryptocracy itself - that the number of people needs to be a culled. Between 1957 and 1990 the world's population doubled in size. Perhaps this became a source of major concern to them, so this might help to explain this de-population agenda, but why are they still talking about it and pushing this idea decades later? Demographers have shown that they expect numbers to decline naturally as economic factors make having many children an unviable

---

[255] King and Schneider, *The First Global Revolution*, 1991.

[256] Donella Meadows was the lead author of *Limits to Growth*, a Club of Rome publication, page 183. A PDF version can be found at http://www.donellameadows.org/wp-content/userfiles/Limits-to-Growth-digital-scan-version.pdf

The Club of Rome also wrote; 'The Earth has a cancer and man is the cancer.' From 'Mankind at the Turning Point', The 2nd Report of the Club of Rome. 1974.

proposition. This trend we have seen almost all over the world, but the Cryptocracy are still subtly pushing the depopulation agenda. They will, eventually, as always, get what they want, so the world can be under their control and there will be no-one who is not under their control. No dissenters or believers in anything but that which the State authorises.

At the Gorbachev State of the World forum a speaker said: 'We must speak more clearly about sexuality, contraception, about abortion, about values that control population because the ecological crisis, in short, is the population crisis. Cut the population by 90% and there aren't enough people to do a great deal of ecological damage.'[257]

Henry Kissinger in his book *The Final Days* has infamously been quoted as saying that, 'The elderly are useless eaters'. He also said: 'The world population must be reduced by 50%.'

Propaganda specialist Bertrand Russell, wrote in *The Impact of Science on Society*. 'At present the population of the world is increasing ... War so far has had no great effect on this increase ... I do not pretend that birth control is the only way in which population can be kept from increasing. There are others ... If a Black Death could be spread throughout the world once in every generation, survivors could procreate freely without making the world too full ... the state of affairs might be somewhat unpleasant, but what of it? Really high-minded people are indifferent to suffering, especially that of others.'[258] Surely, he means low minded people, but then he's a Eugenicist and conspirator, so he turns everything the other way around like Satanists do, so wrong is right and good is evil.

The Bible further concurs with the depopulation concept where in Revelation 6:9 it states: 'Then I looked and saw a pale horse. Its rider's name was Death, and Hades followed close behind. And they were given authority **over a fourth** of the earth, to kill by sword, by famine, by plague, and by the beasts of the earth.'

---

[257] Gorbachev's State of the World Forum in San Francisco in 1996, New Age writer and philosopher Dr. Sam Keen. Quoted from Stan Monteith. http://www.khouse.org/articles/1997/93/

[258] Bertrand Russell, *The Impact of Science on Society*, chapter 6.

If the population at this time is 9 billion then 25% (a fourth) would be killed (2.25 billion) taking the population down to 6.75 billion. This is not the only purge mentioned in Revelation, in 9:18 it states that: '**A third of mankind** was killed by the three plagues of fire, smoke and sulphur that came out of their mouths'. This is from the 200 million army which is released by the four angels during the Sixth Trumpet, which is the Day of the Lord. From 6.75 billion this would be another third dead (2.3 billion dead) and many others would also be killed in diverse ways such as the death of the saints (Revelation 6:9), or those dieing from starvation due to the scorching of the land (Revelation 8:7). If another half a billion died in this manner this would leave, in the region of 4 billion people remaining.

And this is probably a conservative estimate. If the population were 7.5 billion at the time of the Tribulation and using the same maths (25% and 33.3% = 50%, plus half a billion for other deaths), the end population number is 3.25 billion – a vastly reduced global population.

The Georgia Guidestones is an unusual monument built in 1980, dubbed the 'American Stonehenge.' On its granite monolithic walls are carved the 'Illuminati ten commandments.' The First Commandment is to: 'Maintain humanity under 500,000,000 in perpetual balance with nature'. R C Christian was the person who paid for the building of the stone monument, and this is most likely code for Christian Rosenkreutz, which refers to the Rosicrucians, a secret society similar to Freemasons. No-one knows why they bothered to build this expensive structure – but could it be, that same belief in culpability? That letting people know what they are going to do, and why, in some way allows them to be free from the consequences of what they plan to do? (The culpability doctrine.)

The reference to Christian Rosenkreutz therefore most likely refers to the Cryptocracy again - that thin, tiny layer of people above the government, who are directing everything in our world today. Their first and their last commandment is about depopulation. Their final commandment being: 'Be not a cancer on the earth — Leave room for nature — Leave room for nature.' Again, we can see their religious pantheism in this statement that man should leave room for nature, the environment.[259]

Another high-level member of the Network, Ted Turner, spoke of the optimum number of the population being between 250 - 300 Million. Bill Gates spoke of 500 Million and mentioned the use of vaccines in order to get there. He also went to the 2012 'family planning' Conference in London which commemorated 100 years from the start of the International **Eugenics** Congress. Why would you have a conference on family planning exactly on this date if there wasn't an intentional link?

Even the UN has provided a population number that they think the planet could sustain, and this is between 1 and 3 billion people. From the *Global Assessment Report of United Nations Environmental Program*, the authors quote an un-named 'expert' who writes. *'A reasonable estimate for an industrialized world society at the present North American material standard of living would be 1 billion. At the more frugal European standard of living, 2 to 3 billion would be possible.'* [260] The International Union for Conservation of Nature (IUCNO) was originally set up by high-level conspirator Julian Huxley, brother of Aldous Huxley, writer of Brave New World. This is still a vast population reduction from where we are today.

Why is the number 500 million or 1 billion of significance? Could it be that this number would be enough people to maintain the services, robots and machines that would be needed in the new age? It would be enough to make sure that everybody alive is in 'their system' and no-one will be outside of the government of the future dictatorship. It is also the number of people who will not consume the Earth's resources too fast since in their view these resources belong to them and no-one else.

For the Elite and their families, probably around only 4,000 families at maximum, it would be the new Utopia they have spoken of for centuries, but for the vast majority of the remaining people it

---

[259] Georgia Guidestones, see Wikipedia entry.

[260] Global Assessment Report of UNEP, Phase One Draft, Section 9. From The International Union for Conservation of Nature (IUCN0) which has observer and consultative status at the UN. https://www.iucn.org/theme

will be hell on Earth. An existence without hope, without freedom of expression, job variety, ownership of property or any means of bettering oneself and one's family since money would cease to exist and be replaced with energy credits. There is a certain finality about Sustainable Development, that it is the conclusion of the direction the entire Global Economy and Society is heading towards. There's no document giving us any idea what life will look like POST Sustainable Development. It therefore seems likely that this is their ultimate economic model. Or could it perhaps be yet another deception or a stepping stone leading to the world-wide genocide which will follow?

Defenders of the indoctrinated mainstream media mindset will seek to explain away all these writings and comments as mistakes uttered by top politicians and think tanks who 'make many comments about all sorts of things'. They would argue that these comments have been taken out of context and blown out of proportion by 'conspiracy theorists'. But if this were true and the Elite were *only* interested in gaining more money and power, then why do they back liberal causes such as the New Age, the gay rights movement, women's liberation and reproductive rights and environmentalism? Evidence points incontrovertibly to the fact that the Elite have pushed these beliefs for a reason, and that is all part of their power grab over humanity, who they think they own, and can manipulate into their future 'control grid'. The Cryptocracy's finger prints are also all over the History of the 20th Century with its wars and depressions; all this leading to the eventual roll out of the syncretic New World Religion to underpin their Agenda for the 21st Century. Their religious concepts fit in with their long-term plan, of which, depopulation is only one part of what will be happening later this century. Why are they not *just* interested in maximizing their profits for their families and friends and leaving a good legacy for future generations? Why do they believe in reducing the earth's population and taking away all property rights making the survivors of the onslaught live at pre-industrial levels of consumption? The reason is that the people at the top of the pyramid are not interested in sharing anything, they are greedy to the point of stupidity and want it all for themselves. The ten Kings 'will devour the whole earth'. (Daniel 7:23.)

Emergence of the New World Religion

As part of this, in the final analysis, the New World Order is not so much about politics and economics but the politicization of their religion as the final revolution (or take over), the conclusion of which is the emergence of 'the beast' system. The previous 'take overs' being economic and political, where the institutions in charge of regulating political and economic power were completely infiltrated into the Network's hands, as mentioned in Chapter 1. Although most people still have no idea that this has indeed happened.

In the New System, 'The dragon (Satan) gave power to the beast' - Revelation 13:2b - and, 'All the inhabitants of the earth will worship the beast'. Revelation 13:8. This is the ultimate conclusion of the entire agenda we have elucidated. To bring Satan down to earth and to enforce the worldwide worship of him as the capstone of the All-Seeing Eye. It is there depicted on the one-dollar bill as the New Religion is brought down onto the 13-layered pyramid. It will be enforced to the death, and anyone who does not fit in or agree with it will be killed and be unable to buy or sell any of the necessities of life. Without the mark of the beast our existence will become impossible. Many will openly welcome the Luciferic initiation with open arms in a spirit of unity and deception that Lucifer 'isn't so bad after all'. This may seem quite theoretical, or even far-fetched bearing in mind where we are in society at the moment, but this is what the Bible and the New Age writers have spoken about. And it is also in direct line with the plans of the hidden government that really runs everything. Satan is the driving force behind the Cryptocracy and the Cryptocracy is where evil is made tangible. After all, why are some of the richest and most powerful people so interested in creating a New Religion?

Underpinning the entire system would be the Gnostic Earth-worship religion of the Luciferian Elite who would command their subjects at their whim to do their bidding. This is the emergence of the neo-feudal State which they planned for the second half of this Century. Survivors of the onslaught will live in a scientific, technocratic dictatorship as slaves, no doubt enmeshed into the transhumanist hive neural network. The Elite will no longer live as

Cryptocrats since they will no longer need to hide from public view, but they will live as worshipped gods with every modern convenience, whilst the vast majority, only 500 million or a billion people will be their slaves. This is the conclusion to their Luciferian religion. Coupled with this, eventually, will be the appearance of their one world Masonic Messiah, who will be the Anti-Christ, and will force everyone to take the mark.

This is the aim of the Cryptocracy, depopulation and to be worshipped as gods, make no mistake. It is also one of the reasons they remain hidden controlling events from behind supposed elected ministers. Their agenda is so frightening that they daren't make it known. It has come out in their statements and some of their publications mentioned above as they try to find their way to their destination without arousing the populace's suspicions. It was also written about in the Bible and from the opposite point of view in the writings of Theosophists, Satanists and Luciferians. A religion in which they will be worshipped as god, and in which Satan has free reign over mankind. This is the culmination of the New World Order and the point at which their power is revealed for all the world to see. It is the accomplishment of the 'Great Plan' which they have been speaking about from time immemorial.

What can be done? Political concepts

We could research the political scientific methods of state subversion as explained by Gene Sharp and the Albert Einstein Institute.[261] He espoused political methods of civil unrest to remove a dictator from power in typically second and third world states. Via a popular non-violent uprising, his methods have been successful in slowly breaking the potency of political institutions to such an extent that a dictator's power becomes untenable. For example, through peaceful non-violent means of interruption and non-compliance, similar to those used by Gandhi, these methods have had some results in removing tyrants in

---

[261] Gene Sharp's concepts of non-violent resistance to dictators is explained in, *From Dictatorship to Democracy*, 1993.

the last 40 years. Although there is cause for concern that Gene Sharp's political systems were used by the Cryptocracy to advance their 'Colour Revolutions' in Yugoslavia, Ukraine and elsewhere.

The problem with this method is that the masses of people have to know who the enemy is, and which political institutions are causing the problems. But if those institutions are so entrenched and unknown to everyone that they are hidden from the populace, there is no way for those actions to take hold and work against a hidden agent. In other words, a popular uprising cannot take hold if the agents are not exposed. It is proving difficult for most people to understand who the Cryptocracy are, yet alone take any meaningful action to oust them. So, this method is unlikely to work at the current time unless many more people know and understand who the hidden government are, and what they're agenda really is. If everyone knew who the conspirators were, such as the CFR, the Trilateral Commission, and other groups mentioned in Chapter 3, then there is a chance. So we need to expose them as much as we can, so please mention this book to other people so they can learn and understand who really rules them. But, at the moment, the Cryptocrats hide behind our ignorance! This is why they are hidden in the first place, so no-one can take a swipe at them! Even if they were ousted, a new State based on Satan's earthly power would soon emerge. So, on a political basis we ideally need a new method of control or a **new Magna Carta** to put these elite controllers into place and limit their power so they cannot cause any more harm.

In many areas, such as the case of Eastern Europe, the people have known for decades who and what their enemy is, but this knowledge arrived too late. They have already been taken over so completely that fighting back is futile. We will soon be entering into a similar position in the West, but we still don't understand or know who our hidden enemy is at the moment. We are like blind men in a room on fire, feeling our way to a door! We need to wake up and take responsibility before our world burns!

It's a massive deception. They are taking us down the wrong path and since it's already too late to get off this path, the deeper the deception, the harder it is find your way back - don't even take that path! To a degree we are victims, but we need to wake up, and wake up quickly. We need to throw away, entirely, our treasured worldviews, which were sold to us anyway, and not be afraid to seek the truth with a totally fresh perspective. We need to have the wisdom and strength of character to look again at what really is going on in the world today. We need to stop listening and looking at the mainstream media since this is where most of the programming and disinformation is coming from. We need to ignore their programming and make them an irrelevance. If you do continue to review the mainstream media, you need to consider yourself like an Intelligence Officer, filtering and checking every piece of information to make sure it is correct or even happened. Currently there are still a few outlets which provide unfiltered information on the Internet, but this is under increasing threat as we see freedom of speech become more and more constricted. With correct knowledge we may be able to make an impact and affect change.

Neither should you let this subject 'eat you up' and destroy your joy and laughter! There is freedom and peace which eventually comes from understanding this agenda, but it really comes from knowing God's purposes and walking the life of faith. For those further along this path we also need to realise that we could possibly be the last generation to live in the material and mental comfort which we enjoy today. Conversely, perhaps we should try not to be too fatalistic that this really is the future we are entering into.

Final message

There is one major issue which the Cryptocracy have not accounted for, and one major power they have not made allowance for, and this is the power of the Lord Jesus Christ, who will make a stand against this onslaught of evil in the world. Remember, they have become so deluded that they believe that Satan really is the ruler of the Earth. Our battle is therefore in the spiritual realm since it is Satan who is driving the Cryptocracy and so to defeat the Cryptocracy we need to fight against the dark spiritual forces of evil in the heavenly realms. We can't do this without Christ. 'For our struggle is not against flesh and blood, but against the rulers, against the authorities, against the powers of this dark world and against the spiritual forces of evil in the heavenly realms.' Ephesians 6:12. Our battle is therefore against the kingdom of darkness.

But, thanks to Christ and the Holy Spirit as Christ's Comforter, there is still hope in what is a hopeless situation. As Jesus said; 'You are Peter, and on this rock I will build this church, and the gates of Hell will not overcome it'. (Matthew 16:18.) Christ will eventually be victorious when the story of human history is concluded, and He will set up his Heavenly Kingdom in 'the regeneration'. Even before the Cryptocracy even existed God had already ordained the end of things, and the Cryptocracy and their schemes are doomed to failure.

It is by faith, and by faith alone, that we walk with Christ, and so we need to continue to seek Him in faith until we have a powerful revelation of the reality of God. With a true encounter of the living God everything else will pale into insignificance.

Therefore, we need to seek God, have faith, and pray for changes in our society and in ourselves; this is why we need God more than ever in this Century. If you still haven't made a commitment to Christ now is as good a moment as any to make the decision to follow the Lord Jesus and never look back.

We therefore need to love Christ and follow Him, never conforming to the Religion of the New World Order or bow down to the Beast system. The worship of the beast will become mandatory and will be enforced by worldwide legislation brought into effect by the Second Beast. Those who refuse to bow to this image will killed. Revelation 13:15: 'the image would also speak and cause all who refused to worship it to be killed.'[262] But it's better to die than to worship the beast, since 'If anyone worships the beast and its image, and receives its mark on his forehead or hand, he too will drink the wine of God's anger', Revelation 14:9-10. In other words, it is better to die than to forfeit your Salvation. As Jesus said: Do not be afraid of those who kill the body but cannot kill the soul. Instead, fear the one who is able to destroy both soul and body in hell. (Matthew 10:28.)

---

[262] Then I saw a second beast, coming out of the earth. It had two horns like a lamb, but it spoke like a dragon. It exercised all the authority of the first beast on its behalf, and made the earth and its inhabitants worship the first beast... Revelation 13:11-12.

They may tell us that, for the sake of unity, we need to compromise, and that if we are unwilling, they will brand us as terrorists, lock us up and even kill us. We therefore need to love Christ more than politically correct beliefs which are an indoctrination. At that time the Lord will tell us what to say.[263]

We need to know who we are, and **speak out in authority**, not anger, about the situation that is before us. Don't entertain fearful thoughts since lack of faith can be a blind spot, and **'Greater is He that is in you, than he that is in the world.'** 1 John 4:4. The best way to overcome fear is by knowing who you are in Christ. Let the Holy Spirit and the words of the Bible bring you that insight. 'All authority on earth has been given' to Christ, which He passed onto believers.[264] This includes authority over the devil and ALL his schemes. Step out in faith, since it is impossible to please God other than by faith. Hebrews 11:6. Also try not to show them a 'red flag, like to a bull,' but let the wisdom and love of the Holy Spirit guide you. Love the person, dislike the religion, trust God, and be prepared to tell people the reason for your hope in Christ, and tell them why they should stop believing in 'the Lie'. Resist the devil and he will flee from you.

Jesus Christ is the culmination of human History. **Jesus will be victorious** over Satan and the Satanic forces of the Cryptocracy. Trust in God, do not be afraid, and be wise at all times. Love God and your fellow human and keep the faith.

Please join my Facebook group
The Regeneration

Twitter:
New World Rel

---

[263] When you are brought before the synagogues, rulers, and authorities, do not worry about how to defend yourselves or what to say, For at that time the Holy Spirit will teach you what you should say. Luke 12:11-12. Also see Matthew 10:19-20.

[264] Matthew 28:18-20. Then Jesus came to them and said, "All authority in heaven and on earth has been given to me. Therefore go and make disciples of all nations, baptizing them in the name of the Father and of the Son and of the Holy Spirit, and teaching them to obey everything I have commanded you. And surely I am with you always, to the very end of the age."

APPENDIX

NEW WORLD RELIGION CHRONOLOGY

1893   1st World Parliament of Religions held in Chicago. The world's first wide-ranging interfaith meeting in modern history.

1908   World Council of Churches was set up as an ecumenical outreach.

1920   League of Nations set up by Milner group. Failed attempt to create the League of Churches to parallel the League of Nations.

1930   World Congress of Faiths. Sir Francis Younghusband wrote 'a religious basis is essential for the new world order.'

1937   World Council of Churches formed but officially announced in 1948. It is ecumenical not interfaith.

1943   The Three Faiths Declaration of Dr George Bell, Bishop of Chichester starts an interfaith group.

1945   24th October, United Nations formed.

1948   World Council of Churches becomes official and marks the beginning of the world ecumenical movement. It is funded by the Rockefeller Foundation.

1952   World Parliament of Religions founded to work with the United Nations to stop war and the causes of war.

1960s   World Alliance of Religions.

1965   Second Vatican Council (Vatican II) the Catholic Church supremacy over other religions opened the way for interfaith dialogue.

1970   The World Alliance of Reformed Churches (WARC) ecumenical grouping for Presbyterian and other Reformed Churches.

1970   World Conference of Religions for Peace started: a multi-faith group that meet for inter religious co-operation. It has consultative status with the United Nations Economic and Social Council (ECOSOC), UNESCO and UNICEF.

1970   Earth Day was instituted on 22nd April (notice the Master number). A day to honour the Earth.

1972   Club of Rome, *Limits to Growth* publication starts the new mythology of global warming (climate change) as the method to bring all the nations together into the New World Religion.

1974   2nd World Conference of Religions for Peace

1979   3rd World Conference of Religions for Peace

1984   4th World Conference of Religions for Peace

1986   Vatican calls for all religions to pray for Peace

1986   World Council of Faiths is proposed but it fails to gain traction.

1989   5th World Conference of Religions for Peace

1992   United Nations Conference on Environment and Development (UNCED). Rio de Janeiro Earth summit. The emergence of the post capitalist vision.

1993   2nd World Parliament of Religions - at that time the largest gathering of world's religious leaders who decide that a united religion is beyond their capabilities.

1993   The Parliament of World Religions publishes '*The Declaration of the Global Ethic*'. An interfaith declaration promoting the merging of religions for the good of preserving the Earth and looking forward to the new global order.

1993   The concept of the United Religious Initiative was promoted by the UN by Gillian Sorenson (CFR member) who invited Bishop Swing to hold an interfaith service for

1995.

1994   6th World Conference of Religions for Peace. Dr William Fray Vendley (CFR member) become the Secretary General of (WCRP).

1995   Bishop Swing holds the interfaith service at Grace Cathedral to celebrate the 50th Anniversary of the signing of the UN Charter – this is basically the founding of the *United Religions Initiative* (URI).

1995   Alliance of Religions and Conservation. Prince Charles starts UN based secular group to develop Sustainable Development for the UNDP based on unified religious beliefs.

1996   The San Francisco Summit Meeting for a Global United Religions initiative set itself the task of peace for all life and a target date for its Charter of 2000.

1997   The Charter for the United Religions Initiative (URI) via Stanford University, California, is started with Bishop Swing, Dee Hock and 14 others.

1999   7th World Conference of Religions for Peace

1998   European Congress of Ethnic Religions (ECER) starts to promote ethnic and pagan 'old' European religions.

2000   United Religions Initiative (URI) Charter signed by most of the world religions June 26th. George Shultz is a URI Trustee.

2000   World Peace Summit of religious and spiritual leaders. The Millennium World Peace Summit was held at the UN. Signing of commitments to global peace and creation of World Council of Religions and interfaith declarations. Ted Turner was one of the keynote speakers giving a message that 'maybe there's one god who manifest himself in different ways to different people. You know, what about that huh.' (Ted Turner also said that 300,000 was enough people for the planet.)

2000   United Nations Millennium Summit- the world's leaders signed the UN Millennium Declaration which is an international treaty setting up the infrastructure empowering the UN to eventually become a world government.

2000   Earth Charter document is released to the world - variously called the Sermon on the Mount by Mikhail Gorbachev, or the 10 Commandments or the Magna Carta for Planet Earth by Maurice Strong. This document has been said to be the prototype New World Order constitution.

2001   World Conference on the preservation of religious diversity.

2001   The Religions For Peace Global Women of Faith Network is launched. Linked to the UNHCR. The Religions For Peace Global Youth Network is also launched and comprises six regional inter-religious youth networks in Asia, Africa, Europe, Latin America and the Caribbean, the Middle East and North America.

2002   Vatican calls for another meeting to come and pray for peace and overcome conflict.

2002   First meeting of World Council of Religions. Development of the European Council of Religious Leaders (ECRL), it is an interreligious council for cooperation between senior European leaders of Judaism, Christianity, Islam, Buddhism, Hinduism, Sikhism and Zoroastrianism.

2002   World Council of Women religious leaders and Spiritual Teachers meeting.

2002   World Peace site established by World Conference of Religions for Peace.

2002   United Religions Initiative first global assembly in Rio de Janeiro.

2003   2nd World Peace Summit.

2003   Pope commends the peace of the world to Mary.

2003   Pope urges unity among world religions.

2003   Inter-religious tribute given on behalf of Mother Theresa.

2000   3rd World Peace Summit.

2004   Vatican holds interfaith concerts.

2004   Pope says all religions must unite for peace.

2005	4th World Peace Summit.
2005	World Council of Churches asks for more renewed commitment to ecumenicalism.
2005	Global Day of Prayer unites diverse Churches.
2005	Vatican promotes unity at world mission conference.
2005	Alliance of World Civilizations started to help bring the West and Islam together.
2005	1st meeting of World Congress for Imams and Rabbis for Peace (WCIRP).
2006	World Conference of Religions for Peace/ Launch of Global inter faith Youth Network.
2006	Pope encourages more inter-religious prayer meetings.
2006	5th World Peace Summit.
2006	World religions unite over global warming.
2006	2nd Global Day of prayer.
2006	Pope and Dalai Lama meet for peace between Catholics, Buddhists, and Hindus.
2006	Popes' praying in a mosque deemed a new horizon in interfaithism.
2006	2nd meeting of World Congress for Imams and Rabbis for Peace (WCIRP).
2007	6th World Peace Summit.
2007	Interfaith Council established for Jerusalem.
2007	3rd Global Day of Prayer.
2007	Groups in US declared that all paths lead to God.
2007	World Council of Churches encourages different religions to unify in diversity.
2007	URI has consultative status at the UN.
2008	7th World peace Summit.
2008	World Council of Churches and Pope seek cooperation.
2008	Pope meets with Jewish, Islamic, Buddhist, Jain and Hindu

leaders in Washington.

2008   3rd meeting of World Congress for Imams and Rabbis for Peace (WCIRP).

2008   4th Global Day of Prayer.

2008   Oprah Winfrey begins openly promoting New Age thought and One World Religion ideals specifically saying that Jesus is not the only way to heaven.

2008   Tony Blair launches the Tony Blair Faith foundation to help unite the world religions and counter extremism via his Global Citizenship.

2008   Rick Warren (CFR member) via his Saddleback Church launches the PEACE Coalition, acronym (plant, equip, assist, care, educate).

2009   World Parliament of Religions is held in Melbourne Australia. Up to 8000 people participated in discussions about climate change and the eradication of poverty.

2009   The Earth Charter Initiative pushes the green aspect of Agenda 21 – respect for the Earth. One of the Elite's key power grabs.

2010   Tony Blair begins to become allied with Rick Warren (CFR member since 2005) in uniting the world's religions.

2010   Interfaith meetings in Manhattan begin to be held twice a month by Christian, Jewish, Muslim and other religious leaders. It is supported by the Obama administration which identified interfaith work as a public policy goal.

2010   The G8 World Religions Summit was held where a sacred fire was lit, and participants were told the Mother needs to hear that we hear her, and they offered to a prayer of gratitude. Other rituals were performed to invoke the spirits to encourage that "there is not only one way, there are many ways."

2011   Another interfaith global day of prayer.

2011   World Peace Summit.

2012   Rick Warren (CFR member) begins promoting 'King's Way' as an attempt to bring evangelical Christians and

Muslims together as an overall part of his peace plan. A document was produced that stressed points of agreement between the two basic beliefs including belief in one God, and it also called for sharing their faith with one another, but not for the purpose of conversion.

2012   The Global Charter of Conscience was drafted by a group of 50 international academics, politicians, and NGO leaders representing all the religions. It is to encourage the world to 'live together in peace without religious differences.'

2012   Pope urges religions to root out "fundamentalism".

2012   Vatican calls for the establishment of a One World Government and a new world order that will 'serve the common good of the human family' and be a 'moral force' that will have 'the power to influence.'

2013   Pope Francis calls for all religions to unite together.

2013   9th World Assembly of Religions for Peace in Vienna, Austria. Creation of the Vienna Declaration which is yet another inter-faith infiltration exercise.

2014   September 4th Shimon Peres announces the world is ready for a United Religion.

2014   World Alliance of Religions for Peace Summit held. All the world's religious leaders signed the agreement to bring into international law, 'peace agreements' between the religions. The meeting's slogan was: 'We are one'.

2014   November 29th Pope Francis holds a meeting with Benjamin Netanyahu and Palestinian leader Mahmoud Abbas for peace in the Middle East at the Vatican. Pope Francis prays that God would accept the unification of Christianity and Islam.

2015   Pope Francis declares that 'fundamentalism is a disease across all religions'.

2015   November Encyclical. Pope Francis visits the US and UN where he is hailed as the potential leader of the religious world. He 'beats the environmentalist drum!'

2016   March. Pope says all religions are different paths to the same God.

2016   World Alliance of Religions for Peace Summit sign 'Declaration of Peace Cessation of War'. Attempts to make into a legally binding agreement.

2017   500th Year after the Reformation. World Alliance of Religions for Peace Summit during which all religions signed the 'Unity of Religion Agreement' for peace.

2018   7th Parliament of World Religions Meeting in Toronto. Celebration of 125 years from their first meeting in 1893.

2018   World Alliance of Religions for Peace Summit.

Forecasts (Based on the conspirators' writings and extrapolating forward the parts of the agenda which still need to be put in place, and the amount of time it would take for their *gradualist* psychological programming techniques to bring these events into fruition, here are some forecasts.)

2020s   Continuing psychological programming and deceptions to further divide us up and bring us into the 'masonic managed society'. The surveillance State is all-encompassing.

2030s   The end of the 30 Years' War will bring about a new set of mythologies. Ongoing 'decoupling' of economies into the 'Green Economy' and psychological preparation for the post capitalist society. Further reduction in the Sovereignty of nation states. Possibly the rebuilding of the Third Temple in Jerusalem.

2040s and 50s.   The merging of Christian denominations and promotion of the Utopian State with new creeds. Emergence of the post capitalist era, cashless society and trading blocks. Recognition of new political institutions. The rise of Transhumanism, AI, Nanotechnology and Robotics and the emergence of the 'central neural hive network'.

2060s – 2090s.   Posthumans no longer need physical bodies. Continual merger of Religions to form Chrislam. Emergence of the Luciferian New World Religion. End of property ownership. All of this leading to the depopulation strategy of the Cryptocracy, and the Anti-Christ being worshipped as god, leading to the Battle of Armageddon in which God will be victorious. God is Sovereign!

2100   The end of Agenda 21.

BIBLIOGRAPHY

Books in bold particularly relate to the New World Religion

Antelman Marvin	*To Eliminate the Opiate.* Zahavia.
Bains S K	*The Most Dangerous Book in the World. 9/11 as Mass Ritual.* Trine Day LLC.
Bailey Alice A	*Externalisation of the Hierarchy. The Unfinished Autobiography. The Reappearance of the Christ. The New Group of World Servers. Esoteric Psychology.* Lucis Trust.
Barruel August	*Memoirs Illustrating the History of the Jacobinism.* Amazon.
Bernays Edward	*Propaganda.* IG Publishing.
Blavatsky Helena	*The Secret Doctrine,* and *Isis Unveiled.* Tarcher Pedigree.
Brooke Tal	***One World.*** Amazon.
Carter Dallas	***Mystery Babylon Rising.*** CNG Publications.
Carr William	*Pawns in the Games.* Dauphin Publications.
Carrington H. Andrew	*The Synagogue of Satan.* Rivercrest Publishing.
Chomsky Noam	*Media Control.* Seven Stories Press.
Cumbey Constance	*The Hidden Dangers of the Rainbow.* Huntington House 1983.
De Chardin Tielhard	*The Phenomenon of Man.*

De R. Robin & S. Fritz.   *Worldwide Evil and Misery. The Legacy of the 13 Satanic Bloodlines.* Mayra Publications. *Worldwide Evil and Misery 2.*

Dice Mark   *The Illuminati.* Fact and Fiction,

Estulin Daniel   *The Bilderberg Group* Independent Publishers Group 2006.

Kah Gary   **New World Religion.** Hope Int Publishing 1998.

Kah Gary   **En Route to Global Occupation.** Huntington House Publishers 1991.

Geering Lloyd   *The World to Come.* Polebridge Press 1999.

Gonzalez Servando   *Psychological Warfare and the New World Order. The Secret War Against the American People.* Spooks Books 2016.

Gonzalez Servando   *I Dare Call It Treason: The Council on Foreign Relations and the Betrayal of America.* Spooks Books 2016.

Gore Al   *Earth in the Balance.* Earthscan.

Greer Michael   *The Element Encyclopaedia of Secret Societies.* Harper Collins 2006.

Guyenot Laurent   *9/11: 50 Years of the Deep State.*

Hamer John   *The Falsification of History.* Amazon.

Hays Micha-el Thomas   **Rise of the New World Order, The Culling of Man.** Amazon.

Hoffmann Michael II   *Secret Societies and Psychological Warfare.* Independent History & Research.

J. Faith, B. Dusty   *Numerology and The Divine Triangle.* Whitford Press.

Jaspar William F   *Global Tyranny… Step By Step.* Appleton.

King MS   *Planet Rothschild Volume 1 & 2.* Create Space 2015

Kissinger Henry   *World Order. Reflections on the Character of Nations and the Course of History.* Penguin.

Lake Michael	*The Shinar Directive. Preparing the Way for the Son of Perdition.* Amazon.
Levenda Peter	*Sinister Forces: The Nine: A Grimoire of American Political Witchcraft.* Independent Publishers Group.
Lewin Leonard	*Report from Iron Mountain,* The Dial Press Inc.
Marrs Texe	*Dark Secrets of the New Age.* Crossway Books.
Marrs Texe	*Circle of Intrigue.* Rivercrest Publishing.
Marrs Jim	*Rule by Secrecy.* Harper Collins.
Meadows Donella	*Limits to Growth.* (Club of Rome.) Potomac Associates.
Melanson Terry	*The Perfectibilists. The 18ᵗʰ Century Bavarian Order of the Illuminati.* Trine Day 2009
Monteith Stan	**Brotherhood of Darkness.** Hearthstone Publishing.
Muller Robert	*New Genesis: Shaping a Global Spirituality.* Image Books 1984.
Mullins Eustace	*The Curse of Canaan.* Ibad Press. *World Order – Our Secret Rulers.* Omnia Veritas Ltd.
Penn Lee	**False Dawn, The United Religions Initiative, Globalism, and the Quest for a One-World Religion.** Sophia Perennis.
Ratiu Ioan	*The Milner-Fabian Conspiracy.* Print on Demand 2012.
Rockefeller David	*Memoirs.* Random House 2003
Robison	*Proofs of a Conspiracy to Destroy all Governments and Religions.* Amazon.

Russell Bertrand	*The Impact of Science on Society.* Routledge.
Schimel Annamarie	*The Mystery of Numbers.* Oxford University Press 1993.
Schnoebelen William	*Masonry: Beyond the Light.* Chick Publications.
Sutton Anthony	*America's Secret Establishment. Skull and Bones.* Progressive Press.
Sutton Anthony	*Western Technology and Soviet Economic Development.* Hoover Institution Publications 1968.
Swing William Bishop	*The Coming United Religions.* CoNexus Press 1998
Tarpley Webster	*Synthetic Terror 9/11. Made in the USA.* Progressive Press.
Taylor Bron	*Dark Green Religion.* University of California Press 2010.
Thorn Victor	*Made in Israel. 9-11 and the Jewish Plot against America.* Sisyphus Press.
Thorn Victor	*9/11 On Trial, The World Trade Center Collapse.* Progressive Press.
Quigley Carroll	*The Anglo-American Establishment.* Dauphin Publications
Quigley Carroll	*Tragedy and Hope.* Macmillan.
Wood Patrick	***Technocracy Rising: The Trojan Horse of Global Transformation.*** Convergent Publishing.
Wood Judy	*Where did the Towers Go?* The New Investigation 2010
Young Zoe	*A New Green Order?* Pluto Press.
Zilinsky Sheila	*Green Gospel, The New World Religion.* Redemption

INDEX

29494669R00177

Printed in Great Britain
by Amazon